EU Consumer Law and Policy

ELGAR EUROPEAN LAW

Series editor: John Usher, *Professor of European Law and Head, School of Law, University of Exeter, UK*

European integration is the driving force behind constant evolution and change in the laws of the Member States and the institutions of the European Union. This important series will offer short, state-of-the-art overviews of many specific areas of EU law, from competition law to consumer law and from environmental law to labour law. Whilst most books will take a thematic, vertical approach, others will offer a more horizontal approach and consider the overarching themes of EU law.

Distilled from rigorous substantive analysis, and written by some of the best names in the field, as well as the new generation of scholars, these books are designed both to guide the reader through the changing legislation itself, and to provide a firm theoretical foundation for advanced study. They will be an invaluable source of reference for scholars and postgraduate students in the fields of EU law and European integration, as well as lawyers from the respective individual fields and policy-makers within the EU.

EU Consumer Law and Policy

Stephen Weatherill

Jacques Delors Professor of EC Law, Somerville College, Oxford, UK

ELGAR EUROPEAN LAW

Edward Elgar
Cheltenham, UK • Northampton, MA, USA

© Stephen Weatherill 2005

Published by
Edward Elgar Publishing Limited
Glensanda House
Montpellier Parade
Cheltenham
Glos GL50 1UA
UK

Edward Elgar Publishing, Inc.
136 West Street
Suite 202
Northampton
Massachusetts 01060
USA

A catalogue record for this book
is available from the British Library

ISBN 1 84376 963 8 (cased)

Typeset by Cambrian Typesetters, Camberley, Surrey
Printed and bound in Great Britain by MPG Books Ltd, Bodmin, Cornwall

Contents

Series editor's preface

It is a great pleasure to welcome this new and expanded edition of Professor Weatherill's book on *EU Consumer Law and Policy* as the first volume to appear in the Elgar European Law Series. The subject is one which, as the author explains, can no longer be regarded as a peripheral area of EU law; indeed it has been a major element in leading the EU into the heartlands of private law. This new edition reflects not only the considerable growth of EU legislation and case-law in the area of consumer law and policy but also the burgeoning academic and political debates on the policy issues involved. Some of these issues are specific to consumer law, but others, such as the division of competence between the EU and its Member States, underlie many areas of EU activity.

Professor Weatherill is a leading writer on EU law in general and is also well-known for his special interest in EU Consumer Law. This book provides comprehensive yet readable coverage of EU Consumer Law and Policy within a manageable compass.

John A. Usher
April 2005

Preface

I began the Preface to the first edition of this book, published in 1997, by observing that

> I have always believed that a lot of interesting research has been and is being conducted into EC consumer law and policy. And yet it seems to me that many EC lawyers and students have tended to treat consumer policy as peripheral.

Do they still? Not to the same extent, I think. EC consumer policy has ever more energetically developed its own body of scholarship. And I warmly welcome that.

My purpose in writing this book has not changed between the first and second editions. It remains to construct a bridge between basic EC law principles and the particular context in which they are applied in consumer policy. To this end, I assume a basic grasp of the pattern of the EC legal order, but do not assume any advanced knowledge. So the book should be readily accessible to anyone who has followed an introductory EC law course, covering institutional and constitutional law and the basic framework of trade law. The book should be perfectly intelligible on its own, although the reader could usefully have the texts of relevant Treaty provisions, Directives and Resolutions to hand. And naturally I provide plenty of sources of further reading.

I deliberately wrote the first edition as a short book. It was designed to set out the main themes in EC consumer policy. It did not immerse the reader in a highly technical research agenda, though it did make clear where the difficult areas requiring further theoretical and empirical analysis lie. My initial intention on approaching this second edition was to hold the book to the same length. So whatever material I added, I would subtract the same amount. But this proved impossible. There is a great deal of legislative and judicial development to take into account. There are Treaty revisions – already in force and, in the shape of the Treaty establishing a Constitution for Europe, pending. But I could just about have coped with this updating without extending the book. I was, however, defeated by the vast increase in scholarly examination of EC consumer law and by the rise of major questions of policy – to what extent does the market serve the consumer? Is the Commission's shift away from minimum to maximum harmonization justified? Is EC consumer law the driving force for European private law? Should it be? I concluded that if I wrote a second edition that was no longer than the first I would not do justice to the profound nature of the debates that attend the evolution of consumer policy in the EU – and I would cheat the reader. So this second edition is longer than its predecessor. But I hope it is no less readable. Most of all, I have maintained a concern to trace the trends in the evolution of consumer policy in the belief that they illustrate much about the evolution of the EU generally.

Any book on 'consumer law', whether national or transnational, has to make difficult choices about its subject matter. Consumer law is notoriously fuzzy-edged. I have picked the areas which I think would normally be regarded as the core of consumer policy. Separate treatment of detailed areas such as food and pharmaceuticals has been omitted with reluctance largely because to include them would have left me with too much detailed explanation, which would have precluded discussion of policy. There are two new chapters in this second edition. A new Chapter 3 devotes attention to the rhythms of harmonization in the EC. There are important questions about the constitutional reach of harmonization and its impact on national regulatory competence which deserve to be examined separately from the general sweep found in Chapter 1 and the sector-specific examination in the individual chapters that follow. I have also added a new Chapter 7 dealing with European private law. This ranges beyond the normal map of consumer law, but it is predominantly consumer law that has driven the EC deep into private law and so the wider horizons deserve inspection.

I owe thanks to many people, most of all, in the EC consumer field, to Geoffrey Woodroffe, Hans Micklitz, Norbert Reich, Thomas Wilhelmsson and Geraint Howells. All have inspired me, and I am grateful to them.

Stephen Weatherill

Table of cases

Table of legislation

1. The evolution of consumer policy in the European Union

THE CHALLENGE OF CONSUMER POLICY IN THE EUROPEAN UNION

> Consumer protection . . . has a bearing on what is probably the most central issue of European economic integration, for it brings into very sharp relief the dialectics of open borders, protectionism, and bona fide intervention of the Member State to protect legitimate societal values and goals even if at the expense of interrupting the free flow of goods on which the idea of a common marketplace is postulated. To understand the problematics of consumer protection in the common market context is to understand the core issue of European market integration.[1]

This challenging observation remains as pertinent today as when it was written, two decades and four formal revisions of the Treaty ago. Why should there be a consumer policy at EU level? Isn't the quest to create a more efficient, competitive, border-free economy for Europe itself amply beneficial to the interests of consumers? From this standpoint one would celebrate the EC Treaty provisions governing the free movement of goods, persons and services across borders coupled to the competition rules as in themselves vibrant instruments of consumer policy (see Chapter 2 of this book). Perhaps this is so – but where does this leave the scope for states to select patterns of market regulation that suit their own consumers' particular preferences? And can there truly be a common market without a comprehensive framework of common rule-making established at European level? These are deeply intriguing questions, and they are not cleanly answered by the EC Treaty. They go to the very heart of the nature of the process of European economic integration, built on legal rules and institutions but resistant to the construction of a European state to underpin a European market.

In fact, the capacity of consumer policy to provide insights into some of the fundamental tensions that beset the evolution of the European Union is today even more enticing than when Bourgoignie and Trubek penned the quote that introduces this book. At Maastricht, it was agreed to create a European Union

---

[1]   T. Bourgoignie and D. Trubek, *Consumer Law, Common Markets and Federalism* (Berlin: De Gruyter, 1987), p. vi.

(EU) of which the European Community (EC), first established by the Treaty of Rome in the 1950s, would form part. This came into being with effect from 1993. Of direct relevance to this book, it was agreed at Maastricht to add to the EC Treaty a provision which for the first time would explicitly empower European Community action in the consumer protection field. The relationship between this 'positive' commitment to market regulation at European level and the 'negative' emphasis on removing national laws that act as trade barriers in pursuit of market integration was obscure when the Maastricht Treaty came into force in 1993. The ambiguity has not been dispelled since. Neither the Amsterdam Treaty, which came into force in 1999, nor the Nice Treaty (2003) make any contribution to clarifying the balance to be struck between integration, deregulation and re-regulation. It is not overstating the case to claim that striking this balance is the most controversial economic issue facing the European Union today. In this vein shaping the landscape of European labour market regulation asks how much should be done at state or at sub-state level and how much should be done at European level. Similar questions of regulatory design attend the matter of social policy more generally and of environmental protection. But consumer policy too is a richly illustrative area of inquiry.

An emphasis on market deregulation breeds opposition to active regulatory policies at Community level; such a perspective is suspicious of EC consumer policy as anti-competitive. One might be tempted to suppose that supporters of such a viewpoint were routed at Maastricht, where an explicit consumer protection Title was inserted into the EC Treaty. However, the simultaneous inclusion of the subsidiarity principle guaranteed a persisting debate about the appropriate intensity of Community intervention, and in practice the new Title has been little used since the Union Treaty entered into force in 1993 (see further below). Most of the legislative activity conducted by the EC which affects the consumer has been pursued in the name of economic integration achieved by harmonizing national laws. Harmonization entails a transfer of regulatory competence from state to Community in the area subjected to the discipline of harmonization and, accordingly, where laws of consumer protection provide the focus of harmonization activity the EC assumes a role in choosing standards of consumer protection (Chapter 3). But how should it select among available regulatory techniques? What vision of the consumer is revealed by the EC's legislative *acquis*? Lately intense attention has been devoted to the supplementary question of whether, whatever type of rule is chosen by the EC, there is or should be scope for Member States to assert a competence to set stricter rules of consumer protection than those chosen as the harmonized EC standard. Legislative practice has long been accommodating of such flexibility, but the Commission's policy preferences have been switched towards a model that insists on maximizing the contribution of legislative harmonization to levelling the regulatory playing field in the EU by excluding such stricter national standards. Bourgoignie and Trubek were indeed far-sighted when they spotted the fundamental collision between open borders and Member State concern to protect locally cherished societal values and goals.

Beyond debate about the appropriate reach of harmonization as a basis for a level commercial playing field, there are arguments about the extent to which regulation at Community level is needed for reasons other than ironing out differences between national legal systems. It is argued that a wider market needs a wider regulatory system to achieve, loosely, social justice, not just an integrated free market. No one doubts that the EC is deregulatory – knocking down national regulations that impede trade is a key part of its economic success – but there is plenty of doubt about the appropriate aims and intensity of European-wide re-regulation. Here too examination of consumer policy opens a window on a broader landscape marked by conundrums about the shape the European Union should assume in future if it is live up to the motto allocated it by the draft Constitutional Treaty signed in 2004 – 'united in diversity'.

CONSUMER POLICY UNDER THE TREATY OF ROME

The Treaty of Rome was agreed in 1957 and entered into force in 1958. The text contains only five explicit references to the consumer. Article 39 contains a list of five objectives of the common agricultural policy, the fifth of which is 'to ensure that supplies reach consumers at reasonable prices'. Article 40 requires that the common organization of agricultural markets exclude 'any discrimination between producers or consumers within the Community'. Under Article 85(3) one of the conditions for exempting an agreement between firms from the prohibition of Article 85(1) is the requirement that it allow consumers 'a fair share of the resulting benefit'. Article 86 provides an illustrative list of abusive conduct perpetrated by dominant firms, including 'limiting production, markets or technical development to the prejudice of consumers'. Article 92(2)(a) identifies aid granted by a Member State that has a social character and is 'granted to individual consumers' as compatible with the common market. These provisions, containing incidental reference to the consumer, are still to be found in essentially unamended form in the text of the EC Treaty today, although the Amsterdam Treaty, which entered into force in 1999, renumbered the whole of both the EC and the EU Treaties from start to finish. Articles 39, 40, 85, 86 and 92 are today Articles 33, 34, 81, 82 and 87 – and the reader must always be fully aware that 'pre-Amsterdam' legal texts may be using a different numerical 'currency' from those that apply today.

None of the original Treaty's five explicit references to the consumer represents an attempt to develop a sophisticated structure of consumer rights or interests. In fact the assumption of the original Treaty pattern is that the consumer will benefit from the process of integration through the enjoyment of a more efficient market, which will yield more competition allowing wider choice, lower prices and higher-quality products and services. The substantive provisions of the Treaty, such as those designed to remove barriers to the free circulation of goods, persons and services (which were Articles 30, 48 and 59 and are now Articles 28, 39 and 49 respectively), are designed indirectly to improve the lot of the consumer. In this sense, they are themselves instruments of consumer policy – but of an inexplicit, 'hidden' type. These Treaty provisions are examined further from this perspective in Chapter 2. Moreover, there existed no explicit basis in the original Treaty for making European Community legislation in the area of consumer protection and, since the Community can act only in areas in which it is attributed powers by the Treaty (Article 5(1) EC), legislative action affecting the consumer could only be indirect.

Despite this barren Treaty background, a type of 'EC consumer policy' took shape not only through the application of the core provisions of EC law on market integration but also through two other routes. The first route was through 'soft law' initiatives in the field of consumer protection. The second was through the harmonization of national laws in the field of consumer protection, leading to a form of 'indirect' consumer policy at Community level. Gradual expansion of Community activity beyond narrowly defined Treaty limitations has been a characteristic feature of the evolution of the Community since its inception.[2] These features contributed to the shaping of an EC consumer policy well in advance of the formal recognition of consumer protection as a legislative competence enjoyed by the EC, which occurred only in 1993 on the entry into force of the Maastricht Treaty. From 1993 onwards the constitutional status of the EC as an actor in the field of consumer protection has been secure, although, as will be explained, the practical impact of this change has not been profound, and the main emphasis of EC consumer policy remains rooted in the process of market integration, including the commitment to legislative harmonization affecting consumer law, buttressed by 'soft law' policy statements.

A theme of this book is exploration of the extent to which it is possible to talk of a European consumer law and policy in spite of this unfavourable background in the Treaty. The thesis of this book holds that it is possible to iden-

---

[2]   J. Weiler, 'The Transformation of Europe' (1991) 100 *Yale Law Journal* 2403; A. Stone Sweet, W. Sandholtz and N. Fligstein (eds), *The Institutionalisation of Europe* (Oxford: Oxford University Press, 2001).

tify notions of the role of the consumer through examination of Community judicial and legislative activity. It has been necessary for the institutions to elaborate their own perceptions of the consumer in order to develop a range of other Community policies, most notably, but not exclusively, the process of building an integrated market. In this sense, the shaping of an 'EC consumer policy' cannot be simply depicted as an exercise in constitutionally over-ambitious interpretation of the scope of the Treaty by the Community institutions, but rather must be assessed as a part of the evolution of the Community towards its current *sui generis* status as something more than a market, but less than a state. The structure of this chapter is designed to sustain this theme. It covers the development of EC consumer policy before the entry into force of the Maastricht Treaty, which introduced consumer protection as a formal EC legislative competence for the first time; then it explains the impact of the Maastricht Treaty and the policy developments which followed in its train; and finally it traces the current preoccupations of the EC in the consumer field, including enlargement of the Union and the impact of the Treaty establishing a Constitution for Europe, as well as the new emphasis on a model of 'maximum harmonization'.

THE GROWTH OF A POLITICAL COMMITMENT TO CONSUMER PROTECTION AT EU LEVEL

Although it may be tempting to assume that an integrated market for Europe inevitably brings with it an integrated regulatory strategy underpinning that European market, it is simply the case that the EC Treaty does not provide for this. Article 5(1) EC declares that 'The Community shall act within the limits of the powers conferred upon it by this Treaty and of the objectives assigned to it therein.' This is commonly referred to as the principle of 'attributed competence'. The EC cannot 'self-authorize' an increase in its own competence. It may act in the areas in which the Member States have given it a mandate, and extension of the grant rests with the Member States acting at times of periodic Treaty revision. Article 5(1) was formally introduced into the EC Treaty by the Maastricht Treaty with effect from 1993 but, as a general statement of the law of Treaties, it has always been a foundation stone of the EC's constitutional order.

Accordingly, and as mentioned above, the original Treaty of Rome contained several provisions that were directly and indirectly relevant to the consumer, including the provisions governing the free movement of goods and services and the competition rules. The former exercise a control over public action hostile to the objectives to the EC, while the latter exercise a control over private action of this type. But nothing offered the EC an explicit authorization to adopt its own secondary legislation in the name of consumer protection.

However, by the 1970s the political commitment to the establishment of a consumer protection programme for the EC had grown irresistible. This formed part of a general trend in Community policy-making at the time. Following the largely successful transitional period within which many obvious trade barriers had been first reduced and then eliminated in accordance with timetables set out within the Treaty, political importance was increasingly attached to widening the Community's focus beyond economic integration alone. At the 'Paris Summit' in October 1972 the Member States expressed a general desire to broaden the appeal of the Community beyond economic affairs and into the social sphere. As one element in this policy, the heads of state and government called for the submission of a programme of consumer protection policy.

The 'soft law' initiative that emerged from this new political atmosphere was the Council Resolution of 14 April 1975 on a preliminary programme of the European Economic Community for a consumer protection and information policy.[3] This Resolution constituted the formal inauguration of a consumer protection and information policy for the Community. The Annex, a 'Preliminary Programme of the European Economic Community for a Consumer Protection and Information Policy', provides a relatively extended assertion of the place of the consumer interest in Community law. It is a relatively ambitious agenda, built on the perception that the consumer interest represents a distinctive element in society. In Point 3, it is explained that

> [t]he consumer is no longer seen merely as a purchaser and user of goods and services for personal, family or group purposes but also as a person concerned with the various facets of society which may affect him directly or indirectly as a consumer.

Point 3 encapsulates consumer interests in a statement of five basic rights:

(a) the right to protection of health and safety,
(b) the right to protection of economic interests,
(c) the right of redress,
(d) the right to information and education,
(e) the right of representation (the right to be heard).

The assertion of this notion of consumer 'rights in the Resolution, which is transparently inspired by US President Kennedy's similar declaration in March 1962, suggests an acceptance by the Council that the consumer interest transcends a purely economic, open-border focus. However, Point 4 provides

---

[3] *Official Journal* (henceforth *OJ*) 1975 C92/1.

an immediate reminder that, in conformity with the formal terms of the EC Treaty as they stood at the time, no consumer protection policy exists independently of other Community policies. Consumer policy will be amplified 'by action under specific Community policies such as the economic, common agricultural, social, environment, transport and energy policies as well as by the approximation of laws, all of which affect the consumer's position . . .'. Here, then, the principle of attributed competence now contained in Article 5(1) EC came to the fore in the admission that consumer policy could not be treated in itself as falling within the Community's legislative gift.

So action designed to achieve consumer protection *per se* cannot be pursued in the absence of a separate consumer protection Title in the Treaty, a constitutional deficiency which persisted until Maastricht (considered below). Appendix 2 to the Resolution, 'A Selection of Council Directives of Interest to Consumers', confirms the limited progress made at that time. The list is largely devoted to measures in the field of harmonization of laws concerning foodstuffs, animal health, textiles and motor vehicles. Important though such measures may be, they do not come close even to a glimpse of a comprehensive consumer policy. Therefore, the first Council Resolution on a preliminary programme for a consumer protection and information policy reveals a gap between policy aspiration and available constitutional foundation.

The 1975 Resolution on the preliminary programme was followed in 1981 by the Council Resolution of 19 May 1981 on a second programme of the European Economic Community for a consumer protection and information policy.[4] The 1981 Resolution is based on the same essential premises as those which underlie the first Resolution. It repeats the five basic rights. The Resolution expresses a priority for action in the field of the quality of goods and services, the conditions affecting their supply and the provisions of information about them. It also places rather firmer emphasis than the first Resolution on improving consultation between consumer representatives, producers and distributors.

These 'soft law' initiatives were of significance in the gradual development of a political atmosphere conducive to recognition of the distinctive function that may be performed by consumer policy. Moreover, although Article 249 (ex 189) EC makes it plain that Resolutions are not binding legislative acts, such initiatives are not wholly devoid of legal effect. For example, the Court has drawn on the emphasis placed on the value of providing information to the consumer in the 1981 Resolution in interpreting Article 28 in the context of a national measure restricting the provision of information to consumers.[5] And,

---

[4] *OJ* 1981 C133/1.
[5] Case C-362/88 *GB–INNO–BM* v. *Confédération du Commerce Luxembourgeois* [1990] ECR I–667, examined in Chapter 2.

as a general proposition, non-binding acts are capable of providing assistance in the interpretation of binding provisions of EC law.[6] 'Soft law' has a real significance in patterns of policy development in the consumer field and beyond. Nevertheless, legislative elaboration of EC consumer policy *per se* remained foreclosed by the absence of any explicit base in the Treaty.

From the middle of the 1980s, the EC's focus was the completion of the internal market by the end of 1992.[7] This project was presented as a method of accelerating integration in order to realize the substantial economic benefits which were suppressed by the fragmented pattern of 'non-Europe'. It was also a shrewd device for re-invigorating the EC itself, which had by this time become short of momentum and inspiration. The advantages that were identified, most prominently in the Cecchini Report,[8] were based on deeper market integration as a stimulus to competition and an encouragement to specialization, permitting the realization of economies of scale. The process was generally designed to achieve enhanced economic efficiency. Theory assumes that the ultimate beneficiary in such a process will be the consumer as the recipient of a wider choice of goods and services at a higher quality level and a lower price level. To this extent, the perceived advantages of the internal market for the consumer were comparable to those already expected to flow from the programme designed to construct a common market. Common market theory places the consumer as the ultimate beneficiary of the whole process, albeit as a passive recipient of the advantages of cross-border commercial activity.[9] From this perspective, economic integration in Europe is in itself a form of consumer policy, although it is not explicitly presented as such by the Treaty.

Once the Community had set in train the project of completing the internal market as defined by Article 14 EC by the end of 1992, which was given constitutional impetus by the entry into force of the Single European Act in 1987, initiatives in the field of consumer protection rapidly came to be viewed within the framework of internal market strategy. This theme was taken up in the 'soft law' expressions of consumer policy. Following the first and second Resolutions of 1975 and 1981, mentioned above, the third Council Resolution, of 23 June 1986, concerning the future orientation of the policy of the European Economic Community for the protection and promotion of consumer interests was expressed within the context of internal market

---

6   Case C-322/88 *Grimaldi* v. *Fonds des Maladies Professionnelles* [1989] ECR 4407.
7   The pattern of the project was initially advanced in the Commission's 'White Paper' on Completing the Internal Market, COM (85) 310.
8   Summarized in P. Cecchini, *The European Challenge: 1992, the Benefits of a Single Market* (Aldershot: Wildwood House, 1988).
9   M. Artis and F. Nixson, *The Economics of the European Union* (Oxford: Oxford University Press, 2001).

policy.[10] The Council Resolution welcomed a Commission paper entitled 'A New Impetus for Consumer Protection Policy'.[11] In that paper, the Commission had reviewed progress. The Commission's view was that progress towards the realization of the objectives of the 1975 Resolution fell short of what had been expected. It was certainly true that if one measured the success of the programmes by the number of Directives adopted, then the progress was slow indeed. In the first ten years since 1975, a very small number of consumer-related measures had been adopted. Those which had been adopted lay primarily in the rather technical field of food labelling.

The Commission determinedly attempted to impose a positive outlook on the prevailing situation. It rejected the idea that consumer protection should be a 'fair-weather' phenomenon and asserted that because national consumer laws may affect market integration, they must accordingly be taken into account by Community policy-makers. The Commission also took the opportunity in its paper to explain its future preoccupation with the more flexible 'New Approach' to technical harmonization (Chapter 9). The Commission proposed a new impetus in consumer protection policy, aiming at three main objectives: products traded in the Community should conform to acceptable safety and health standards; consumers must be able to benefit from the common market; and consumer interests should be taken more into account in other Community policies.

The Council Resolution which welcomed the Commission's paper was relatively brief. It stressed the objective of improving the ability of consumers to benefit from the Community's internal market. Moreover, it adopted a theme contained within the Commission's paper by linking the consumer interest with the notion of a 'People's Europe'. The Council Resolution called on the Commission to prepare proposals.

Perhaps the most striking overt change between the 1986 document, the third in the series, and the earlier programmes of 1975 and 1981 is the diminution in assertion of consumer 'rights'.[12] The discussion treated the consumer as the beneficiary of the process of market integration. Consumer choice, rather than consumer rights, emerged as the dominant theme.

In December 1986, the Council adopted a Resolution on the integration of consumer policy in the other common policies.[13] This readdressed the themes already set out in the resolution of June 1986, most prominently the objective of taking greater account of consumers' interests in other Community policies. The series of 'soft law' declarations continued with a Council Resolution of

[10]   *OJ* 1986 C167/1.
[11]   COM (85) 314.
[12]   N. Reich, 'Protection of Consumers' Economic Interests by the EC' (1992) 14 *Sydney Law Review* 23.
[13]   *OJ* 1987 C3/1.

November 1989 on future priorities for relaunching consumer protection policy.[14] In essence, this amounted to no more than a consolidation of pre-existing policy. It emphasized once again the consumer benefit which would accrue from the completion of the internal market. An annex to the Resolution contained a list of priority areas, covering the integration of consumer protection policy into other common policies; improving consumer representation; promoting general safety of goods and services and better information on their quality; encouraging Member States to promote access to legal redress; and pursuing work on other specified initiatives.

Focus on the perceived virtues of the internal market illuminates the first of the Commission's three-year action plans for consumer policy, covering 1990–92.[15] Part A of the document offered a brief summary of *Consolidation of Progress*. Part B provided a *Three Year Action Plan*. There were four main areas of focus within the plan, which were selected because of their contribution to building the consumer confidence necessary to support the realization of the internal market. The four chosen areas were consumer representation; consumer information; consumer safety; and consumer transactions.

The end of 1992 was the deadline for the completion of the internal market. At the end of 1992, it was vividly apparent that the consumer was in a better position. The completion of the internal market in accordance with the Treaty had in principle established the right of private consumers to move freely across borders and to return home with whatever they pleased for their private consumption. Although in the past consumers had typically been regarded as the passive beneficiaries of free trade through enhanced choice, they are now increasingly able actively to enjoy the benefits of an integrated market. The Court too has made plain its view that the consumer has the right to treat the Community as border-free and to 'travel freely to the territory of another Member State to shop under the same conditions as the local population'.[16] Large differences between applicable tax rates have ensured that British consumers of tobacco products and alcoholic drinks in France have been among the most enthusiastic shoppers who have exploited these economic freedoms.

LEGISLATIVE HARMONIZATION AND THE PROTECTION OF THE CONSUMER

By the beginning of the 1990s a string of 'soft law' commitments to the virtues of a consumer protection policy at EC level had been forthcoming. These were

14   *OJ* 1989 C 294/1.
15   COM (90) 98.
16   Case C-362/88, note 5 above.

surveyed in the previous section. Market integration, itself designed to foster a competitive economy in the service of the consumer interest, had been vigorously promoted as central to the EC's activities. But the Treaty remained deficient in any explicit provision equipping the EC with a legislative competence in the field of consumer protection. This would arrive only on the entry into force of the Maastricht Treaty in 1993, and even then – as will be discussed below – only in a carefully restricted form. However, the gulf between political rhetoric favourable to the protection of the consumer by the EC and the unfavourable constitutional underpinnings was not as wide in practice as it seemed in theory. The bridge was provided by the Treaty's conferral on the EC of a competence to legislate to harmonize laws in pursuit of the integration of markets. This has always been a competence attributed to the EC by its Treaty. And a batch of measures of legislative harmonization has been directly concerned with the protection of the consumer. The harmonization programme has acted as an indirect consumer policy.

The original Treaty of Rome included a provision which provided 'for the approximation of such provisions laid down by law, regulation or administrative action in member states as directly affect the establishment or functioning of the common market'. This was Article 100 EEC, and it is today Article 94 EC (in consequence of the Amsterdam Treaty's renumbering of the EC Treaty effective from 1999). After the entry into force of the Single European Act (SEA) in 1987, a new provision inserted by the SEA began to be used to harmonize national laws in the field of, *inter alia*, consumer protection. This was Article 100a, and it is today (after amendment) Article 95. It provides for the adoption of measures 'for the approximation of the provisions laid down by law, regulation or administrative action in member states which have as their object the establishing and functioning of the internal market'. Article 95 (ex 100a) has largely superseded Article 94 (ex 100) as an instrument of harmonization. This is not because of its reference to the creation of an 'internal' market, in contrast to Article 94's concern with a 'common' market, because in practice little, if anything, has turned on the distinction between an internal market and a common market. The key point is that harmonization legislation adopted pursuant to Article 95 requires only a 'qualified majority vote' (QMV) among the Member States acting in Council whereas Article 94 is subject to a requirement of unanimity in the Council.

The nature and purpose of the harmonization programme will be explored more fully in Chapter 3. However, the key general point is that harmonization of national laws has been conducted in the name of promoting the establishment and functioning of the EC's unified trading space, as envisaged by Articles 94 and 95. Variation between national laws was typically presented as an impediment to market integration, prompting a need for harmonization at Community level – 'common rules for a common market'. In so far as economic integration improves the consumer's position by promoting a more efficiently functioning market, then harmonization is a pro-consumer policy. In this vein Articles 94 and 95 are supplemented by Articles 47(2) and 55 EC which permit the adoption of measures designed to liberalize the free circulation of persons and services. Such harmonization, yielding, for example, liberalization in markets for financial services, also counts as an indirect aspect of EC consumer law and policy. But that is not all. More specifically, in so far as the national laws subjected to the discipline of harmonization affect consumer protection, the EC, by harmonizing, assumes the function of setting its own rules of consumer protection. Harmonization therefore has a dual function. It sets common rules for the European market but it also involves a choice of the appropriate common standard of regulatory protection. This is how harmonization policy also becomes an exercise in selecting a pattern of consumer protection for the EU.

This is reflected in the Treaty. Article 95(3) provides that

> The Commission, in its proposals envisaged in paragraph 1 concerning health, safety, environmental protection and consumer protection, will take as a base a high level of protection, taking account in particular of any new development based on scientific facts. Within their respective powers, the European Parliament and the Council will also seek to achieve this objective.

Since the entry into force of the Maastricht Treaty in 1993 this has been buttressed by a 'horizontal' provision which is now found in Article 153(2) (see further below). This provides that 'Consumer protection requirements shall be taken into account in defining and implementing other Community policies and activities' – which must include market integration. So the harmonization programme has embedded within it by Articles 95(3) and 153(2) EC a responsibility cast upon the EC's political institutions to pay attention to the quality of the consumer protection policy to be developed in common at EU level. The intimate connection between legislative harmonization and the consumer interest has also been highlighted by the Court. It has accepted that harmonization Directives are capable of generating *rights* vested in consumers in the event that a Member State fails to put in place the envisaged protective regime.[17]

Driven by this dual function, Article 94 (ex 100) and, since 1987, Article 95 (ex 100a) have generated a substantial body of measures of legislative harmonization that are also measures which reveal choices about the EC's preferred techniques of consumer protection. This provides this book with much of its detailed subject matter. And although the internal market was scheduled for

---

[17]   E.g. Case C-91/92 *Paola Faccini Dori* [1994] ECR I-3325, Cases C-178/94 et al. *Dillenkofer* [1996] ECR I-4845. See further Chapter 10.

completion by the end of 1992, its maintenance remains an evolving process and harmonization measures affecting consumer protection continue to be adopted pursuant to Article 95 (ex 100a) today. Exploring how the programme of legislative harmonization, which the Treaty identifies as constitutionally tied to market-making, has been used to shape a consumer policy for the EC is thematically central to this book's concern to demonstrate that the intricacies of policy-making are a good deal more intriguing than the bare bones of the Treaty might suggest. It is too simplistic to assert a sustainably neat divide between the Community's interest in market integration and the role of the Member States in matters of market regulation in the sphere of consumer protection. The Community's role has inevitably spread, blurring this initially appealing division of function.[18] The Community has developed a form of consumer policy, both in judging the validity of national consumer laws which impede trade (the subject matter of Chapter 2 of this book) and also through the need to elaborate the substantive content of legislative harmonization. The general lesson – which extends far beyond consumer policy – is that a programme presented as an exercise in securing market freedom inevitably involves a sustained commitment to rule-making.[19]

This rationalization of the spread of EC consumer law must be capable of meeting the objection that even though harmonization might have impinged on consumer law, it has not done so in any coherent fashion. The measures that will be reviewed in this book disclose a range of different techniques and assumptions. One must be wary of overstating the case for treating the Community as possessing a thematically coherent consumer policy. But there are more fundamental constitutional objections too. Many harmonization measures are perfectly obviously based on the perception that legislative diversity damaged integration, and that, in matters such as product safety (Chapter 9) and advertising (Chapter 8), common rules were required. But several Directives were adopted pursuant to the Treaty-conferred competence to harmonize with no serious expectation that they would advance the process of market integration. Some will be encountered in this book. One of the more blatant examples of this type of unconvincing harmonization is provided by Directive 85/577 on 'doorstep selling'.[20] It was based on Article 100 EC (now Article 94). The Preamble states that the practice of doorstep selling is the subject of different rules in different Member States. This is perfectly true. The Preamble proceeds to declare that 'any disparity between such legislation may directly affect the functioning of the common market'. This is far from obviously true, and the claim is not supported by any

---

[18] For early recognition of this phenomenon see L. Krämer, *EEC Consumer Law* (Brussels: Story Scientia, 1986), pp. 7–25.
[19] M. Egan, *Constructing a European Market* (Oxford: Oxford University Press, 2001).
[20] *OJ* 1985 L372/31. See Chapter 4.

evidence. The Preamble also makes revealing reference to the Council Resolutions of 1975 and 1981 on consumer protection and information policy, mentioned above, and observes that consumers may be 'unprepared' in negotiations for contracts away from business premises. This gives the political game away. It was plain that the Member States were unanimously committed to developing a richer texture to EC policy-making, beyond mere trade integration in the narrow sense. In the absence at the time of any formal Treaty revision giving effect to these wider aspirations by extending the list of available legislative competences, harmonization was used as the chosen route.

What was at stake here is what has been labelled 'competence creep'.[21] It strays close to an expansion in the EC's competence achieved not by Treaty revision, but by over-ambition practised by the EC's legislative institutions. This is in principle entirely impermissible, for it subverts the constitutional constraint of attributed competence, now found in Article 5(1) EC. In practice the unanimous support of the Member States in Council nudged this proviso aside. The 'soft law' Resolutions setting out the importance of consumer protection at European level which were examined above were accompanied by the adoption of binding legislation that was presented for the purposes of constitutional respectability as market-making harmonization but which was really an expression of consumer policy.

The voting rule in Council applicable to harmonization was altered from unanimity to 'QMV' in 1987 on the entry into force of the Single European Act. Thereafter a Member State opposed to a proposed measure of harmonization could not simply veto it. It could vote against it but, if in a sufficiently small minority in Council, it could find itself outvoted and bound by legislation adopted pursuant to Article 95 (ex 100a) to which it was opposed. The temptation to proceed to the Court and argue that the legislation was invalid as an improper exercise of the competence to harmonize laws is obvious. Eventually the Court was provided in 2000 with the opportunity to clarify its view of the scope of legislative harmonization granted by the Treaty. This is the *'Tobacco Advertising'* judgment, *Germany* v. *Parliament and Council*.[22] The Court for the first time annulled a harmonization Directive on the basis that it failed to make an adequate contribution to the establishment and functioning of the internal market. Discussion of the judgment, the light which it sheds on the validity of previous legislative practice and its impact on the future of consumer policy is reserved for Chapter 3. The point of current relevance is that *Tobacco Advertising* confirms that the Treaty confers no competence to harmonize *per se*: the competence is more limited than that. A measure

---

[21] E.g. M. Pollack, 'Creeping Competence: The Expanding Agenda of the European Community' (1994) 14 *Journal of Public Policy* 95.

[22] Case C-376/98 [2000] ECR I-8419.

of harmonization must actually contribute to eliminating obstacles to the free movement of goods or to the freedom to provide services, or to removing appreciable distortions of competition. And the Court will police this. Harmonization, long treated with benevolence at EU level, has become a more fiercely contested process.[23] At relevant points this book will therefore raise the question: is it constitutionally valid for the EC to intervene in the name of consumer protection? In some instances the answer will be unavoidably uncertain.

THE ESTABLISHMENT OF CONSUMER PROTECTION AS A FORMAL EC COMPETENCE

The three intermingled streams of consumer protection continued to irrigate the EC through the 1980s and into the 1990s. The promotion of market integration under the influence of the rules of EC trade law, in particular free movement and competition law, combined with the lengthening list of 'soft law' resolutions and similar policy instruments and, in addition, the growing body of measures of legislative harmonization affecting the consumer to permit commentators to talk perfectly convincingly about the reality of an 'EC consumer policy'. But there was still no explicit legislative competence granted to the EC in the field of consumer protection as such.

This breakthrough arrived in 1993 on the entry into force of the Maastricht Treaty. This for the first time created a separate Title devoted to 'Consumer Protection' which conferred on the EC a legislative competence in the field of consumer protection which was not tied to the imperative of market integration. The relevant provision was Article 129a. Since the renumbering and amendment effected in 1999 by the Amsterdam Treaty, it has become Article 153 EC.

> 1. In order to promote the interests of consumers and to ensure a high level of consumer protection, the Community shall contribute to protecting the health, safety and economic interests of consumers, as well as to promoting their right to information, education and to organise themselves in order to safeguard their interests.
> 2. Consumer protection requirements shall be taken into account in defining and implementing other Community policies and activities.
> 3. The Community shall contribute to the attainment of the objectives referred to in paragraph 1 through: (a) measures adopted pursuant to Article 95 [ex 100a] in the context of the completion of the internal market; (b) measures which support, supplement and monitor the policy pursued by the Member States.
> 4. The Council, acting in accordance with the procedure referred to in Article 251 [ex 189b] and after consulting the Economic and Social Committee, shall adopt the measures referred to in paragraph 3(b).

---

[23] S. Weatherill, 'Why Harmonise?'in P. Tridimas and P. Nebbia (eds), *European Union Law for the Twenty-First Century, Volume 2* (Oxford: Hart Publishing, 2004).

5. Measures adopted pursuant to paragraph 4 shall not prevent any Member State from maintaining or introducing more stringent protective measures. Such measures must be compatible with this Treaty. The Commission shall be notified of them.

The arrival of such a provision in the Treaty is plainly a major landmark in mapping the EC's consumer policy. It was supplemented at Maastricht by the corresponding addition of consumer protection to the list of the Community's activities set out in Article 3. This now provides that the activities of the Community shall include 'a contribution to the strengthening of consumer protection' (Article 3(t)). This was subsequently reinforced by the EU Charter of Fundamental Rights, which was proclaimed as a (non-binding) instrument at Nice in December 2000.[24] In Article 38, under the sub-title 'Consumer Protection', it states that 'Union policies shall ensure a high level of consumer protection'.[25] According to Article 5(1) EC the Community 'shall act within the limits of the powers conferred upon it by this Treaty and of the objectives assigned to it therein': since the entry into force of the Maastricht Treaty in 1993 the EC has had conferred on it an explicit power to act in the service of the consumer.

The creation of this legal base pursuant to the Maastricht Treaty was therefore a novelty, but inspection of the supporting paragraphs in Article 153 reveals obvious connections with the trajectory of pre-existing policy. The reference in Article 153(1) to the contribution of the Community 'to protecting the health, safety and economic interests of consumers, as well as to promoting their right to information, education and to organize themselves in order to safeguard their interests' echoes the general ambitions mapped out by the 'soft law' Resolutions on consumer policy that have proliferated since the first in 1975.[26] Article 153(2)'s direction that 'Consumer protection requirements shall be taken into account in defining and implementing other Community policies and activities' acts as a 'horizontal' or 'mainstreaming' provision, lending weight to consumer protection not only as a Community competence in its own right but also inserting it into the wider framework of policy-making. Article 153(2), as mentioned, ensures that consumer protection shall be taken into account *inter alia* in the shaping of the programme of legislative harmonization. Finally, it is striking that Article 153(5) provides for *minimum* rule-making. Article 153(5) requires Member States to put in place the floor of protection mandated by an adopted Community rule but it permits them to set more stringent protective measures above that floor, up to the ceil-

[24]   *OJ* 2000 C364.
[25]   Cf. A. Kiss, 'Environmental and Consumer Protection', ch. 10 in S. Peers and A. Ward (eds), *The EU Charter of Fundamental Rights: Politics, Law and Policy* (Oxford: Hart Publishing, 2004).
[26]   Note 3 above.

ing fixed by the Treaty itself, most prominently by the Treaty provisions governing free movement.

The entry into force of the Maastricht Treaty in 1993, and the emergence of what is now Article 153 EC, is unquestionably important in formal terms, for it embraced consumer protection for the first time as an explicit EC competence. It provides a potential constitutional basis for the development of an EC strategy on consumer protection which is independent of harmonization policy in particular and the process of market integration in general.[27] An institutional consideration hinted at a further basis for optimism that consumer policy might have come of age with its 'constitutionalization' in the Treaty as a result of the Maastricht amendments. The Commission had first granted institutional recognition to its functions with regard to the consumer in 1968 when it established an administrative unit as part of the Competition Policy Directorate General. Thereafter responsibility for consumer policy had drifted among different entities. Between 1981 and 1989 it was part of a rather loosely conceived Directorate General XI alongside Environmental and Nuclear Affairs. From 1989 consumer policy was driven by a Consumer Policy Service within the Commission, which lacked the status of a Directorate General. Consumer policy suffered from a low budget and vulnerability to the policy concerns of more powerful Directorates General, most notably those dealing with agriculture and the internal market. In 1995, for the first time, a separate Consumer Policy Directorate General was established within the Commission. The transformation of the Consumer Policy Service into a Directorate General (then known as DG XXIV, headed by Emma Bonino) did not necessarily remedy such weaknesses, but it was readily capable of being viewed as a step up for consumer policy. This stand-alone institutional status within the Commission has now been preserved for a decade. The relevant Directorate General is now known as 'Consumer Affairs' and since the internal adjustments made to the Commission in 2001 it is more commonly referred to as 'DG SANCO'.[28] An Irishman, David Byrne, was the responsible Commissioner until late in 2004, since when the post has been held by a Cypriot, Markos Kyprianou.

Moreover, the Commission has endeavoured over time to establish methods of consumer input through a series of differently constituted consumer representative bodies.[29] The risk is that the consumer voice within the

---

[27] T. Bourgoignie, 'European Community consumer law and policy: from Rome to Amsterdam' [1998] *Consumer Law Journal* LJ 443.

[28] The acronym derives from the French for Health and Consumer Protection.

[29] The Consumers' Consultative Committee, Dec. 73/306/EEC, *OJ* 1973 L283/18, the Consumers' Consultative Council, Dec. 90/55/EEC, *OJ* 1990 L38/40, and the Consumer Committee, Dec. 95/260 *OJ* 1995 L162/37. For comment see M. Nevenko, '(Re)constructing the Consumer Committee: glossae marginalis' (2000) 8 *Consumer Law Journal* 25. The most recent version is the European Consumer Consultative Group, Dec. 2003/709, *OJ* 2003 L258/35 (composition altered on enlargement, *OJ* 2004 C150/21).

Commission may be drowned by those of other, less diffuse interest groups, especially sector-specific players in the commercial sphere. But here too the significance of Article 153 is that, as a minimum, there is no scope for denying the proper place of the consumer interest in the formulation of policy.

And yet how much has really changed since Maastricht?[30] Judged by its addition to the practical reach of the legislative competence of the EC, Article 153 did remarkably little. Article 153(3)(a) cross-refers to the existing competence to act pursuant to Article 95 in the context of the completion of the internal market. As mentioned above, this has been used to develop a body of consumer-related legislative harmonization, although the *Tobacco Advertising* judgment makes clear that Article 95 is available only for measures which actually contribute to eliminating obstacles to the free movement of goods or to the freedom to provide services, or to removing appreciable distortions of competition. If that threshold is not crossed, the EC's competence to act in the field of consumer protection is supplied by Article 153(3)(b). Although this envisages EC action which is not tied to the market-making imperative, it is a tightly confined provision. Only measures which 'support, supplement and monitor the policy pursued by the Member States' may be adopted. The Member States were evidently willing to equip the EC with an explicit competence to act in the field of consumer protection but they were bent on keeping a short rein on what could be done in its name. The practical record of lawmaking pursuant to Article 153(3)(b) bears out the impression of caution underpinning the new legislative competence conferred at Maastricht. Article 153(3)(b) has been little used. The first occasion was as a basis for Decision 94/3092 of the Parliament and Council concerning the collection of data on home and leisure accidents with a view to promoting accident prevention, improving the safety of consumer products and informing and educating consumers so that they make better use of products.[31] It was also the legal basis for Directive 98/6 on the indication of prices offered to consumers[32] and it has been cited in the Preambles to some 'soft law' instruments in the field of access to justice, such as Recommendation 2001/310 on the principles for out-of-court bodies involved in the consensual resolution of consumer disputes (Chapter 10). But an exhaustive list would be little longer. And none of the occasions on which the Community legislature has acted pursuant to Article 153(3)(b) can be described as strikingly important in policy terms.

---

[30] G. Howells and T. Wilhelmsson, 'EC Consumer Law: has it come of age?' (2003) 28 *European Law Review* 370; J. Stuyck, 'European Consumer Law after the Treaty of Amsterdam: Consumer Policy in or beyond the internal market?' (2000) 37 *Common Market Law Review* 367.

[31] *OJ* 1994 L331/1, amended by Dec. 95/184, *OJ* 1995 L120/36 to take account of the accession of Austria, Finland and Sweden in 1995. See further Chapter 9.

[32] *OJ* 1998 L80/27.

In practice the principal motor of legislation affecting the consumer interest remains the long-standing competence to harmonize laws in pursuit of market integration, found in Article 95 and the subject of cross-reference in Article 153(3)(a). The Maastricht Treaty's elevation of consumer protection to an explicit competence with effect from 1993 has not altered the central role of harmonization in giving shape to EC consumer policy.

SUBSIDIARITY AND CONSUMER POLICY

The EC must not overstep the limits of the competences attributed to it by the Treaty. This principle is found in Article 5(1) EC. A competence granted need not necessarily be exercised. Article 5(2) contains the principle of subsidiarity. This provides that:

> In areas which do not fall within its exclusive competence, the Community shall take action, in accordance with the principle of subsidiarity, only if and in so far as the objectives of the proposed action cannot be sufficiently achieved by the member states and can therefore, by reason of the scale or effects of the proposed action, be better achieved by the Community.

The principle of subsidiarity was introduced into the EC Treaty as a general principle by the Maastricht Treaty. Its focus is on efficient administration. Sir Leon Brittan helpfully described it as a method for identifying the 'best level' for regulatory activity in the Community.[33] This rendition is important and, it is submitted, helpful, because it brings out the point that subsidiarity is not based on preconceptions about centralization or decentralization. Instead it is a matter of efficiency. And it is hard to disagree with the notion that lies at the heart of Article 5(2), which is that the Community should act where it adds value to action taken by the Member States – and not otherwise.

This core of the objection to subsidiarity lies in its lack of precision and predictability. Much will depend on how one calculates whether the objectives can be 'better achieved by the Community'. This is problematic in its practical application, by politicians and, even more so, by judges. The quest to convert subsidiarity from catchphrase into a reliable set of principles for guiding the exercise of Treaty competences progressed via the Conclusions of the Edinburgh European Council in 1992 and the inter-institutional agreement of 1993 to the Amsterdam Protocol on subsidiarity and proportionality which entered into force in 1999.[34] But the shaping of consumer policy has been affected by the rise of subsidiarity as a guiding principle from a very early

---

[33] Sir Leon Brittan, 'Institutional Development of the EC' [1992] *Public Law* 567.
[34] G. De Burca, 'Reappraising Subsidiarity's Significance after Amsterdam', Jean Monnet Working Papers 7/99 (via http://www.jeanmonnetprogram.org/).

stage. In fact the Commission employed the vocabulary of subsidiarity even before its arrival as a general principle of the EC legal order courtesy of the Maastricht Treaty. In the consumer policy action plan 1990–92[35] the Commission declared under the heading 'Subsidiarity Principle' that

> Practical consumer policy must be effectively managed in the member states on an ongoing basis with the management and control of safety, information and redress being adapted in each instance to local needs. It would be unrealistic to undertake such tasks continuously at a Community level.

A report submitted to the European Council by Jacques Delors, the President of the Commission, was annexed to the Conclusions of the Presidency issued after the meeting of the European Council in Edinburgh in December 1992. The report declared that the Commission had withdrawn three proposals for Directives in the light of the demands of the principle of subsidiarity. One of these impinged on consumer policy, a Directive dealing with compulsory indication of nutritional value on the packaging of foodstuffs. Consideration was being given to withdrawing several further proposals. A third group of proposals was singled out because of the inclusion of excessive detail. These Directives were to be revised and drafted in a more general style. This batch included proposals relating to the liability of suppliers of services (Chapter 6) and comparative advertising (Chapter 8).

The Commission made three commitments with regard to the application of the subsidiarity principle in a further report to the European Council in Brussels in December 1993. In relation to consumer policy, it would justify all new legislative proposals with reference to subsidiarity; withdraw or revise certain pending proposals; and continue work on the proposals in the field of liability of suppliers of services and comparative advertising.

These trends, combined with a general impression that Member States were adopting a more sceptical attitude to EC rule-making, fuelled anxieties that subsidiarity might be used to slice away a Community contribution to consumer policy-making. This apprehension was placed on the political agenda by the Parliament's Committee on the Environment, Public Health and Consumer Protection. In 1992 it complained that the advantages of Community consumer policy had been inadequately presented. This, it diagnosed, had led to calls for 'repatriation under the guise of the subsidiarity doctrine'.[36] The Committee refers explicitly to the risk of 'regulatory gaps'. Such gaps yawn where the Member States are precluded from taking action by Community law but where the Community itself is unable to take action (either because it lacks competence or because political support is not forthcoming).

[35]   COM (90) 98.
[36]   PE DOC A3-380/92.

It appears that some Member States have used the vocabulary of subsidiarity in seeking to block Community action. For example, it is known that in the early 1990s the German government issued a list in which it proposed a radical reduction in Community measures touching on consumer policy,[37] although Directive 93/13 on unfair terms in consumer contracts was adopted soon afterwards (Chapter 5), so one should not overestimate the depth of German intransigence. In April 1993 the House of Commons European Standing Committee, discussing the proposed Distance Selling Directive (Chapter 4), was told by the Minister that one Member State, which he was unprepared to name on grounds of confidentiality, had proposed the abandonment of the Directive on the basis that it violated the subsidiarity principle.[38] It would not be incautious to guess that Germany was the unnamed state in question. But the proposal was eventually adopted: it is Directive 97/7, considered in Chapter 4.

The Community has continued to legislate in the field of consumer protection since the rise to prominence of the subsidiarity principle in the early 1990s. In fact, quite contrary to the expressions of alarm that subsidiarity might be used to undermine the scope and potential of EC rule-making, the general impression is that subsidiarity has done little, if anything, to shake an EC institutional culture of law- and policy-making perceived to be too ready to fall prey to a centralizing impulse. The Commission's first report on the application of the subsidiarity principle, released in 1994, raised this concern by including the wry remark that 'one cannot help observing that principle and practice are often far apart with Member States meeting within the Council often adopting positions on individual cases at variance with their respect in principle for Article 3b [now 5]'.[39] Rarely, if ever, are legislative proposals rejected for perceived violation of the subsidiarity principle. In 2001 Alain Lamassoure MEP went so far as to complain that 'No European institution is in reality willing to comply with the principle of subsidiarity.'[40]

It is in this vein conspicuous that explained compliance with the principle in legislation is on occasion at best perfunctory. For example, the Preamble to Directive 2000/31 on electronic commerce[41] asserts that 'by dealing only with certain specific matters which give rise to problems for the internal market, this Directive is fully consistent with the need to respect the principle of subsidiarity' but it makes no serious attempt to substantiate this claim.

---

[37] Printed in *Verbraucher und Recht*, 1/1993.
[38] H.C. EC Standing Committee B, 28 April 1993.
[39] COM (1994) 533.
[40] Evidence given to the Scottish Parliament's European Committee on 30 October 2001, available via: http://www.scottish.parliament.uk/S1/official_report/cttee/europe-01/eu01-1202.htm# Col1211. (SP Paper 466 *The Governance of the European Union and the Future of Europe* Session 1 (2001)).
[41] *OJ* 2000 L178/1.

Directive 97/55 on comparative advertising[42] offers another example of a rhetorical insistence on compliance with subsidiarity which is lacking in detailed elaboration. In other circumstances subsidiarity is used as an argument in favour of legislative intervention at EC level, not against it. When Recommendation 90/109 on the transparency of banking conditions relating to cross-border financial transactions was shown to have generated negligible improvement in the malfunctioning market in question, the subsequent more ambitious step to introduce binding EC rules in Directive 97/5 on cross-border credit transfers was justified explicitly as in conformity with the principle of subsidiarity.[43] This confirms that subsidiarity is not loaded in favour of decentralization. Subsidiarity, properly understood, fully supports Community rule-making provided it is shown to improve the pre-existing pattern of diversity founded on state regulatory autonomy. The Protocol introduced by the Amsterdam Treaty makes this plain in declaring that

> Subsidiarity is a dynamic concept and should be applied in the light of the objectives set out in the Treaty. It allows Community action within the limits of its powers to be expanded where circumstances so require, and conversely, to be restricted or discontinued where it is no longer justified.

Subsidiarity's impact should of course be judged with reference to more than the record of adopted secondary legislation. The Consumer Policy Action Plan of 1999–2001[44] uses the language of subsidiarity to emphasize the virtues of better, not more, lawmaking, and better enforcement of existing laws. As a general observation, subsidiarity has become embedded within the debate about EC consumer policy but for many critics it fares poorly as an operationally useful means to allay anxieties that the Community has contributed to over-centralization in Europe.

At a specifically legal level, no legislative act has ever been annulled by the European Court for non-compliance with the subsidiarity principle in Article 5(2) EC. The impression that subsidiarity is bark but not bite is strengthened by the Court's ruling in *R* v. *Secretary of State ex parte BAT and Imperial Tobacco*,[45] in which the Court found that the challenged Directive, a measure of harmonization, took as its objective the elimination of the barriers raised by the differences between state laws. This objective cannot be sufficiently achieved by the Member States individually – indeed it is the variety of

---

[42] *OJ* 1997 L290/18 (corrig. *OJ* 1998 L194/54). See Chapter 8.

[43] Rec. 90/109 *OJ* 1990 L67/39, Dir. 97/5 on cross-border credit transfers, *OJ* 1997 L43/25. See now Reg. 2560/2001 on cross-border payments in euro, *OJ* 2001 L344/13, lacking any reference to subsidiarity.

[44] COM (98) 696. See also on 'Better lawmaking', COM (97) 626, COM (98) 715, COM (02) 275.

[45] Case C-491/01 [2002] ECR I-11543.

approaches taken that causes the problem! The Court concluded that the matter therefore called for action at Community level. It appears that the Court has neatly sustained subsidiarity as a legal principle on paper while conceding much in practice to legislative discretion.[46] As far as harmonization affecting the consumer interest is concerned, compliance with Article 5(1) EC is vital, and is policed by the Court. This is *Tobacco Advertising*.[47] Compliance with Article 5(2) is in principle vital too, but in the light of *R* v. *Secretary of State ex parte BAT and Imperial Tobacco* the Court seems unlikely to interfere with a legislative assertion that the subsidiarity principle is satisfied.

In summary, subsidiarity is an unavoidable feature of the debate about the pattern of EC consumer policy, as it is in other areas of EC regulatory competence. But it is in truth an invitation to engage in debate about how to achieve effective governance for the European market. The principle of subsidiarity does not in itself offer concrete answers.

THE CURRENT SHAPE OF EU CONSUMER POLICY

The importance of securing an integrated market has been at the heart of the Commission's policy documents concerning consumer protection since the internal market moved to political centre stage in the mid-1980s. The first of the Commission's three-year action plans on consumer policy, to cover 1990–92,[48] selected its points of focus with reference to their contribution to building consumer confidence necessary to support the realization of the internal market. The second three-year action plan for 1993–95 carried as a subtitle 'Placing the single market at the service of European consumers'.[49] The plan declared a commitment to concentrate on areas which are crucial for consumer confidence in the internal market. These included consumer information, access to justice and consumer health and safety. The third three-year action plan covered the period 1996–98 and discussed *inter alia* the need to tie up the loose ends of the internal market.[50] Subsequent Commission policy documents – the Consumer Policy Action Plan for 1999–2001,[51] the report on the *Action Plan for Consumer Policy 1999–2001* and on the *General Framework for Community activities in favour of consumers 1999–2003*[52] and most recently the Consumer Policy Strategy for 2002–2006[53] – retain an

---

[46] See similarly Case C-103/01 *Commission* v. *Germany* [2003] ECR I-5369 para. 47.
[47] Case C-376/98 note 22 above.
[48] COM (90) 98.
[49] COM (93) 378.
[50] COM (95) 519.
[51] COM (98) 696.
[52] COM (2001) 486, 23 August 2001.
[53] *OJ* 2002 C137/2.

emphasis on the advantages that should accrue to the consumer from an integrated market. It is evident that since the end of 1992 the process of market-making has not come to an end. The Commission itself has confessed that 'The Internal Market will never be "completed". The effort to maximize its performance is a process, not an event.'[54] The priorities pursued by the Commission (in particular) have shifted. It is more overtly concerned to emphasize the need for the effective application of the existing rules of the internal market rather than to pursue significant new legislative initiatives. This process of managing the internal market is directed at promoting belief that its rules are respected in practice as well as on paper. So in 2003 the Commission declared that

> Free movement of goods (and services) in the Internal Market is above all based on confidence. Confidence of businesses that they can sell their products on the basis of a clear and predictable regulatory framework. Confidence of Member States' administrations that the rules are respected in practice throughout the EU and that the competent authorities in other Member States will take appropriate action when this is not the case. And, of course, consumers' confidence in their rights and that the products they buy are safe and respect the environment. . . .[55]

As part of its drive to promote a predictable regulatory framework the Commission has increasingly identified harmonization which sets only minimum rules as inadequate to provide the basis for a smoothly functioning internal market. Preference is for a full or maximum model – whereby the Community sets both floor and ceiling of regulatory protection. The Commission's Consumer Policy Strategy for 2002–2006[56] advocates a 'move away from the present situation of different sets of rules in each Member State towards a more consistent environment for consumer protection across the EU'. As far as protection of consumers' economic interests is concerned, it is stated that there is a need 'to review and reform existing EU consumer protection directives, to bring them up-to-date and progressively adapt them from minimum harmonisation to full harmonisation measures'. A key priority in this move to full or maximum harmonization is 'to minimise variations in consumer protection rules across the EU that create fragmentation of the internal market to the detriment of consumers and business'.

For all the pre-existing policy linkage established between consumer policy and the completion of the internal market, the emphasis on maximum harmonization as a device to accelerate the integration of product and services

---

[54] Internal Market Scoreboard No. 11, November 2002, http://europa.eu.int/comm/internal_
    market/en/index.htm.
[55] Commission Communication of May 2003, Internal Market Strategy, Priorities 2003–2006,
    COM (2003) 238 final.
[56] COM (02) 208, *OJ* 2002 C137/2.

markets will, if maintained by the Commission and accepted by the Council and the Parliament, bring about a considerable re-shaping of the bargain that has hitherto underpinned the development of a consumer policy for the EC. The creation of a more efficient, competitive market in Europe is in the consumer interest. The rules of the internal market – governing free movement and competition policy – operate in this sense to promote the welfare of the consumer in Europe. The programme of legislative harmonization entails the setting of common rules of consumer protection which ought to provide a supplementary impetus towards a more smoothly functioning market. However, the development of the EC's consumer policy in the form of harmonization of measures that protect the economic interests of consumers has been conducted since the 1980s on the assumption that minimum rule-making is the normal style of Community intervention. This generates a pattern of regulation which mixes both Community rules, setting a minimum floor below which Member States may not slip, and national rules, in so far as stricter local standards are preferred. Examples will be met frequently in this book. If the Commission gets its way, this is now to be set aside in favour of a system of maximum harmonization which involves complete transfer of regulatory responsibility from Member States to the Community in the field covered by the measure in question.

The perception that it is not only in the commercial but also in the consumer interest to place such a high priority on eliminating the fragmented regulatory framework that follows from preference for a model of minimum harmonization is far from uncontested.[57] Commercial interests seek a common set of rules for the purposes of gearing up for a pan-European market, thereby reducing transactions costs and releasing economies of scale. This is by no means inevitably inconsistent with the consumer interest. But the risk from the consumer perspective is that common rules will – at least for some groups of consumers, in some Member States – result in a depreciation in standards of protection from market failure and/or market inequities. In so far as Member States are not allowed to set standards that are more stringent than the agreed Community norm, the proponent of effective consumer protection must rely heavily on influencing the political debate in order to ensure that harmonization is pitched at a high standard of protection – and must then seek to ensure that the relevant rules are faithfully interpreted and applied in this pro-consumer manner.

---

[57] T. Wilhelmsson, 'The abuse of the confident consumer as a justification for EC consumer law' (2004) 27 *Journal of Consumer Policy* 317; H.-W. Micklitz, 'De la Nécessité d'une Nouvelle Conception pour le Développement du Droit de la Consommation dans la Communauté Européenne', in J. Calais-Auloy (ed.), *Liber amicorum Jean Calais-Auloy, Études de droit de la consommation* (Paris, Dalloz, 2004). See also M. Dougan, 'Vive La Différence? Exploring the Legal Framework for Reflexive Harmonisation within the Single European Market' (2002) 1 *Annual of German and European Law* 113.

It is appropriate to add a broader horizon. Since the expiry of 'deadline 1992' the internal market has increasingly been presented as only one element in the EU's consumer-related activities. The third three-year action plan was published by the Commission in October 1995 and covered the period 1996–98.[58] The plan endorsed the importance of securing the advantages of the internal market, but the message of the document was that consumer policy should now look beyond the 1992 project. It asserted that (what was then) Article 129a (and is now Article 153) requires the Community to deal with a broad sweep of consumer issues, not simply those connected with the economics of the internal market project. Ten priorities for action were picked out. These relate to improving the education and information of consumers; devoting continued attention to ensuring that consumers' interests are taken fully into account in the internal market; the consumer aspect of financial services; protecting consumer interests in the supply of essential services of public utility; measures to enable consumers to benefit from opportunities presented by the information society; measures to improve consumer confidence in foodstuffs; encouraging a practical approach to sustainable consumption; strengthening and increasing consumer representation; assisting Central and Eastern and European countries to develop consumer policies; and, finally, consumer policy considerations in developing countries. The plan is none the less notable for a relative dearth of concrete legislative proposals.

The period 1999–2001 was covered by a consumer policy action plan published in 1998 by the Commission.[59] This was buttressed in January 1999 by Decision 99/283 of the Parliament and Council establishing a general framework for Community activities in favour of consumers in 1999–2003[60] and, in June 1999, by a Council Resolution on Community consumer policy in 1999–2001.[61] The Commission duly continued the paperchase by releasing its own report on the *Action Plan for Consumer Policy 1999–2001* and on the *General Framework for Community activities in favour of consumers 1999–2003* in August 2003.[62] These policy statements share common and persisting themes – most prominently the anxiety to secure effective application of the rules that have already been agreed at Community level and the concern to situate consumer policy in a broader context than market integration alone.

The Commission's Consumer Policy Strategy for 2002–2006 was communicated to the Parliament and the Council in early 2002.[63] It tracks actual and

---

[58]   COM (95) 519.
[59]   COM (98) 696.
[60]   *OJ* 1999 L34/1.
[61]   *OJ* 1999 C206/1.
[62]   COM (2001) 486, 23 August 2001.
[63]   *OJ* 2002 C137/2.

planned legislative developments in a 'rolling programme' set out in an annex. The Communication prompted a largely approving Council Resolution of 2 December 2002 on a Community consumer policy strategy for 2002–2006.[64] By Decision 2004/20 of the Parliament and Council a general framework for financing Community actions in support of consumer policy for the years 2004 to 2007 was established.[65]

Three priorities are selected in the main body of the 2002–2006 Strategy document. These are first, a high common level of consumer protection; second, effective enforcement (including administrative co-operation and redress); and, third, involvement of consumer organizations in EU policies. None of these three priorities has an obviously controversial flavour, although one might readily question whether the political mood will allow that they be put vigorously into practice. Nevertheless, scratch the surface and there is no doubt that the most central and controversial element in the policy menu set out in these documents is the new commitment to maximum harmonization, surveyed above. This shines a bright spotlight on the first of the three priorities, pursuit of a high common level of consumer protection. Under a model that excludes Member State capacity to choose to set more protective rules than are envisaged under the EC norm, the quality of the EC standard itself becomes crucially important to the nature of consumer protection throughout the integrated market. The model of maximum harmonization makes it vital for public and private actors anxious about a diminution in consumer protection consequent on harmonization to ensure that such concerns, reflected in the Treaty by Articles 95(3) and 153(2), are met in the shaping of a high level of protection in the common rule itself.[66] 'Upgrading' protection by subsequently claiming to wish to promote local preferences for stricter rules is excluded.

ENLARGEMENT

For consumer policy as for other areas of EU activity, recent planning has been heavily influenced by the enlargement of the European Union.[67] On 1 May 2004 ten countries joined the European Union, the largest ever wave of enlargement. There are now 25 Member States. Outside the EU's 'core 25' lies a further ring. The European Economic Area (EEA) came into being at the start of 1994 and now comprises the EU's 25 Member States plus Iceland,

---

[64]   *OJ* 2003 C11/1.
[65]   *OJ* 2004 L5/1.
[66]   Cf. the Opinion of the Economic and Social Committee on the 2002–2006 document, *OJ* 2003 C95/1, para. 1.2.2.
[67]   R. Simpson, 'EU enlargement: ticking the boxes or making history?' (2003) 13 *Consumer Policy Review* 43.

Liechtenstein and Norway. The EEA is based on a body of law that is in many respects comparable to, though not so ambitious as, the EU's system. Switzerland co-operates with the EU according to bilateral arrangements, but has no present intention to apply to join, while several countries in Eastern Europe, such as Bulgaria and Romania, have applied for membership. 'Europe' is not the European Union, but the EU's influence is now felt throughout the continent. And EU consumer policy accordingly carries a very wide and deep influence.

THE EFFECT OF THE DRAFT TREATY ESTABLISHING A CONSTITUTION FOR THE EU

The Nice Treaty was agreed in 2000 and came into force in 2003. It made the necessary detailed adjustments to the institutional architecture to prepare the Union for enlargement to a family of 25. However, a growing mood asserted a need for a fresher approach to reform to the EU. The Nice Treaty itself had attached to it a Declaration on the Future of the European Union which called for 'a deeper and wider debate about the future of the European Union'. In December 2001 the European Council in Laeken agreed to convene a convention on the 'Future of Europe'. It held its inaugural session under the chairmanship of Valery Giscard d'Estaing in February 2002. It was composed of national Parliamentarians, representatives of the EU institutions and other actors including representatives of civil society. The aim was to follow a debating procedure that would be far more transparent than previous practice centred on the 'closed doors' of the intergovernmental conference. It was hoped that this would begin to cure the widespread sense of citizen alienation from the endeavours of the European Union. The Convention itself took on the task of producing a draft 'constitutional Treaty' that would equip the Union with an efficient and comprehensible working method for the future. Even informed citizens can barely grasp the current rules of the Union's game, given the messy incrementally adjusted set of Treaties, and it was hoped that the Convention's text, agreed and released in July 2003, would serve the Union and its citizens better.[68]

The dominant figures of the Convention, most of all Giscard d'Estaing himself, urged that the text be accepted without adjustment by the Member States. Ultimately any proposed amendment to the EU's constituent Treaties must itself take the legal form of a Treaty and must be supported by and ratified by all the Member States. And, in the second half of 2003, it became

---

[68] Texts may be inspected at http://Europeanconvention.eu.int/bienvenue.asp?lang=EN& Content=.

apparent that some aspects of the Convention's agreed text were unpalatable to some of the Member States. In Brussels in December 2003 agreement proved impossible to reach. However, after the astute Irish Presidency that occupied the first half of 2004, a breakthrough was achieved in June 2004, and a constitutional Treaty was agreed by the heads of state and government. This was then signed in Rome on 29 October 2004.[69] It is now open to ratification as an international Treaty. It cannot enter into force until all 25 Member States have ratified it. Ratification depends on national constitutional procedures – some Member States are required to hold a referendum, others will choose to do so, while others again will ratify without resort to the electorate. Even if the ratification process proceeds smoothly in all 25 Member States it is improbable that the new Treaty will enter into force before late 2006. And it is highly likely that one or more Member States will encounter serious domestic difficulty in securing the approval required to underpin ratification. It is perfectly conceivable that the deal struck in June 2004 will never be converted into a binding international Treaty.

The text finally agreed in June 2004 bears the scars of the disagreements that prevented a consensus in December 2003 and which therefore required resolution according to compromises advanced by the Irish Presidency and further tweaked during the endgame in June 2004. These relate in particular to the weighting of voting for the purposes of achieving a qualified majority in Council and the composition of the Commission. However, the framework of the constitutional Treaty that will seek to negotiate the tortuous path to ratification remains visibly that proposed by the Convention on the Future of Europe in 2003. The pre-existing three-pillar structure of the European Union is to be replaced by a single Treaty creating a single Constitution for Europe. There are four parts – the general first part, the Charter of Fundamental Rights as the second part, the detail of the EU's common policies embedded in the third part, and final provisions collected in the fourth and final part. The EU will have legal personality (currently only the EC does). The principal concern is to improve transparency – to make the whole enterprise more intelligible. So much of what is at stake concerns improving the presentation of what is already done in the name of the EU, and not in effecting radical change. This is true of the provisions governing the EU's competence, which collect together existing provisions scattered throughout the Treaties and seek to impose order on them without making any changes of substance that are more than minor.[70] There is very little expansion in the EC's competence – far less

---

[69] The text is available at http://europa.eu.int/constitution/index_en.htm. This also provides information on the progress of ratification.

[70] E.g. P. Craig, 'Competence: clarity, conferral, containment and consideration' (2004) 29 *European Law Review* 323; J. Kokott and A. Rüth, 'The European Convention and its Draft Treaty establishing a Constitution for Europe: Appropriate Answers to the Laeken

than occurred at Maastricht or under the Single European Act. Similarly there
is a reorganization and relabelling of the legal instruments available to the
Union, but no fundamental change in their character. Co-decision between
Council and Parliament becomes the normal method of lawmaking in the EU,
which means that in most areas of EU activity a qualified majority vote in
Council is sufficient. Exceptionally unanimity in Council remains necessary
for action in the field of taxation and, partially, social policy and defence. The
detailed arrangements governing the common policies – tucked away in the
turgid Part III of the text – are very little changed from what already exists,
albeit that there is a helpful degree of reordering (so that, for example, the
horizontal provisions come at the beginning).

These adjustments affect the capacity of the EU to develop consumer
policy in the same way as they touch other areas of EU policy-making. In so
far as the newly agreed system puts in place an EU which is more efficient,
more transparent and less remote from the citizen, the corresponding advantages will be of relevance to the consumer activist as they will be to the envi-
ronmentalist, the advocate of effective transport policy, and so on. However,
at a more specific level, there is rather less that is of concrete interest to the
consumer. The references to the 'consumer' that appear in the text signed in
Rome on 29 October 2004 are perfectly familiar to the connoisseur of the
current basis of EC consumer law provided by the Treaty. This textual congruence confirms the impression that there is relatively little innovation in the
draft constitutional Treaty and that, moreover, some questions that are
currently open, for example the precise scope of the competence to harmonize
laws in the wake of the *Tobacco Advertising* judgment,[71] remain open.[72]

Article I-14 lists consumer protection as one of 11 areas in which the EU
enjoys a competence shared with its Member States. The internal market is on
the same list. An area of 'shared' competence is defined by Article I-12(2) in
the following terms: 'the Union and the Member States may legislate and
adopt legally binding acts in that area. The Member States shall exercise their
competence to the extent that the Union has not exercised, or has decided to
cease exercising, its competence.' Never before has the notion of shared
competence (or any other kind of competence) been defined in the Treaty; this
is part of the quest to make the EU more transparent. The definition is helpful,
although it is warned in Article I-12(6) that the 'scope of and arrangements for
exercising the Union's competences shall be determined by the provisions

Questions?' (2003) 40 *Common Market Law Review* 1315; A Dashwood, 'The Relationship
between the Member States and the European Union/ European Community' (2004) 41
Common Market Law Review 355.
[71]   Case C-376/98 note 22 above.
[72]   Cf. H.-W. Micklitz, N. Reich and S. Weatherill, 'EU Treaty Revision and Consumer
Protection' (2004) 27 *Journal of Consumer Policy* 367.

relating to each area in Part III'. In fact, although Part I of the Treaty provides a generally applicable definition of shared competence, the precise character of the several areas of shared competence varies in accordance with the detailed arrangements made in Part III. In fact, inspection of Part III reveals that the EU's 'shared' internal market competence is not identical to its 'shared' consumer protection competence in the matter of the residual scope allowed to national autonomy. This conforms to the current pattern.

Article II-98 contains the commitment of the Union to a 'high level' of consumer protection. This provision was already contained within the Charter of Fundamental Rights of the European Union proclaimed at Nice by the Presidents of the Parliament, Council and Commission in December 2000,[73] but the consecration of the Charter as Part II of the draft Treaty enhances the constitutional character of this assertion. It was not binding in law; it will, once the new Treaty enters into force, become so. Still, its value in a specifically legal context is limited by its aspirational wording.[74] It is improbable that it could be employed of itself to provide the foundation for a successful challenge to the validity of a legal act, though it certainly forms part of the broader constitutional case that a high level of consumer protection is part of the EU's mission. Much the same comment could be directed at Article III-120. This provides that 'Consumer protection requirements shall be taken into account in defining and implementing other Union policies and activities.' A closely comparable proviso is currently situated in Article 153(2) EC but in the draft Treaty it is promoted to earlier in the text, as part of the reorganization of the horizontal provisions designed to group them together at the start of Part III of the text, which takes 'The Policies and Functioning of the Union' as its title. Its relevance across the whole sweep of Union policy and practice is thereby underlined. The quest to secure a high level of consumer protection also appears in Article III-172(3) in connection with the competence to harmonize national laws, echoing the existing Article 95(3). There is no attempt in Article 172 to reshape the legal base governing harmonization of laws. The ambiguities of the *Tobacco Advertising* judgment were left well alone in this reform process and therefore they remain live issues. A Protocol allocates a formal status to national Parliaments in monitoring the exercise of competences. They are empowered to issue a 'reasoned opinion' objecting to Commission legislative proposals, which forces Commission reconsideration provided at least one-third of national Parliaments are involved. However, this applies only where the existence of competence is claimed under Article I-18(2) – 'flexibility', the successor to the current Article 308 – and where a violation of the

---

[73] Note 24 above.
[74] Kiss, note 25 above.

subsidiarity principle is alleged. So this procedure does not cover use of the legal base authorizing harmonization except in so far as the issue of compliance with the subsidiarity principle is raised.[75]

Articles III-161, 162, 167, 227 and 228 simply repeat the flimsy references to the consumer currently found in provisions concerning competition law, State Aids and CAP, and Article III-424 makes a peripheral reference to the consumer in relation to remote regions. It is well known that the consumer interest is properly seen as an element in the development and application of other common policies even in the absence of any developed articulation of what is at stake in such thematic interconnection. This is simply reflected, unchanged, in the 2004 text.

That leaves only Article III-235, which plays the role currently performed by Article 153 EC, albeit displaying textual changes reflecting the alterations made elsewhere to the vocabulary of EU law and boasting only four, not five, paragraphs because of the migration of the 'horizontal' provision, the current Article 153(2), to the earlier reaches of Part III of the draft Treaty where, as mentioned above, it is numbered Article III-120.

Article III-235, entitled 'Consumer Protection', provides:

1. In order to promote the interests of consumers and to ensure a high level of consumer protection, the Union shall contribute to protecting the health, safety and economic interests of consumers, as well as to promoting their right to information, education and to organise themselves in order to safeguard their interests.
2. The Union shall contribute to the attainment of the objectives referred to in paragraph 1 through: (a) measures adopted pursuant to Article III-172 in the context of the establishment and functioning of the internal market; (b) measures which support, supplement and monitor the policy pursued by the Member States.
3. European laws or framework laws shall establish the measures referred to in paragraph 2(b). Such laws shall be adopted after consultation of the Economic and Social Committee.
4. Acts adopted pursuant to paragraph 3 shall not prevent any Member State from maintaining or introducing more stringent protective provisions. Such provisions must be compatible with the Constitution. They shall be notified to the Commission.

It will be immediately plain that the core of this provision remains true to the pattern of the current Article 153 EC. The Union's objectives, covered in the first paragraph, are essentially unaltered. A cross-reference to the harmonization of laws in pursuit of a well-functioning internal market is preserved (Article III-235(2)(a)), while the consumer-specific competence remains carefully limited in scope (Article III-235(2)(b)). Minimum rule-making is

---

[75] For criticism see S. Weatherill, 'Better Competence Monitoring' (2005) 30 *European Law Review* 23.

preserved by Article III-235(4), but only for measures adopted under Article III-235(2)(b). The provision governing harmonization of laws remains silent on this point of pre-emption, as it is silent now (see Chapter 3).

Were the Treaty establishing a Constitution to secure ratification and enter into force, the amendments made in the area of consumer protection would be largely cosmetic – renumbering, reordering and reorganization, in the main. The principal thematic issues which are the subject of examination in this book would in no sense be 'solved'.

2. Negative law and market integration

MARKET INTEGRATION AND CONSUMER CHOICE

The transformation of relatively small-scale national markets into a large single Community market will stimulate competition and induce producers to achieve maximum efficiency in order to protect, and *a fortiori* to expand, their market share. As a matter of economic theory, this intensification of competition should serve the consumer by increasing the available choice of goods and services, thereby inducing improvements in their quality and reduction in their price.

The law is an instrument in this process. Article 28 (ex 30) EC serves to eliminate national measures that partition product markets. Article 49 (ex 59) EC fulfils the same function in the market for services. Removal of barriers to cross-border trade in goods and services stimulates competition and enhances consumer choice. The Treaty competition rules too have as one objective the prevention of practices that cause fragmentation of the market along national lines. In this sense, the law of market integration is itself a form of (indirect) consumer policy. The achievement of a common market will benefit the consumer, and accordingly the legal prohibition of national measures and practices that impede trade across borders is in the consumer interest. These prohibitions are frequently grouped together as 'negative law': law that forbids action hostile to the interpenetration of national markets.

Consumer choice is an occasional explicit visitor to the Court's judgments. The Court has declared that the legislation of a Member State must not 'crystallize given consumer habits so as to consolidate an advantage acquired by national industries concerned to comply with them'. The Court has made this observation in the context of both fiscal rules which favour typical national products[1] and technical rules which exert a similar protectionist effect.[2] The first case involved the British system of taxing alcoholic beverages, which favoured beer over wine and which accordingly protected the typical domestic product, beer, from competition from a typically imported product, wine. The second case involved German rules which were based on assumptions

---

[1] Art. 90 (ex 95) EC: Case 170/78 *Commission* v. *United Kingdom* [1980] ECR 417.
[2] Art 28 (ex 30) EC: Case 178/84 *Commission* v. *Germany* [1987] ECR 1227.

about beer-making techniques typical in Germany but not the norm elsewhere, which resulted in the German beer market being closed off to brewers based in other states using different recipes. In neither case did the European Court's ruling prevent producers adopting favoured techniques. Rather, the Court was concerned to prevent the public authorities making choices on behalf of consumers. The elimination of the national rule permitted consumers to make their own choice without the distorting influence of state intervention.

A case dealing with the services sector, *Commission* v. *France*,[3] provides a simple illustration of the Court's approach. French rules obliged tourist guides to obtain a licence. This rule exerted a restrictive effect on the ability of tourist guides from outside France to accompany groups who wished to tour France. The Court did not deny the legitimacy of the objective of ensuring proper cultural and artistic appreciation of the host country, but found the rules in question disproportionately restrictive. As the Court observed, the French rules would be likely to have the effect that visiting groups would be denied the opportunity to be guided by someone 'who is familiar with their language, their interests and their specific expectations'. The decision serves to enhance market integration and consumer choice. Much of this chapter is taken up with surveying the implications of the Court's case law which has elaborated the Treaty rules governing the free movement of goods and services into powerful instruments for market restructuring in Europe.

Deregulating the market by abolishing state intervention incompatible with Articles 28 (ex 30) and 49 (ex 59) is accompanied by the use of the Treaty competition rules to control anti-competitive and anti-integrative practices in the private sector. The Court has on occasion explicitly referred to the consumer interest in securing free competition in accordance with Article 81 (ex 85). In *Zuchner* v. *Bayerische Vereinsbank AG*[4] the Court ruled that Article 81 (ex 85) may apply where firms have abandoned their independence in favour of unlawful collusion which suppresses competition, 'thus depriving their customers of any genuine opportunity to take advantage of services on more favourable terms which would be offered to them under normal conditions of competition'. *Cooperatieve vereniging Suiker Unie UA and others* v. *Commission*[5] concerned practices which led to the isolation of national markets from cross-border competition. The Court found that such arrangements were 'to the detriment of effective freedom of movement of the products in the common market and of the freedom of consumers to choose their suppliers'. For agreements that fall within Article 81(1), exemption is available under Article 81(3) only on condition that it, *inter alia*, 'contributes to

3   Case C-154/89 [1991] ECR I-659.
4   Case 172/80 [1981] ECR 2021.
5   Cases 40–48, 50, 54–56, 111, 113 & 114/73 [1975] ECR 1663.

improving the production of goods or to promoting technical or economic progress, while allowing consumers a fair share of the resulting benefit . . .'. This is one of the few explicit references to the consumer in the Treaty, although its impact as a tool of consumer policy is diluted, first, by the point that 'consumer' in this context covers any user of the item, not simply the end user[6] and, second, by the Commission's typical readiness to assume that provided an agreement promotes efficient commercial structures and provided a sufficient level of competition endures, then the consumer will benefit in consequence.[7] The 'consumer benefit' criterion therefore commonly performs no independent function. In 2004 the Commission issued guidelines on the application of Article 81(3).[8] These insist on the role of Article 81 in promoting consumer welfare. The guidelines state that the requirement that consumers obtain a fair share of the resulting benefit as required by Article 81(3) is satisfied provided that the costs to consumers of the restriction of competition which brings the agreement within Article 81(1) are at least neutralized by the benefits accruing to consumers from the arrangements. It seems that the criterion is not satisfied only where the consumer will be worse off. The guidelines seek to map out how to assess efficiencies and how they may be passed on to consumers.[9]

Article 82 (ex 86) has a role to play in sustaining consumer choice. Included in the list of illustrative abuses of a dominant position in Article 82 (ex 86) is 'limiting production, markets or technical development to the prejudice of consumers . . .'. This may be used to require a private firm occupying a dominant position to respond to consumer demand. The Commission's insistence that television companies which printed separate guides to future programmes using copyright over the listings to prevent the publication of a single, integrated guide had breached Article 82 (ex 86) was upheld by the European Court in *RTE and ITP* v. *Commission*, on appeal from the decision of the Court of First Instance. The Court observed that the companies, the sole sources of the raw material needed for compiling a weekly guide, had unjustifiably blocked the appearance of a new product for which a potential consumer demand existed.[10] The Court has subsequently shown itself to be cautious when invited to strengthen the intrusion of Article 82 (ex 86) into the power of dominant firms to decide how to operate in the market. Exercising an exclusive right by refusing to grant a licence may be abusive within the

---

6   This is better reflected in the French text, which refers to *utilisateur*, rather than *consommateur*.
7   Cf. A. Evans, 'European Competition Law and Consumers: the Article 85(3) Exemption' [1981] *European Competition Law Review* 425.
8   *OJ* 2004 C101/97.
9   Paras 83–104.
10 Cases C-241/91 P, C-242/91 P *RTE and ITP* v. *Commission* [1995] ECR II-801.

meaning of Article 82 EC, but in *Oscar Bronner* v. *Mediaprint*[11] the Court described the circumstances that obtained in *RTE and ITP* as 'exceptional'. In *IMS Health*[12] the Court explained that a refusal by a copyright-holder to give access to a product or service indispensable for carrying on a particular business would be treated as abusive if it prevented the emergence of a new product for which there is a potential consumer demand, if it was also unjustified and if, in addition, it excluded any competition on a secondary market. Where such circumstances obtain – which will be rare, but did occur in the case of the television guides – this Treaty provision may be used to extract the supply of products and services that are of appeal to consumers. Article 82 has also been used to condemn practices of dominant firms that discriminate against consumers on the basis of nationality. In *1998 Football World Cup*[13] the Commission concluded that the channelling of the availability of tickets bought 'blind' (in advance of the draw for the tournament) in a manner that favoured French nationals and residents over other EU nationals was a breach of Article 82. It explicitly decided that 'Consumers' interests are protected by Article 82', adding that this may be achieved by prohibiting conduct by dominant undertakings which impairs free and undistorted competition or which is directly prejudicial to consumers.[14] The organizers were fined, and subsequent major sporting events held in the EU have sold tickets to EU nationals without reference to the nationality of individual purchasers.

TOWARDS CONSUMER RIGHTS

The Court has developed EC trade law into a charter of consumer choice. The consumer is able to benefit from the fruits of market integration by buying goods and services imported by traders from other Member States while resident in his or her home state. This may be taken further, into the realms of active consumer rights. In *GB–INNO–BM* v. *Confédération du Commerce Luxembourgeois (CCL)* the Court declared that[15]

> Free movement of goods concerns not only traders but also individuals. It requires, particularly in frontier areas, that consumers resident in one Member State may travel freely to the territory of another Member State to shop under the same conditions as the local population.

[11] Case C-7/97 [1998] ECR I-7791.
[12] Case C-418/01 judgment of 29 April 2004.
[13] Dec. 2000/12/EC, *OJ* 2000 L5/55. See S. Weatherill, '0033149875354: Fining the Organisers of the 1998 Football World Cup', [2000] *European Competition Law Review* 275.
[14] Para. 100 of the Decision.
[15] Case C-362/88 [1990] ECR I-667.

The Court determined in *Luisi and Carbone* v. *Ministero del Tesero*[16] that 'tourists, persons receiving medical treatment and persons travelling for the purpose of education or business' are to be regarded as recipients of services who enjoy the right of free movement under Article 49 (ex 59). So the consumer as an economically active migrant enjoys rights of entry into and residence and non-discrimination in other Member States. The Court has interpreted the right to non-discriminatory treatment within the scope of the Treaty broadly. In *Cowan* v. *Le Trésor Public*[17] the European Court found that a tourist, as a recipient of services, was entitled to compensation for criminally inflicted injuries on the same terms as those applicable to nationals of the host state. This was the product of the combined application of Article 49 (ex 59), the free movement of services, and Article 12 (ex 6), the rule against nationality discrimination within the scope of application of the Treaty. The Court's decision in *Cowan* envisages an extended notion of the need to ensure equal access to social benefits as part of the policy of securing the elimination of impediments to migration.

The notion of consumer rights was bolstered by the post-1992 legislative adjustments which permitted consumers (though not commercial operators) to buy goods duty-paid in another Member State and return with them for private consumption without hindrance by the home state.

It remains questionable how far beyond equal treatment with host-state nationals and open access to markets of other states it is necessary for the law to reach in order to induce consumers actively to explore the advantages of the internal market. The question is: to what extent is 'positive' Community legislation required in support of 'negative' law? This is a key question in the general development of Community consumer policy. Its constitutional dimension is considered in Chapter 3 in connection with fixing the scope of the competence conferred by Article 95 of the Treaty to harmonize national laws, and, more generally, the evolution of a legislative framework of consumer protection law at Community level is traced through the remaining chapters of this book. The concern of the current chapter remains 'negative law' – EC law that controls national practices which impede cross-border trade.

Although the law of market integration is itself a form of consumer policy in the sense that it promotes a more efficiently competitive market for Europe, it is more normal in the field of 'negative law' for the examination of the compatibility of national rules which obstruct trade with substantive Community law to be undertaken without explicit reference to the position of the consumer. For all the hints of consumer as right-holder in the law of the internal market, the consumer is normally cast merely as the passive benefi-

[16]   Cases 286/82 & 26/83 [1984] ECR 377.
[17]   Case 186/87 [1989] ECR 195.

ciary of cross-border commercial activity. Indeed the bold assertion of consumer rights in *GB–INNO–BM* appears in a ruling delivered in the context of a Belgian trader's successful reliance on Article 28 (ex 30) to set aside a Luxembourg rule obstructive of a cross-border commercial strategy.

COMPETING NOTIONS OF THE CONSUMER INTEREST

National rules which obstruct cross-border trade are enforceable only where they serve an interest of sufficient importance to override the principle of free movement and where they are apt and proportionate to achieve that objective. It falls to the regulating state to show that its rules are justified.[18] One justification for obstructive national rules recognized under Community law is the protection of the consumer. There are a number of cases under both Articles 28 (ex 30) and 49 (ex 59) which pit the consumer interest in integration, served by eliminating trade-restrictive national laws, against the consumer interest in protection, which dictates the maintenance of national regulations. National consumer protection law may come into collision with Community law of market integration, which is itself designed to advance the consumer interest. These cases force the Court to develop its own notion of the consumer interest in defining the scope of application of Community trade law. This is in accordance with one of this book's themes that the EC institutions, in this instance the Court, have been forced by the growth of EC law and policy to develop an approach to the consumer interest despite the absence in the Treaty pre-Maastricht of any explicit place for consumer policy (Chapter 1). That is, the simple divide between the Community's interest in securing market integration and the Member States' responsibility to citizens to select appropriate levels of social and economic regulation breaks down as the deepening process of integration calls into question national measures that may initially appear remote from cross-border trade.

This is an especially intriguing inquiry because it involves the Court making an examination of two competing conceptions of the consumer interest. Negative law is based on assumptions about the advantages of cross-border trade as a means of improving the functioning of the economy to the benefit of the consumer. Accordingly, national measures that impair product and service market integration are treated with suspicion. But some such national measures will themselves reflect domestic concern to protect the consumer from perceived failings of the market system. This is the clash of competing consumer interests: the Community-driven notion of free trade

---

[18] Case 227/82 *Van Bennekom* [1983] ECR 3883, Case C-14/02 *ATRAL SA* judgment of 8 May 2003.

versus the national choice about protection. Quite apart from positive regulation of the market in the consumer interest agreed by the political institutions
of the Community, the Court becomes a participant in the debate about the
place of the consumer in a market economy where the application of negative
law forces it to confront the validity of national choices about consumer
protection that confine consumer choice.[19]

ARTICLES 28–30 (EX 30–36): THE BASIC PATTERN OF THE LAW OF THE FREE MOVEMENT OF GOODS

The Court's case law relevant to Article 28–30 (ex 30–36) EC is vast. However,
it can be boiled down to two vital elements. First, what is a barrier to trade for
the purposes of application of Article 28 (ex 30)? Second, what scope is
allowed for justification of national measures that are qualified as barriers to
trade? The readier the Court is to treat national measures as barriers to trade,
the deeper the incursion of EC law into national regulatory autonomy. And vice
versa. The wider the scope allowed to the possibility to justify barriers to trade,
the more room for manoeuvre is handed back to national regulatory autonomy
– and the more weight is placed on the process of legislative harmonization at
EC level as the way to advance integration. And vice versa.

The identification of what is a trade barrier – the first element in the legal
inquiry – and the evaluation of whether a trade barrier is justified – the second
element – has generated a torrent of litigation, charted by a wealth of academic investigation. This chapter deals with the evolution of the law from the
particular perspective of consumer protection, but the reader is encouraged to
be aware of the wider literature on defining a trade barrier[20] and on exploring
the scope and manner of justification,[21] as well as on the broader sweep of the
law of free movement.[22]

---

[19] S. Weatherill, 'The Evolution of European Consumer Law and Policy: from well-informed
      consumer to confident consumer,' in H.-W. Micklitz (ed.), *Rechtseinheit oder Rechtsvielfalt
      in Europa?* (Baden-Baden: Nomos, 1996).
[20] C. Barnard and S. Deakin, 'Market Access and Regulatory Competition,' ch. 8 in Barnard and
      Scott, *The Law of the Single European Market* (Oxford: Hart Publishing, 2002); S.
      Enchelmaier, 'The Awkward Selling of a Good Idea, or a Traditionalist Interpretation of *Keck*'
      (2003) 22 *Yearbook of European Law* 249.
[21] S. Weatherill, 'Recent case law concerning the free movement of goods: mapping the fron-
      tiers of market deregulation' (1999) 36 *Common Market Law Review* 51; M. Poiares Maduro,
      'Striking the elusive balance between economic freedom and social rights in the EU', ch. 13
      in P. Alston (ed.), *The EU and Human Rights* (Oxford: Oxford University Press, 1999).
[22] C. Barnard, *The Substantive Law of the EU: the Four Freedoms* (Oxford: Oxford University
      Press, 2004); P. Oliver and Roth, 'The Internal Market and the Four Freedoms' (2004) 41
      Common Market Law Review 407. J. Snell, *Goods and Services in EC Law* (Oxford: Oxford
      University Press, 2002).

Article 28 (ex 30) covers 'all trading rules enacted by member states which are capable of hindering, directly or indirectly, actually or potentially, intra-Community trade'.[23] This is the 'Dassonville' formula, narrowed in *Keck and Mithouard*,[24] in which the Court, concerned to refocus Article 28 (ex 30) on to the elimination of market-partitioning measures, not simply measures which affect commerce generally, ruled that there is no actual or potential, direct or indirect, barrier to inter-state trade where national laws limit or prohibit certain selling arrangements, provided those laws apply to all traders active on the national territory and provided that they affect in the same way in law and in fact the marketing of national products and those originating in other Member States. This means, in short, that it is not enough to bring Article 28 into play to show that a national rule curtails the volume of sales. It must be shown in addition that the impact is felt more heavily by imports than by domestic production.

According to this approach a ban or restriction on the marketing of a product is in principle capable of being caught by Article 28 (ex 30) where it affects intra-Community trade. More subtly, rules governing product composition are similarly capable of being caught by Article 28 (ex 30) where they impede the access to the market of goods made elsewhere according to different regulatory specifications. It is also possible to find a trade barrier falling within the Article 28 net where a state prohibits the advertising of a product, even if in principle all products suffer the same disadvantage. In *Konsumentombudsmannen* v. *Gourmet International Products*[25] the Court found that a Swedish ban on the advertising of alcoholic drinks harmed imports more severely than home-produced goods because the latter already enjoyed the advantage of familiarity to local consumers. The Court's decision reflected what Advocate General Jacobs had in his Opinion on the case described as the 'primordial' role of advertising in penetrating new markets. But each case must be examined carefully on its facts and the trader will not succeed in forcing the state to justify its regulatory choices if the measure in question lacks a sufficient impact on imports or importers in particular. In *Hünermund*[26] a challenge under Article 28 was directed against a rule preventing pharmacists from advertising particular products outside their pharmacies, even though it was perfectly permissible to sell such products within the shops. The Court accepted that such a rule suppresses opportunities for sales promotion. It may therefore restrict the volume of sales of goods, and that this restriction may be felt by imported goods. But there was no reason to think that the rules would not apply equally to all traders operating within the national territory nor that

---

[23] Case 8/74 *Procureur du Roi* v. *Dassonville* [1974] ECR 837.
[24] Cases C-267 & 268/91 *Keck and Mithouard* [1993] ECR I-6097.
[25] Case C-405/98 [2001] ECR I-1795.
[26] Case C-292/92 *Hünermund* [1993] ECR I-6787.

they would not affect all goods in the same manner. The rule impeded general commercial freedom but it was not a trade barrier within the meaning of Article 28. This had the key jurisdictional consequence that Germany was not required to justify the rule according to standards recognized by EC trade law. It was instead treated as an expression of local choice about how to regulate the market. Similarly in *Herbert Karner GmbH* v. *Troostwijk GmbH*[27] the Court concluded that Austrian restrictions on methods of advertising would likely cause a diminution in the volume of sales of goods but that there was no evidence that this would be felt particularly severely by imports or importers. The Court explained that its ruling was based on different factual findings from those that had underpinned *Konsumentombudsmannen* v. *Gourmet International Products*. In that case the total nature of the Swedish ban had been enough to persuade it that trade in imports would be peculiarly disadvantaged, and that accordingly a justification for the national rule was required.

Assuming a trade barrier of the required kind is identified, justification for obstructive rules under the relevant Chapter of the Treaty is available only under Article 30 (ex 36). This provides that 'The provisions of Articles 28 and 29 shall not preclude prohibitions or restrictions on imports, exports or goods in transit justified on grounds of . . . (inter alia) the protection of health and life of humans, animals or plants.' There is no explicit reference to the consumer in Article 30, but the notion of the protection of the health and life of humans is capable of covering the protection of the physical integrity of the consumer. Accordingly, national rules designed to secure health and safety may be enforced notwithstanding any impediment to integration, provided the conditions under Article 30 are satisfied. Justification under Article 30 encompasses the compatibility with Community law of both the end in view and the means chosen to achieve that end. This is inherent in the second sentence of Article 30, which declares that 'such prohibitions or restrictions shall not, however, constitute a means of arbitrary discrimination or a disguised restriction on trade between member states.' Accordingly, it is incumbent on the Member State to show that the national measure adopted is apt to achieve the end in view and the least restrictive of trade necessary to achieve that end.

The Court is not prepared simply to accept at face value Member State submissions that national measures are required to defend domestic health standards. In some cases the Court has demonstrated vigorous scepticism about an alleged threat to health. In *Commission* v. *United Kingdom*[28] the UK sought to demonstrate that its restrictions on the import of poultry were justi-

---

[27]   Case C-71/02 judgment of 25 March 2004. See J. Stuyck, 'Annotation' (2004) 41 *Common Market Law Review* 1683.
[28]   Case 40/82 [1982] ECR 2793.

fied in the light of the need to tackle the spread of Newcastle disease. The Court remarked on the haste with which the measures had been introduced in the approach to Christmas 1981 at a time when British turkey breeders were appealing for protection. There was scant evidence of a seriously considered health policy, and the UK, acting in breach of Article 28 (ex 30) by obstructing imports, was unable to seek refuge in Article 30 (ex 36). In such circumstances the Court is, in effect, identifying national measures as devious protectionism in favour of home producers. Such a ruling, prohibiting national measures, asserts consumer choice through market integration.

However, Article 28 (ex 30) is not a charter for irresistible deregulation. States may permissibly protect domestic consumers even where this impedes integration. This is possible even where scientific evidence advanced to show a health risk posed by the product subject to control is equivocal. For example, in *Eyssen*[29] Dutch rules banning the use of nisin, a preservative, in processed cheese were presented as measures of health protection, yet other states were prepared to allow the use of nisin, adopting a different view of inconclusive scientific evidence about the safety of the substance. The Court held that a state may take precautions to protect its consumers against health risks in accordance with Article 30 (ex 36) where there is genuine scientific doubt about the safety of the product. Community law does not depress national standards of protection to the lowest common denominator prevailing among the Member States. More recently the Court has adopted the language of the 'precautionary principle' in conceding to Member States the space to maintain rules that restrict trade in goods, especially foodstuffs, on the basis that there is doubt about the effects of particular ingredients on the health of consumers. States enjoy a 'discretion relating to the protection of public health [which] is particularly wide where it is shown that uncertainties continue to exist in the current state of scientific research'.[30] The Court insists, however, that national authorization procedures shall be targeted at identified risks, rather than applying indiscriminately or in cases of purely hypothetical risk, and that they shall be transparent and open to challenge.[31]

An analogous perception of the limits to integration through negative law may be observed in *Aragonesa de Publicidad Exterior SA (APESA)* v. *Departamento de Sanidad y Seguridad Social de la Generalitat de Cataluna (DSSC)*,[32] where the Court found that measures that restricted the advertising

---

[29] Case 53/80 [1981] ECR 4091.

[30] Case C-192/01 *Commission* v. *Denmark* judgment of 23 September 2003. Comparable issues arise in international trade law; see C. Button, *The Power to Protect: Trade, Health and Uncertainty in the WTO* (Oxford: Hart Publishing, 2004).

[31] Case C-192/01 note 30 above; also e.g. Case C-95/01 *John Greenham* judgment of 5 February 2004, Case C-387/99 *Commission* v. *Germany* judgment of 29 April 2004; Case C-41/02 *Commission* v. *Netherlands* judgment of 2 December 2004.

[32] Cases C-1, C-176/90 [1991] ECR I-4151.

of alcoholic drink above a certain threshold strength might impede market integration,[33] but that such intervention in the market might be accepted as part of a seriously considered health policy – even where other Member States were content with more permissive regimes. A comparable approach emerges in the field of free movement of services, where the Court, asked to consider the compatibility of France's *Loi Evin* with Article 49, concluded that the restrictions on trade consequent on the prohibition of advertisements for alcoholic drinks at sports events broadcast on television were a justified expression of concern to contain alcohol abuse.[34] So consumer choice is not the inevitable result of the impact of EC negative law; regulation by the public authorities remains permitted even where it obstructs cross-border trade, provided both ends and means are capable of justification against the standards recognized by Community law.

THE 'CASSIS DE DIJON' PRINCIPLE

National measures which are designed to protect the economic interests of the consumer, yet which impede trade, such as rules against deceptive marketing practices or misleading product description or rules encouraging or requiring the provision of information to consumers, seem to fall beyond the scope of the justifications envisaged by Article 30 (ex 36). However, provided they are origin-neutral, such rules are capable of being defended despite their restrictive effect on trade. The assessment of the compatibility of such national measures with Article 28 (ex 30) takes place against the background of one of the Court's most remarkable creations, the 'Cassis de Dijon' line of authority. This applies where disparity between technical standards in different Member States relating to composition and, more extensively still, relating to marketing are shown to be capable of impeding trade by affecting imported goods more heavily in fact than home-produced goods.

In the case itself French blackcurrant liqueur could not be sold in Germany because it fell below the minimum alcohol requirement for such goods under German law.[35] There was no question of discrimination on the face of the measure: it applied to all such products wherever they were made. But in practice a product made in another state where different technical specifications

---

[33] Although, post-*Keck and Mithouard* above, an importer would have to show, loosely, how the rule affected cross-border commercial strategy (e.g. by preventing an integrated advertising plan) and not merely commercial freedom. Only then would the state be called on to justify its rules.

[34] Case C-262/02 *Commission* v. *France*, Case C-429/02 *Bacardi* v. *TF1* judgments of 13 July 2004.

[35] Case 120/78 *Rewe Zentrale* v. *Bundesmonopolverwaltung für Branntwein* [1979] ECR 649 ('Cassis de Dijon').

prevailed could not gain access to the German market without modification. German products, by contrast, would naturally conform to their domestic regulatory system and would obtain an inevitable competitive advantage in Germany. Out-of-state producers would be unable to devise an integrated strategy for the whole EC market. German consumers would be denied the opportunity to choose products made according to different traditions. Short of harmonization of laws, the market would remain fragmented along national lines. This prospect prompted the Court to draw together and to refine its case law and to devise a formula which has proved an enduring basis for assessing the lawfulness of trade barriers that arise in consequence on diversity between national rules:

> In the absence of common rules relating to the production and marketing of alcohol ... it is for the member states to regulate all matters relating to the production and marketing of alcohol and alcoholic beverages on their own territory.

> Obstacles to movement in the Community resulting from disparities between the national laws in question must be accepted in so far as those provisions may be recognised as being necessary in order to satisfy mandatory requirements relating in particular to the effectiveness of fiscal supervision, the protection of public health, the fairness of commercial transactions and the defence of the consumer.

The subtlety of this statement deserves to be appreciated. The Court begins by appearing to confirm that Member States may regulate as they please on their own territory. This seems to uphold the regulatory competence of the 'host state' – the state into which goods are imported from another state. But then the Court deftly turns this concession right around. Where the host state's rules impede cross-border trade because they are different from laws applied in the home state – the state from which the goods originate – then they may be applied against imported goods only if shown to be justified. This model complies with the structure set out in the Treaty. Articles 28 and 30 similarly put local rules that obstruct trade to the test of justification. But the Court in *Cassis de Dijon* has taken that basic pattern and recrafted it into a more elaborate formula for judging the validity of national measures of market regulation.

The same formula has been increasingly applied by the Court to Article 49 (ex 59) where similar economic issues arise in the services sector and where the Court has accordingly developed a similar legal formula involving an assessment of the balance between the consumer interest in market integration which would follow from the abolition of the national rule and the consumer interest in protection at national level at the expense of integration.

CASSIS DE DIJON: INSTITUTIONAL IMPLICATIONS

The Court's moulding of Articles 28 and 49 in this fashion has significant institutional consequences. Prohibiting a national rule contributes to free trade without the need for the Community to adopt legislation in the area. This has the gratifying consequence that diversity persists. Mutual recognition of diverse national traditions secures wider choice. This consequence of negative law has been termed 'negative harmonization'. Free trade is brought about by removing obstructive national rules. It is a fundamental aspect of the deregulatory impulse that pervades the law of market integration. A range of national rules that act as preconditions to market access are, if shown to be unjustified interference with the market, replaced by no precondition at all. Only where national rules are lawful, because they protect an interest of sufficient weight to override the law of market integration, is a positive response required in order to liberalize the market. This is 'positive law': harmonization – the adoption of common Community rules which replace divergent national rules in the field. Harmonization is both deregulatory in effect and re-regulatory. Up to 25 national rules are replaced by one, established at Community level.[36]

The 'Cassis de Dijon' line of jurisprudence has substantially reduced the Commission's workload in the area of harmonization. Article 28 may now be employed to defeat a great many national technical rules which, before *Cassis de Dijon*, seemed capable of partitioning the market until such time as harmonization legislation could be adopted. Freed of this vast burden, the Commission has been able to concentrate its harmonization work in the remaining areas where national rules act as lawful impediments to trade and where Community intervention is appropriate. The Commission quickly identified the *Cassis de Dijon* judgment as central to its plan for the building of an internal market.[37] Moreover, the extension of the Article 28 prohibition and the consequent diminution in the scope of the legislative programme has attractions beyond the perspective of a reduction in the Commission's workload. By shifting the focus to the circulation of traditional national products and away from the need to adopt common Community rules, the rise of the 'Europroduct' is stifled. The need to sacrifice distinct national regulatory philosophies is averted by the Court's eloquent and imaginative preference for negative over positive Community law.

The placing of the line between lawful and unlawful national measures is fundamentally important. The Court, in its *Cassis de Dijon* formula, claims for

---

[36] The many nuances of harmonization policy, which depart from this simple model, are tracked throughout this book. Chapter 3 covers the issues at a general level.
[37] Commission Communication, *OJ* 1980 C256/2; COM (85) 310, the 'White Paper' on the Completion of the Internal Market, para. 61 *et seq.*

itself the sensitive function of judging the competing merits of integration and national regulation, a choice which is institutionally significant in its implications for the margin between judge-led negative harmonization and the need for positive harmonization by legislative act.

CASSIS DE DIJON: A CRITIQUE

It has been suggested that the Court may prioritize integration over legitimate national initiatives of consumer protection as part of an over-enthusiastic pursuit of an integrative function that should more properly belong with the Community's legislature. This debate will be tracked below in the Court's case law. In part, it depends on perceptions of the capacity of the consumer to look after him- or herself in the market. Among some commentators, there is a perceived risk that even legitimate initiatives of national consumer protection may be inhibited because of the oppressive effect of Community law which creates a climate of uncertainty about the lawfulness of national initiatives. This could lead to a 'regulatory gap' in which national action is deterred, but no Community action occurs either. For some, this drives the deregulatory impulse of Community law too far into the legitimate scope of market regulation. A further aspect to the regulatory gap may arise because of the notorious difficulty in achieving legislative action at Community level even where the need for it is widely recognized. Slow progress at legislative level is frequently not attributable simply to disagreement about the need for a measure, but rather to disagreement about its technical details. Then again, it may be that even where Community rules are agreed, their enforcement in practice is less than rigorous. This too will weaken the protection of the consumer. It is impossible to provide objective, comprehensive verification of the criticism that Community law is liable to lead to a deregulated market in which the consumer is left exposed to practices from which protection should be afforded. However, this critical framework for analysis of the Court's role *per se* and its relationship with the place of legislation should be borne in mind by the reader.[38]

---

[38] M. Van Empel, 'The 1992 Programme: Interaction between Legislator and Judiciary' [1992/2] *Legal Issues of European Integration* 1; H.-C. Von Heydebrand und der Lasa, 'Free Movement of Foodstuffs, Consumer Protection and Food Standards in the European Community: Has the Court of Justice got it wrong?' (1991) 16 *European Law Review* 391; C. MacMaolain, 'Free movement of foodstuffs, quality requirements and consumer protection: have the Court and Commission both got it wrong?' (2001) 26 *European Law Review* 413.

CASSIS DE DIJON: STRAIGHTFORWARD APPLICATIONS OF THE RISE OF CONSUMER CHOICE

Many cases decided under Articles 28 and 49 are quite straightforward and uncontroversial. It is hard to disagree with the view that the consumer is better served by being able to choose between liqueurs of differing alcoholic strengths rather than being 'protected' from unexpectedly weak drinks (the situation in *Cassis de Dijon* itself). Choosing between differently packaged margarines is surely better than only being able to buy cube-shaped packs – a situation which, as the Court commented and as economic theorists would expect, led to Belgian consumers paying more for their margarine than consumers in neighbouring states.[39] Community law liberalizes the market for products and services, thereby expanding the consumer's choice.

The Court relies on the capacity of the consumer to process information and thereby to make informed choices about available products and services as a basis for ruling against national measures that go so far as to suppress the appearance on the market of imported products and services. In the application of the proportionality principle, the Court has frequently held unlawful stricter measures which suppress products where information provision might have sufficed to achieve consumer protection. These are cases which demonstrate the principle that even where the *end* of consumer protection may provide a justification for a trade-restrictive measure, the *means* employed must be the least restrictive of trade available which are capable of meeting the end in view.

The principle emerges from the *Cassis de Dijon* ruling itself, where the Court swept aside the alleged need for a statutory minimum alcohol content 'since it is a simple matter to ensure that suitable information is conveyed to the purchaser by requiring the display of an indication of origin and of the alcohol content on the packaging of products'. In the 'Beer Purity' case, *Commission* v. *Germany*,[40] the Court explicitly identified the availability of consumer information as a regulatory device which is less restrictive of trade than mandatory composition requirements. The Court commented that even where beers are sold on draught information may be provided 'on the casks or the beer taps'. This is an application of the proportionality principle which is familiar in EC trade law, and through it EC law indirectly encourages information disclosure as part of the process of market integration. The intended result is that the informed consumer is enabled to exercise choice in accordance with his or her own (informed) preferences, rather than have that choice confined by governmental intervention. The transfer of decision-making

---

[39] Case 261/81 *Walter Rau* v. *de Smedt* [1982] ECR 3961.
[40] Case 178/84 [1987] ECR 1227.

powers away from the public authorities to the consumer is the key to these rulings.

This is not to say that national measures requiring that items be labelled are themselves necessarily compatible with Community law. Mandatory origin-marking is likely to violate Community law as a result of the hindrance to market interpenetration which flows from consequent consumer prejudice in favour of domestic goods.[41] Even where a labelling requirement relates to a product's qualities, rather than its origin, an impediment to market integration is caused by the obligation imposed on an out-of-state producer to modify production runs in order to conform to the labelling law of the target state.[42] Where information relevant to a product's composition can be conveyed on a label in a way which is adequate to alert the consumer to the nature of the product, then a rule which forbids the marketing of the product is dispropor-tionate and cannot be justified, but a state must still show a justification for the labelling requirement. The Court has accepted that, as a general proposition, it is not incompatible with Article 28 to require that labelling must not mislead the consumer, but it has added that it is not permissible for a state to require use of a particular language where it is possible for the information to be provided to the consumer by other means that are less restrictive of trade, such as use of another language readily comprehensible to buyers or other devices such as, for example, symbols or pictograms.[43] So the mandatory use of one particular language is not accepted at face value as inevitably lawful. One might suppose that in practice the relative absence of linguistic competence beyond the mother tongue of most consumers in Europe will readily justify intervention to require use of the local language on labels, especially in rela-tion to detailed information about products that are complex or costly or dangerous.[44] It may be more awkward for a regulating state to justify the suppression of other languages. This would cause market fragmentation by precluding the increasingly orthodox commercial practice of printing labelling

---

[41] Case 207/83 *Commission* v. *UK* [1985] ECR 1202.

[42] Case C-33/97 *Colim* v. *Biggs* [1999] ECR I-3175; Case C-169/99 *Hans Schwarzkopf GmbH* [2001] ECR I-5901.

[43] See, e.g., Case 27/80 *Fietje* [1980] ECR 389; Case C-369/89 *Piageme* v. *Peeters* [1991] ECR I-2971, which provoked a Commission Communication on the issue, COM (93) 532, *OJ* 1993 C345/3; Case C-85/94 *Piageme* v. *Peeters* [1995] ECR I-2955; Case C-366/98 *Geffroy* [2000] ECR I-6579. The cases typically interpret Directive 79/112 on labelling alongside Article 28. See further J. Usher, 'Disclosure Rules (Information) as a Primary Tool in the Doctrine on Measures having Equivalent Effect', in S. Grundmann, W. Kerber and S. Weatherill (eds), *Party Autonomy in the Internal Market* (Berlin: De Gruyter, 2001).

[44] A separate question, unaddressed by the Court hitherto, asks whether there may be good *cultural* reasons for insisting on use of a particular language, even where a trade barrier is the result: C Boch, 'Language Protection and Free Trade: the Triumph of the Homo McDonaldus', 4 *European Public Law* 379 (1998); Candela Soriano, 'Les Exigences Linguistiques: une entrave legitime à la libre circulation?' (2002) 38 *Cahiers de Droit Européen* 9.

bearing the same information in several different languages. One would find a justification only where a sufficient level of consumer confusion flowing from over-supply of information could be demonstrated. But this would be rare. Suppression of truthful information requires a powerful justification.[45]

It remains true that where protection cannot be achieved by information provision, measures of a more restrictive nature may be justified. As suggested, situations where there is a health risk provide the most obvious examples. The rulings in *Eyssen* and *APESA* v. *DSSC*, discussed above, demonstrate how EC law does not require public authorities to retreat totally from the task of market regulation, provided they are able to show a sufficient justification for not leaving a matter to unfettered consumer choice. Community law in this area retains a notion of the consumer who is inadequately protected by the free market and for whom even mandatory information disclosure is inadequate.

In summary, the Court's *Cassis de Dijon* formula involves a judicial assessment of national regulatory measures which obstruct trade informed by the ills of protectionism, yet which reflects in the mandatory requirements an appreciation of the role of national protective measures.

THE RULING IN *DREI GLOCKEN* v. *USL CENTRO-SUD*

A splendidly vivid illustration of the grey areas that lie between lawful and unlawful national rules is provided by *Drei Glocken* v. *USL Centro-Sud*.[46] Italian rules required the use of durum wheat alone in the manufacture of pasta products. Such rules had the effect of excluding pasta made according to different recipes using different types of wheat in other Member States. This was a classic *Cassis de Dijon* case of market fragmentation caused by disparity between national laws.

Advocate General Mancini delivered a remarkably vigorous Opinion in which he asserted that the rules should be regarded as justified despite their restrictive effect on trade in pasta products. He explained that Italians like their pasta *al dente*, 'glissant des deux côtés de la fourchette'.[47] These properties derive from manufacture using durum wheat alone, as envisaged under the challenged Italian law. But should this be enough to justify the Italian authorities denying consumers a choice of rather more prosaic pasta? The Advocate General referred to the principle that it is impermissible to ban a particular

---

[45]   E.g. Case C-362/88 *GB–INNO–BM* v. *CCL* [1990] ECR I-667; Case C-126/91 *Schutzverband gegen Unwesen in der Wirtschaft* v. *Y. Rocher GmbH* [1993] ECR I-2361, both considered further below.

[46]   Case 407/85 [1988] ECR 4233.

[47]   Mr Mancini draws this description from the Journal of André Gide, 22 June 1942; ECR 4253.

type of product where the consumer can be adequately informed about its composition by labelling rules. He inspected four packets of pasta, Italian, Belgian, German and Swiss, acquired in a Luxembourg supermarket. All bore the word spaghetti; all had a range of further information about their varying composition, some 'in microscopic letters'. Mr Mancini concluded that an Italian consumer could *not* be adequately informed by labels about production of differently constituted pasta in other states, given the depth of cultural expectation in Italy about pasta, its many forms of presentation and the exclusive use of durum wheat. Mr Mancini was keenly aware of the institutional choices at stake. His view was that the matter should be resolved through the introduction of common rules by legislative act. Market liberalization achieved through negative law would wreck the market structure for durum wheat production, while also causing undue consumer confusion (the other side of the coin from consumer choice).

Mr Mancini's view did not prevail. The Court came to the opposite conclusion. It found the Italian rules unjustified. It did not investigate in any depth the matters that had so troubled its Advocate General. It observed that it remained open to the Italian authorities to restrict the description 'pasta made from durum wheatmeal' to pasta products made exclusively from durum wheat, and thereby to inform the consumer. The consequence of the ruling is that non-Italian producers could sell their goods in Italy and the Italian consumer could choose from a wider range of pastas. It appears to be assumed by the Court that a consumer will be able satisfactorily to grasp the differences between available pasta products. The Court's ruling applies the *Cassis de Dijon* principle as a means of achieving market integration without waiting for the slow wheels of the Community legislative machinery to turn. Whereas the Advocate General doubted the workability of a market based solely on mutual recognition and would have upheld state decisions taken on behalf of consumers pending Community legislative intervention, the Court's ruling is based on an implied expectation that an informed consumer is capable of making a proper choice.

CHOICE IN THE DEREGULATED WIDER MARKET VERSUS PROTECTION AT NATIONAL LEVEL

National rules designed to protect consumers' economic interests may impede trade where they differ state by state. This may affect several different techniques of national consumer protection, including the suppression of misleading product descriptions, the exclusion of unfair competition and the prohibition of misleading advertising. The impediment arises where the use of a technique employed in state A is forbidden in state B, which forces the trader to pursue a different strategy especially for state B. Where that happens, the importer into state B is forced to adapt. Where he or she is placed at a disadvantage compared to state B's own traders, the impediment to cross-border trade is sufficient to trigger Article 28. The regulator in state B is required to justify its rules according to justifications recognized by Community law.

National rules are based on notions of deception which differ state by state. 'Hard sell' in one state may be 'unfair sell' in another. The Court's jurisprudence provides a window on distinct national views of what should and should not be allowed of traders seeking to drum up business. This then allows an appreciation of the Court's own view of the permitted level of legal protection that may be afforded by the national system in an integrating market. The case law vividly portrays the problematic collision between competing aspects of the consumer interest. The examination that follows contrasts a batch of decisions in which the Court prioritized the consumer interest in integration and wider choice by ruling national measures of (alleged) consumer protection incompatible with Article 28 with another batch of decisions in which the Court reached the opposite conclusion by upholding national measures of market regulation despite the damage they caused to the elaboration of an integrated commercial strategy for the Community market. In all these cases, directly or indirectly, the Court is forced to engage in an assessment of how the market serves the consumer.

UNLAWFUL NATIONAL RULES OF CONSUMER PROTECTION

GB–INNO–BM v. *CCL*[48] involved a challenge to a Luxembourg law which controlled the provision by a trader of information about prices of goods. Advertising practices permitted in Belgium were precluded by this stricter Luxembourg law. This disparity between national laws made it difficult for *GB–INNO–BM* to develop an integrated marketing strategy for the Belgo-Luxembourg market. It fell to Luxembourg to justify the laws. It was unable to convince the European Court. The Court was unpersuaded by the notion that the consumer might benefit from suppression of information. The Court referred to the 1981 Resolution adopting a consumer protection and information policy in asserting the close connection between consumer protection and consumer information (Chapter 1). It is of constitutional interest that the Court drew in this way on a 'soft law' instrument adopted a long time before the formalization of Community competence in the field of consumer protection.

[48]   Case C-362/88 [1990] ECR I-667.

Schutzverband gegen Unwesen in der Wirtschaft v. *Y. Rocher GmbH*[49] displays a similar policy preference in favour of a free market in information allied to a free market in goods. German law prohibited advertisements in which individual prices were compared, except where the comparison was not eyecatching. Rocher showed that the rule inhibited its ability to construct an integrated marketing strategy because it could not export to Germany techniques used elsewhere in states with more liberal laws. The European Court focused on the fact that the German law controlled eyecatching advertisements whether or not they were true. The law suppressed the supply of accurate information to the consumer. The Court's ruling leaves no room for doubt that such a restriction cannot find justification under Community law.

The interplay between judicial decisions and legislation in the Community is well illustrated here. Directive 84/450 harmonizes national laws concerning misleading advertising (Chapter 8). That, however, was all that remained of a more ambitious original proposal to regulate misleading and unfair advertising and to liberalize comparative advertising.[50] The unfair and comparative elements had to be deleted because of inability to achieve agreement on a Community regime in the face of severe heterogeneity among national laws. German law was strict in its control; English law, for example, much less so. Yet comparative advertising was opened up by the Court's 'negative law' rulings in *GB–INNO–BM* and *Rocher*. This shows how national systems may be forced to adjust under the influence of EC law even where legislative initiatives are blocked. And moreover, once the grip of the Member States over the pattern of permitted comparative advertising had been loosened by the Court's intervention into national law pursuant to Article 28, the resistance among Member States to legislative action at EC level was weakened. Directive 97/55 was adopted subsequently. It amends Directive 84/450 by setting standards that must be met for comparative advertising to be allowed throughout the territory of the EU (Chapter 8).

The third case in this illustrative series is *Verband Sozialer Wettbewerb eV* v. *Clinique Laboratories SNC*.[51] German law prohibited the use of the name 'Clinique' for cosmetics, because of an alleged risk that consumers would be misled into believing the products had medicinal properties. *Klinik* is the German word for hospital. This ban was held to impede trade in goods marketed in other Member States under the Clinique name. It fell to Germany to show justification for the rule, but it was unable to do this to the Court's satisfaction. The Court was not persuaded that there was sufficient likelihood of consumer confusion for a barrier to trade to be justified. Cosmetics were not

---

[49]   Case C-126/91 [1993] ECR I-2361.
[50]   *OJ* 1978 C70/4, amended proposal *OJ* 1979 C194/3.
[51]   Case C-315/92 [1994] ECR I-317.

sold in outlets specializing in pharmaceutical products. Consumers in other states, with less restrictive regimes, did not seem to encounter confusion. The Court here invites the retort that consumers in other states do not face the risk of confusing Clinique and Klinik, for this is peculiar to the German language. This point could be developed into a more general criticism that the Court is making sweeping assumptions about the capacity of the 'European consumer' to operate confidently in the market which are divorced from special circumstances that may prevail in particular parts of the Community. German law, in particular, has been exposed as 'over-regulatory' in the view of the Court, but there have been disgruntled responses from some German lawyers accusing the Court of failure to take adequate account of national experience in identifying commercial practices which may prejudice at least some consumers.[52] The European Court seems to envisage a rather robust, self-reliant consumer in the market who is able to enjoy the fruits of integration. Such a perspective requires the relaxation of the grip of national laws based on a conception of a consumer more gullible than the European Court will acknowledge.

The Court's vision of the smart consumer is especially prominent in its ruling in *Verein gegen Unwesen in Handel und Gewerbe Köln eV* v. *Mars GmbH*.[53] Mars found that its ambitions to create a pan-European marketing strategy for its ice-cream bars were undermined in Germany. A 'flash' on the wrapper advertised the bar as 10 per cent larger in size for the period of a short publicity campaign. This was accurate. The bar was 10 per cent bigger. But the 'flash' on the wrapper covered a surface area of more than 10 per cent and court proceedings were initiated in Germany with a view to preventing Mars using this device. It was alleged that it would mislead consumers about the size of the bar.

The practice that was suppressed was advertising, but it was physically connected to the product, and so the Court concluded that the German intervention constituted a trade barrier within the meaning of Article 28. This was not excluded from the reach of Article 28 by the *Keck* judgment.[54] So Germany was called on to justify its intervention. It could not do so. The Court stated that 'reasonably circumspect consumers' are aware that there is no necessary link between publicity markings relating to the size of increase in a product and the size of the increase itself.

The judgment in *Mars* is punchy, even terse. One may wonder whether the Court had become rather fed up of the German-sourced stream of indefensible

[52] E.g. O. Sosnitza, *Wettbewerbsbeschränkungen durch die Rechtsprechung* (Baden-Baden: Nomos, 1995), ch. 4; H. Piper, 'Zu den Auswirkungen des EG-Binnenmarktes auf das deutsche Recht gegen den unlauteren Wettbewerb' [1992] *Wettbewerb in Recht und Praxis* 685.
[53] Case C-470/93 [1995] ECR I-1923.
[54] Cases C-267 & 268/91, note 24 above.

examples of over-regulation spuriously depicted as measures of consumer protection. Perhaps so: the vigour of the Court's formula is striking. It was simply not impressed by the German claims that consumers needed such protection and preferred instead to decide the case in a manner apt to promote market integration which should itself serve to improve consumer choice. But the Court is not setting its face against the possibility that a state could justify restrictive rules: it was simply unpersuaded that *these* rules could be justified. Other cases, considered in the next section, suggest a greater readiness on the part of the Court to accept that a free flow of product-related marketing practices may not be achieved by virtue of the application of Article 28. These cases suggest less faith in the competence of the individual consumer in the market to take care of his or her own interests.

LAWFUL NATIONAL RULES OF CONSUMER PROTECTION

Oosthoek's Uitgeversmaatschappij[55] involved rules imposed in the Netherlands which controlled the offer of free gifts as an inducement to purchase encyclopedias. Sellers from outside the Netherlands who were accustomed to using such marketing methods were forced to alter their strategy for the Dutch market. Integration was impeded.[56] The Court conceded that the banned marketing techniques may result in consumers being misled. It ruled that it was accordingly possible to justify the Dutch rules as measures necessary to prevent deception and to enhance consumer protection and fair trading, encompassing the protection of the honest trader from unfair competition. National rules which prevent producers pursuing unfair commercial practices may be compatible with Article 28 even where they forbid the deployment of tactics that are permitted elsewhere in the Community. The ruling confirms that Community law does not drive down standards of protection to the lowest common denominator among the Member States.

The same acceptance on the part of the Court that the consumer may be unable properly to process information and that accordingly Member States may be able to offer protection even where that impedes the process of market integration emerges from the ruling in *Buet* v. *Ministère Public*[57] in which the Court held that a French law which prohibited 'doorstep selling' of educational material was not incompatible with Article 28 in view of its contribution to the protection of consumer from pressure selling tactics. Nor was the legislation

---

[55] Case 286/81 [1982] ECR 4575.
[56] This is probably enough to cross even the *Keck and Mithouard* threshold for the invocation of Art. 28, especially in the light of the *Clinique* ruling.
[57] Case 382/87 [1989] ECR 1235.

pre-empted by the Doorstep Selling Directive, for that Directive is 'minimum' in character (see Chapter 4 on the detail of Directive 85/577: and see Chapter 3 for reflection on the nature of 'minimum harmonization').

It is obviously the case that laws which suppress deliberately misleading practices will survive scrutiny in the light of Article 28. Indeed the Community has itself been active in the field of legal control of misleading advertising for over 20 years (Chapter 8). However, the laws at issue in *Oosthoek* and in *Buet* controlled techniques which need not be deceptive to an alert consumer, but which might have misled a consumer unfamiliar with the technique. The cases display a more permissibly interventionist approach to the protection of the consumer at national level than that which emerges from *GB–INNO–BM*, *Rocher*, *Clinique* and *Mars*.

In *Alpine Investments* v. *Minister van Financiën*[58] a rather different situation arose. The ruling is significant on many levels, including the important reminder that market regulation may pursue the objective of consumer protection at the same time as establishing standards of proper conduct in order to forestall rogue traders undermining the reputation of the majority of participants in the market. The case concerned Dutch rules placing a restriction on the practice of 'cold-calling' potential consumers of financial services. The rule applied to all providers of services established in the Netherlands and restricted the opportunity to drum up business from customers both in the Netherlands and beyond its borders. The Court declared that 'such a prohibition deprives the operators concerned of a rapid and direct technique for marketing and for contacting potential clients in other member states. It can therefore constitute a restriction on the freedom to provide cross-border services.' Given this impediment to direct access to the market of another Member State, the rule required justification. One might have supposed that protection of the consumer from unsolicited telephone calls would form the basis of a justification, which would have required consideration of the extent to which consumers can be expected to look after themselves when confronted by such marketing. However, the Court refused to adopt this approach. It would not accept that the Netherlands could claim jurisdiction to protect consumers in other states, even though it was forced to concede that a home state regulator is much better placed to achieve supervision than a target state regulator. But, viewing the Dutch rules from a different perspective in order to avoid treating them as extraterritorial in effect, it found that the protection of the reputation of Dutch firms in the sector could count as a justification for the rules. The Court did not accept that the fact that authorities in other Member States were more liberal in their approach to supervision of such marketing techniques rendered the Dutch ban disproportionate. From this perspective,

---

[58]   Case C-384/93 [1995] ECR I-1141.

the ruling rejects negative law as a method for fixing the permissible regulation of the Community market at the lowest common denominator of national protection. In effect, the Court was prepared to permit the Dutch authorities to put their own traders at a disadvantage by denying them the capacity to use 'cold-calling' as a method of building a cross-border commercial strategy. However, it is plain that the establishment of a Community-wide system of consumer protection could be achieved only by positive law, through Community legislative action. Moreover, effective enforcement of regulation of such activity would require close co-operation between authorities in different states in view of the technology involved, which transcends physical borders.

TOWARDS A EUROPEAN CONSUMER?

One must appreciate the context in which the Court makes these assessments in order to avoid overstating the potential for drawing a common European notion of the consumer from these cases. The Court is assessing the validity of national choices, not directly imposing its own standard. So, for example, *Buet* represents an acceptance that the French authorities may protect their consumers where other states see no such need. The Court is not saying in *Buet* that the French consumer is particularly gullible, but rather that the French authorities are entitled to take that view in conformity with Community law. Perceptions of the consumer vary between the different legal systems of the Member States and this remains permissible within the limits which the Court has evolved for checking national regulatory choices. That limit is reached where the Court identifies 'over-regulation' of the market – where, as in *GB–INNO–BM*, *Rocher*, *Clinique* and *Mars*, the Court believes consumer choice in the wider market should prevail over perceived risk of prejudice to economic interests. In such circumstances, the Court's expectation of basic consumer competence in the market prompts it to find such national rules incompatible with Community law. Accordingly, the presence of a large block of prudent consumers who will not be duped by a particular practice undermines the legitimacy of national measures designed to suppress that practice, even where some gullible consumers would be prejudiced. It is critically important to the thesis of this book that a Community notion of the 'consumer' is beginning to emerge, albeit indirectly in this instance in the context of checking the validity of national measures which restrict trade.

In some cases where the Court has upheld national rules of consumer protection in spite of its more typical assumption of a 'reasonably circumspect' consumer,[59] the Court has mentioned that a special type of consumer is

---

[59] Para. 24 of the ruling in *Mars* note 53 above.

the subject of protection. So it was of significance that in *Buet* the national law was designed to protect consumers behind with their education and wishing to improve it. By contrast, in *Rocher*, for example, there were no such special considerations: the national rule simply prevented consumers finding out (accurate) information. Further illumination of the Court's stance may be gleaned from *Säger* v. *Dennemeyer*,[60] in which the Court refused to accept that German rules which had the effect of restricting choice of out-of-state providers of services connected with patent renewal could be justified, pointing out that in any event a flawed service would not severely prejudice the buyer. Even a failure to renew a patent by the deadline did not exclude the possibility of subsequent renewal, albeit subject to payment of a small penalty fee. By analogy, one would presume that the graver the risk of harm to the consumer, the stronger the case for regulation of a particular commercial practice or activity. Indeed, in cases concerning insurance provision, the Court has been noticeably more receptive to the permissibility of national regulations even where they impede the activities of out-of-state companies.[61] These are matters of great sensitivity and, where miscalculations are made, potentially economically catastrophic for consumers. This bears heavily on the Court in assessing the virtues of national protective standards, even where they impede cross-border trade. Removal of trade barriers caused by divergence between justified national systems of supervision is a matter for the EC legislature. Common Community-wide rules governing the standards required of providers of financial services have been agreed in a number of sectors in recent years.

It is undeniable that the European Court seems to envisage a rather robust, self-reliant consumer in the market. It is not slow to insist on the setting aside of national rules that serve to restrict cross-border trade where it finds no compelling justification. *GB–INNO–BM*, *Rocher*, *Clinique* and *Mars* provide vivid illustrations. They are not isolated examples. The Court has used its construction of the 'average consumer' as a benchmark in finding a number of other national choices about how to regulate local markets to be incompatible with Article 28.[62] For example, *Commission* v. *Spain*[63] concerned rules setting a minimum chlorine content for bleach. Spain argued that its consumers expected bleach to be no weaker than the Spanish norm – and that they would be confused to find imported bleach containing less chlorine appearing on the market. This offered an amusing echo of the argument that German consumers expected drinks of the *Cassis de Dijon* type to be stronger than those originat-

[60]   Case C-76/90 [1991] ECR 4221.
[61]   E.g. Case 205/84 *Commission* v. *Germany* [1986] ECR 3755.
[62]   L. González Vaqué, 'La notion de "consommateur moyen" selon la jurisprudence de la Cour de justice des Communautés européénnes', *Revue du Droit de l'Union Européenne* 1/2004, 69.
[63]   Case C-358/01 judgment of 6 November 2003.

ing in France. And, 25 years later, the Spanish submissions met the same fate as Germany's in *Cassis de Dijon*. In the Court's view, 'The reference consumer is an average consumer who is reasonably well informed and reasonably observant and circumspect.'[64] This consumer can adapt to new products. The Spanish rules were not compatible with Article 28.

One may criticize the Court for its eagerness to place its view of how the consumer is best served by an integrated market above local regulatory preferences which, in some cases, may be the product of particular democratically legitimated decisions. And yet the Court ostentatiously refuses to make any such assumption in favour of deregulation. The Court has issued a standing invitation to the regulating state to show justification for its rules. And sometimes states have succeeded. *Buet* involved protection aimed at a particular group of vulnerable consumers. In *Alpine Investments*[65] the Court declined to hold the Dutch restrictions incompatible with the law of free movement even though other states did not feel the need to regulate their markets so intensively. It is possible for states to justify a tighter regulatory regime than is preferred elsewhere. And the Court is not unreceptive to submissions in favour of laws designed to reflect local peculiarities. In *Estée Lauder Cosmetics*[66] it redeployed its formula based on 'the presumed expectations of an average consumer who is reasonably well informed and reasonably observant and circumspect' in judging whether a challenged state measure could survive the application of Article 28, but it added that 'social, cultural or linguistic factors' may justify special local anxiety about particular practices tolerated elsewhere.[67] Articles 28 and 49 do not automatically sweep aside national rules of market regulation. They put those national rules to the test of justification.

The Court has therefore concocted a framework within which Member States are allowed room to explain why they have special needs that dictate a need for unusually strict rules. When one inspects the lazy, even absurd, submissions advanced in support of trade-restrictive rules in cases such as *Cassis de Dijon*, *Walter Rau* v. *de Smedt* and *Mars*, one may be tempted to conclude that the chief problem here is not the Court's unwillingness to address justifications advanced by Member States, but rather the Member States' persistent failure to engage constructively in consideration of what degree of regulatory protection a consumer requires in an integrating European market.[68]

---

64 Para. 53 of the judgment.
65 Note 58 above.
66 Case C-220/98 [2000] ECR I-117.
67 A.G. Fennelly's Opinion in the case explores factors that may lead to variation state by state. Cf. on linguistic factors Case C-313/94 *Graffione Snc* v. *Ditta Fransa* [1996] ECR I-6039.
68 Cf. S. Weatherill, 'The Internal Market', ch. 7, pp. 183–210, in S. Peers and A. Ward (eds), *The EU Charter of Fundamental Rights: Politics, Law and Policy* (Oxford: Hart Publishing, 2004).

THE PRINCIPLE OF NON-ABSOLUTE MUTUAL RECOGNITION AND THE PROCESS OF MARKET INTEGRATION

The *Cassis de Dijon* principle is one of non-absolute mutual recognition. A pure model of mutual recognition would hold that once goods and services are produced or marketed on the territory of one of the Member States, in conformity with the rules that prevail in that 'home state', then they are entitled to access to the markets of all the other Member States. The *Cassis de Dijon* principle does not go quite so far. It envisages the possibility that the state of destination – the 'host state' – may maintain its rules, even if they impede cross-border trade, provided they are shown to be justified according to the standards recognized by EC law. This is justification according to what the Court termed 'mandatory requirements' in the *Cassis de Dijon* judgment itself and which, more generally, invites attempts to justify rules as serving the wider public interest in a way that prevails over the interest in market integration. The matter of justification draws the Court into some difficult choices about whether the consumer interest is better served by the retention of national protective rules, even where they restrict trade, or the promotion of a deregulated, more competitive European market.

This pattern of non-absolute mutual recognition has replaced positive harmonization established through Community rules in many circumstances as a consequence of the Court's vigorous renovation of Article 28 beginning with the *Cassis de Dijon* ruling. National methods of consumer protection must be adjusted in the light of the impermissibility of maintaining the isolation of national markets. However, in pursuit of market integration, there remains a need for Community legislative initiatives in the field of consumer protection where national rules remain justified. Broader still, there may be arguments in favour of consumer protection laws that are disconnected from the imperatives of market integration. Much of the rest of this book examines legislative developments. However, the nature and purpose of 'positive' Community consumer policy will be seen to be affected by the background impact of 'negative law' on national competence to maintain consumer protection laws.

3. The law and practice of harmonization

It was explained in Chapter 1 that the bulk of the material which is treated in this book as 'EC consumer policy' has its source in the EC's programme of legislative harmonization. The purpose of Chapter 1 was to place that important strand in the evolution of EC consumer policy in its proper wider context. The entry into force of the Maastricht Treaty in 1993 was the landmark date for the explicit formal recognition of consumer protection as an EC competence, however, not only before but also after that date the EC's legislative track record relevant to the consumer has been predominantly composed of the harmonization of national laws of consumer protection. The purpose of this chapter is to focus more closely on some of the ambiguities and controversies that attend the crafting of a programme of consumer protection in the name of market-making harmonization. These concern issues relevant to the quality of the legislative *acquis* as well as the deeper constitutional questions about whether what has been done is legally valid.

THE EC TREATY AND LEGISLATIVE HARMONIZATION

The original Treaty of Rome included a provision which provided 'for the approximation of such provisions laid down by law, regulation or administrative action in member states as directly affect the establishment or functioning of the common market'. This was Article 100 EEC, and it is today Article 94 EC (in consequence on the Amsterdam Treaty's renumbering of the EC Treaty effective from 1999). This legislative power is subject to a requirement of unanimity in the Council. It was used during the 1970s and early part of the 1980s as the basis for a number of pieces of secondary legislation that harmonized national laws in the name of promoting the establishment or functioning of the common market, but which – in so far as the national measures subjected to the discipline of harmonization were consumer protection laws – are also examined in this book for their contribution to the shaping of a European consumer policy.

After the entry into force of the Single European Act (SEA) in 1987, a new provision inserted by the SEA began to be used to harmonize national laws in the field of, *inter alia*, consumer protection. This was Article 100a, and it is today (after amendment) Article 95. It provides for the adoption of measures 'for the approximation of the provisions laid down by law, regulation or administrative action in member states which have as their object the establishing and functioning of the internal market'.

Article 95 (ex 100a) refers to the creation of an 'internal' market, which is defined in Article 14 EC as 'an area without internal frontiers in which the free movement of goods, persons, services and capital is ensured in accordance with the provisions of this Treaty'. By contrast, Article 94 (ex 100) refers to the creation of a 'common' market, which goes undefined in the Treaty. Moreover Article 95 (ex 100a) permits the adoption of 'measures' of harmonization, which could conceivably extend beyond Directives, to which Article 94 (ex 100) is limited, to include *inter alia* Regulations. These two features appear to distinguish Article 95 (ex 100a) from Article 94 (ex 100).

Nevertheless, in practice, little, if anything, has turned on the distinction between an internal market and a common market. And, in practice, the Directive typically remains the most appropriate instrument for consumer policy-making, as the Community seeks to construct a Community framework built on and strengthened by existing, well-established national structures. It will be seen in this book that the pattern of Community consumer policy largely comprises Directives and, in some instances, 'soft law' instruments such as Recommendations. The principal reason why Article 95 (ex 100a) has replaced Article 94 (ex 100) as the normal Treaty basis for the adoption of harmonization legislation does not lie in subtle textual differences between the two provisions. It relates to the differences in the applicable legislative procedure, and above all to the voting rules in Council. Harmonization legislation adopted pursuant to Article 95 (ex 100a) requires only a 'qualified majority vote' (QMV) among the Member States acting in Council. QMV is based on the allocation of weighted votes to Member States according to their population, with a threshold figure which must be crossed before a measure is deemed adopted by QMV.[1] The key point is that a single state is unable to block adoption of a measure subject to QMV in Council. A minority of three or more dissentient states (depending on their identity and voting power) must be assembled to prevent the adoption of an initiative. Article 94 (ex 100), which in stark contrast demands unanimous support among the Member States, has been left politically marooned as superfluous. Today the legislative procedure applicable to legislation adopted on the basis of Article 95 (ex 100a) is the Article 251 'co-decision' procedure requiring a qualified majority vote in favour in Council coupled to the support of the Parliament.

The removal of the national veto over Community legislative action in the

[1]   The detail is set out in Article 205(2) EC.

field of harmonization with effect from 1987 was intimately tied to the political commitment to deepening the integrative process by completing the internal market by the end of 1992 (Chapter 1). The Single European Act's insertion of qualified majority voting in Council for this type of legislation was the legal means to achieve this objective. It permitted an acceleration in the intensity of lawmaking.

Despite the reference to the 'internal market' in Article 95 (ex 100a), in contrast to the 'common market' mentioned in Article 94 (ex 100), the rationale for Community action is comparable under both provisions. Variation between national laws impedes market integration, prompting a need for harmonization at Community level – 'common rules for a common market'. Free trade is facilitated because protection is achieved according to a common EC standard which irons out trade-restrictive differences between national systems. In so far as economic integration improves the consumer's position by stimulating a more competitive market, harmonization is in general to be viewed positively from the consumer perspective. But the claim that harmonization is correctly portrayed as a form of consumer policy runs deeper. In so far as the national laws which are swept within the harmonization net affect consumer protection, the EC assumes the function of setting its own – common – rules. Community laws come into existence in order to integrate the market, but their incidental effect is additionally to regulate it – or more pertinently to 're-regulate' it, in the sense that the Community is not acting as a *de novo* regulator but rather is responding to the pre-existing diverse regulatory choices among the Member States. Advocate General Fennelly made the point crisply in his Opinion in *Tobacco Advertising*: 'the Community is not acting in a policy vacuum'.[2] Harmonization therefore has a dual function: it sets common rules for the European market but, against a background of diverse national sources of regulatory inspiration, it also involves a choice of the appropriate standard of re-regulatory protection that will apply in common throughout the EC. This is how harmonization policy also becomes an exercise in selecting a pattern of consumer protection for the EU.

The purpose of measures of legislative harmonization not simply to prise open markets but also to serve the consumer interest has been granted vivid confirmation by the Court. It has accepted that harmonization Directives are apt to produce rights held by those envisaged as enjoying regulatory protection in the event that a Member State fails to put in place the envisaged regime.[3] The Court has also nourished the capacity of measures of legislative harmonization to promote the consumer interest by ruling that derogations

---

[2] Paras 64–66 of AG Fennelly's Opinion in *Tobacco Advertising*, Case C-376/98 [2000] ECR I-8419.

[3] E.g. Case C-91/92 *Paola Faccini Dori* [1994] ECR I-3325, Cases C-178/94 et al. *Dillenkofer* [1996] ECR I-4845.

from Community rules for the protection of consumers must be interpreted strictly.[4]

Driven by this dual function, Article 95 (ex 100a) has since 1987 increased the size of the package of Community consumer protection legislation that had already begun to evolve up until 1987 pursuant to Article 94 (ex 100). This provides this book with much of its subject matter. And although the internal market was scheduled for completion by the end of 1992, its maintenance remains an evolving process and harmonization measures affecting consumer protection continue to be adopted pursuant to Article 95 (ex 100a) today.

HARMONIZATION AND A HIGH STANDARD OF CONSUMER PROTECTION

The constitutional breakthrough to 'QMV' in Council in connection with harmonization legislation was vital to the ability of Article 95 (ex 100a) to serve as a cornerstone of the internal market project. Unanimity is not a realistic voting rule for an EC that was growing not only in its functional ambition but also in the size of its membership. Nevertheless, even though one might suppose that the Member States were prepared to surrender a veto in Council which they valued in some areas in anticipation of greater gains consequent on other states losing their own veto in other areas, it was judged politically necessary at the time of the Single European Act to include qualifications to the basic and enduring rule of QMV in Council. By virtue of Article 95(2) (ex 100a(2)), 'fiscal provisions, ... those relating to the free movement of persons [and] ... those relating to the rights and interests of employed persons', lie beyond the scope of Article 95 (ex 100a) and the possibility of adoption thereunder by QMV. National measures of this type may conceivably be harmonized – but only pursuant to Article 94 (ex 100), under which the requirement of unanimity among the Member States in Council secures a veto for any state dissatisfied with the incursion of common rule-making into such sensitive areas of regulatory activity. But, aside from the areas specified by Article 95(2), the scope of harmonization envisaged by the Treaty is functionally unlimited. Any national measure is susceptible to harmonization provided that the process contributes to the establishing and functioning of the internal market – and this has included national measures of consumer protection.

The anxiety of Member States that a harmonization programme driven by qualified majority voting may lead to a depreciation in the standards of regu-

---

[4] Case C-203/99 *Veedfald* [2001] ECR I-3569, para. 15; Case C-481/99 *Heininger* [2001] ECR I-9945.

latory protection enjoyed by some states is reflected in Articles 95(3) and 95(4)–(9). These provisions are more subtle than the brutal exclusion of some areas from the reach of QMV-driven harmonization asserted by Article 95(2), and they are of more direct significance to consumer policy. Article 95(3) has been amended since it was first introduced by the SEA. It now provides that

> The Commission, in its proposals envisaged in paragraph 1 concerning health, safety, environmental protection and consumer protection, will take as a base a high level of protection, taking account in particular of any new development based on scientific facts. Within their respective powers, the European Parliament and the Council will also seek to achieve this objective.[5]

This is significant, first of all, for the addition it makes to the relatively small number of Treaty provisions which include explicit reference to the consumer. It reflects awareness of the risk that the drive for common standards could cause a reduction in existing standards in some Member States. The provision is plainly designed to allay fears that the Community rules may undercut existing national standards of, *inter alia*, consumer protection. Indeed, since the entry into force of the SEA, measures made on the basis of Article 95 (ex 100a) that touch consumer protection routinely include an explanation of their content in the light of Article 95(3) (ex100a(3)). For example, Directive 90/88, amending Directive 87/102 in the field of consumer credit, includes in its Recitals an explicit reference to the desirability of ensuring 'that consumers benefit from a high level of protection' (Chapter 4). Article 95(3) represents a recognition of the link between internal market policy and consumer protection. The harmonization programme envisaged by Article 95 may take the market-making imperative expressed in Article 95(1) as its dominant concern, but Article 95(3) insists that consumer protection forms a component in the shaping of the harmonization programme. The Treaty provisions envisaging legislative action to promote the right of establishment and the freedom to provide services lack any explicit provision comparable to Article 95(3), but in the 'Deposit Guarantee' case the Court took the view that they too should none the less be interpreted to involve pursuit of a high level of protection.[6] The integration of consumer policy into the quest to secure an internal market is further strengthened by the 'horizontal clause', Article 153(2), which provides that 'Consumer protection requirements shall be taken into account in defining and implementing other Community policies and activities.' This embeds consumer protection requirements into – *inter alia* – the quest to secure a internal market, which features in both Articles 3(1)(c) and 14 EC.

---

[5] The original version contained no reference to the Parliament and Council.
[6] Case C-233/94 *Germany* v. *Parliament and Council* [1997] ECR I-2405, para. 48 of the judgment.

Harmonization is not only a technical matter of fixing common rules *but also* a matter of choosing the quality of the harmonized regime.

Both Article 95(3) and Article 153(2) make a contribution to dictating the content of measures that emerge from the harmonization process. However, the textual limitations of these provisions as guarantees of high standards should be noted. Article 95(3) requires only that a high level of protection be taken 'as a base', which implies that it may be adjusted downwards in subsequent negotiation. In any event, the notion of a 'high level' lacks precision and its interpretation may vary between Member States. In the 'Deposit Guarantee' case the Court insisted that no provision of the Treaty requires harmonization at the highest level found in a Member State.[7] The fact that an EC harmonization Directive may cause a diminution in regulatory protection in some Member States is not of itself grounds for annulment. The justiciability of Article 95(3) is accordingly of limited value to those concerned about perceived inadequate regulation of the market asserted by an EC legislative act. Similar reservations may be directed at Article 153(2). The stipulation that consumer protection requirements shall inform the definition and implementation of other Community policies and activities is deficient in both precision and institutional specificity. Its flavour, like that of Article 95(3), is more political aspiration than independently enforceable legal norm. This points to the importance of influencing the political negotiation which fixes the content of the harmonized rule.

MANAGED DEROGATION FROM THE HARMONIZED STANDARD

Articles 95(4)–(9) represent an even more direct assertion of the fear at national level of the consequences of yielding legislative competence to the Community under a QMV regime based on the abandonment of the national veto. They provide a carefully confined 'escape clause' for states wishing to set stricter standards than the agreed Community norm. The provisions deserve to be set out in full.

> 4. If, after the adoption by the Council or by the Commission of a harmonisation measure, a Member State deems it necessary to maintain national provisions on grounds of major needs referred to in Article 30 [ex 36], or relating to the protection of the environment or the working environment, it shall notify the Commission of these provisions as well as the grounds for maintaining them.
> 5. Moreover, without prejudice to paragraph 4, if, after the adoption by the Council or by the Commission of a harmonisation measure, a Member State deems it neces-

---

[7] Case C-233/94 note 6 above.

sary to introduce national provisions based on new scientific evidence relating to the protection of the environment or the working environment on grounds of a problem specific to that Member State arising after the adoption of the harmonisation measure, it shall notify the Commission of the envisaged provisions as well as the grounds for introducing them.

6. The Commission shall, within six months of the notifications as referred to in paragraphs 4 and 5, approve or reject the national provisions involved after having verified whether or not they are a means of arbitrary discrimination or a disguised restriction on trade between Member States and whether or not they shall constitute an obstacle to the functioning of the internal market.

In the absence of a decision by the Commission within this period the national provisions referred to in paragraphs 4 and 5 shall be deemed to have been approved.

When justified by the complexity of the matter and in the absence of danger for human health, the Commission may notify the Member State concerned that the period referred to in this paragraph may be extended for a further period of up to six months.

7. When, pursuant to paragraph 6, a Member State is authorised to maintain or introduce national provisions derogating from a harmonisation measure, the Commission shall immediately examine whether to propose an adaptation to that measure.

8. When a Member State raises a specific problem on public health in a field which has been the subject of prior harmonisation measures, it shall bring it to the attention of the Commission which shall immediately examine whether to propose appropriate measures to the Council.

9. By way of derogation from the procedure laid down in Articles 226 and 227, the Commission and any Member State may bring the matter directly before the Court of Justice if it considers that another Member State is making improper use of the powers provided for in this Article.

Articles 95(4)–(9) have similarities to Article 95(3) in that they too manifest fear about the propensity of Community rules to depress national standards. However, the technique used is quite distinct. Articles 95(4)–(9) are addressed to the capacity of states to escape the limits imposed by the Community norm, rather than to the development of the content of the Community norm. The procedure envisages circumstances in which free trade may yield to national standards which are pitched above the agreed Community norm. Its inclusion was evidently a key feature of the bargain struck at a very late stage in the Single European Act negotiations that persuaded the Member States to surrender their veto of harmonization legislation,[8] and it has been extended in subsequent Treaty revision. In particular, Article 95(5) was added only by the Amsterdam Treaty with effect from 1999.

Nevertheless the procedure is subject to Commission management, and authorization is to be granted only in defined circumstances. Approval of stricter rules would upset the pursuit of an integrated market and, according to

---

[8] C.-D. Ehlermann, 'The Internal Market following the Single European Act' (1987) 24 *Common Market Law Review* 361.

the Court, it is therefore to be treated as exceptional.[9] It has proved to be relatively infrequently invoked and, since the Commission follows the Court in treating it as exceptional,[10] its use even less frequently authorized, although the procedure is no dead letter.[11]

Consumer protection is not explicitly mentioned in Articles 95(4)–(9), but Article 30, which *is* mentioned, refers to the protection of the health of humans. Accordingly, national measures concerned with consumer safety may be applied in derogation from a Community rule adopted under Article 95, provided that the Article 95(4) *et seq.* procedure is followed. However, there seems to be no scope for reliance on this procedure as a basis for the application of measures concerned with protection of the economic interests of consumers which go beyond a Community measure made under Article 95.

These provisions are highly instructive in an understanding of the shaping of regulatory policy in Europe generally. The attraction of establishing common rules is initially strong, yet in a European Union enjoying both functional and geographic expansion, a unidimensional insistence on harmonization as a tool of trade liberalization alone fails to take account of the range of interests which are intimately affected by market integration. Recognition that the adoption of a rigid, uniform and immutable Community norm is not the necessary and inevitable consequence of Community intervention in a particular field is highly significant. This issue is not new,[12] but the stakes are getting higher.[13] It is neither politically feasible nor economically desirable to expect all 25 Member States to advance as a single bloc in all the sectors of economic activity now affected by EC policy. This trend away from the single Community rule carries the potential to cause the fragmentation of the Community market, yet it may be seen as a realistic attempt to accommodate diverse national traditions and consumer expectations within the process of integration. For consumer policy, however, the new emphasis on 'maximum harmonization', considered in Chapter 1 and further below in this chapter, will, if sustained, leave Article 95(4) *et seq.* as the only means for a state to escape 'upwards' from an agreed harmonized rule.

---

[9]   Case C-41/93 *France* v. *Commission* [1994] ECR I-1829; Case C-319/97 *Antoine Kortas* 1999] ECR I-3143 (the problem that arose in *Kortas* was removed by the Amsterdam Treaty's introduction of the 'six-month rule' now found in Article 95(6)). For analysis see N. De Sadeleer, 'Procedures for Derogations from the Principle of Approximation of Laws under Article 95 EC' (2003) 40 *Common Market Law Review* 889.

[10] E.g. Comm. Dec. 2003/653, *OJ* 2003 L230/34 (Austrian rules on release of GMOs that were stricter than Dir. 2001/38 not authorized).

[11] E.g. Case C-3/00 *Denmark* v. *Commission* judgment of 20 March 2003 (Commission refusal of authorization annulled by the Court).

[12] C.-D. Ehlermann, 'How Flexible is Community Law? An Unusual Approach to the Concept of "Two Speeds" ' (1984) 82 *Michigan Law Review* 1274.

[13] G. De Burca and J. Scott (eds), *Constitutional Change in the EU: from uniformity to flexibility?* (Oxford: Hart Publishing, 2000); B. De Witte, D. Hanf and E. Vos (eds), *The Many Faces of Differentiation in EU Law* (Antwerp: Intersentia, 2001).

HARMONIZATION AND THE THEMATIC UNDERPINNING OF EC CONSUMER PROTECTION

So far, so good. The programme of legislative harmonization is not presented in direct terms as an instrument of consumer policy. But its contribution to improving the functioning of the internal market identifies it as a feature that must appear on the map of EC consumer protection. And in so far as the national measures that are subjected to the discipline of harmonization are themselves measures of consumer protection, the result is a brand of consumer protection developed by the EC as a 're-regulator'. This pattern is central to the claim that a sharp divide between the Community's interest in market integration and the role of the Member States in matters of market regulation cannot be feasibly sustained. The one inevitably spills over into the other. It is in fact constitutionally recognized that the tendency of harmonization to prompt assessment of what type of regulatory strategy is appropriate at EC level is not purely incidental. Articles 95(3) and 153(2) EC in particular inject the need to reflect on considerations of consumer protection into the EC's legislative process. This in turn means that even though the legislative *acquis* in the field of harmonization affecting consumer protection has a rather rough-edged feel to it and is in part the product of periodic political opportunism, it is nevertheless important to examine the techniques of regulation which are commonly used within it. This helps to understand what has been achieved hitherto in the name of 'EC consumer policy' and it helps to provide insight into possible future trends. Accordingly the sub-discipline of 'EC consumer policy' has grown, spilling over from the functionally broad programme of harmonization.[14] Features such as mandatory information disclosure, concern for the weaker party and protection of legitimate expectations help to provide an account of the themes of EC consumer policy which transcends mere detailed examination of individual Directives.

---

[14] E.g. – and by no means adopting the same outlook – H.-W. Micklitz, 'Principles of Social Justice in European Private Law' (2000) 19 *Yearbook of European Law* 167; S. Weatherill, 'Consumer Policy', in P. Craig and G. de Burca (eds), *The Evolution of EU Law* (Oxford: Oxford University Press, 1999); J. Stuyck, 'European Consumer Law after the Treaty of Amsterdam: Consumer Policy in or beyond the Internal Market?' (2000) 37 *Common Market Law Review* 367; G. Howells and T. Wilhelmsson, 'EC Consumer Law: has it come of age?' (2003) 28 *European Law Review* 370; N. Reich and H.-W. Micklitz, *Europäisches Verbraucherrecht* (4. Auflage. Baden-Baden: Nomos, 2003); R. Schulze and G. Ajani (eds), *Gemeinsame Prinzipen des Europäischen Privatrechts* (Baden-Baden: Nomos, 2003); H. Rösler, *Europäisches Konsumentenvertragsrecht* (Munich: C.H. Beck, 2004); S. Grundmann, W. Kerber and S. Weatherill, *Party Autonomy and the Role of Information in the Internal Market* (Berlin: De Gruyter, 2001); S. Grundmann, 'The Structure of European Contract Law' (2001) 9 *European Review of Private Law* 505. H.-W. Micklitz, 'De la Nécessité d'une Nouvelle Conception pour le Développement du Droit de la Consommation dans la Communauté Européenne', in J. Calais Auloy (ed.), *Liber amicorum Jean Calais-Auloy Études de droit de la consummation* (Paris: Dalloz, 2004).

Moreover, this is a rolling process of deepening 'Europeanization' which does not involve only academic deconstruction of legislative texts. The European Court, allowed the opportunity to interpret measures of harmonization, has on occasion chosen to do so in a strikingly expansive, even intrusive, manner. Instances will be encountered on several occasions in this book. A helpful illustration is provided by *Oceano Grupo Editorial SA* v. *Rocio Murciano Quintero*.[15] This concerns the interpretation of Directive 93/13, a measure harmonizing laws controlling the use of unfair terms in consumer contracts, considered more fully in Chapter 5. The European Court was asked by a Spanish court whether a national court is empowered to consider of its own motion whether a term is unfair within the meaning of Directive 93/13 on unfair terms in consumer contracts. The Court took the view that effective protection of the consumer may be attained only if the national court acknowledges that it has such a power to evaluate terms of this kind of its own motion. The Court was accordingly prepared to use the harmonization Directive as a springboard to interpret rules of civil procedure relevant to the vindication of consumer rights. Subsequently, in *Freiburger Kommunalbauten* v. *Hofstetter*[16] the Court made clear its readiness to interpret 'general criteria' found in a harmonization Directive. The general message holds that the programme of legislative harmonization may be broad in its scope, and be broadened yet further by judicial interpretation.[17]

These thematically important techniques will be observed on several occasions in the chapters that follow.

THE RISE OF 'COMPETENCE SENSITIVITY'

This, in a sense, is the bright side of the EC's policy of consumer protection. Harmonization of laws generates a modestly coherent pattern of consumer protection. But there is a dark side. As explained in Chapter 1, the entry into force of the Maastricht Treaty in 1993 provided a breakthrough for consumer protection. For the first time it was formally recognized as a legislative competence conferred on the EC – albeit, in what is now Article 153(3)(b), in carefully textually restricted guise. But in practice the new provision has been of pale significance. The heartland of consumer policy remains legislative harmonization. This has been, and frequently still is, driven by unanimity among the Member States in Council. And given that fair political wind,

---

[15]   Cases C-240/98 to C-244/98 [2000] ECR I-4941.
[16]   Case C-237/02 judgment of 1 April 2004.
[17]   An attempt to develop a more systematic account of when the Court is and should be ready to provide detailed interpretation is provided by O. Gerstenberg, 'Private Law and the New European Constitutional Settlement' (2004) 10 *European Law Journal* 766, 782–6.

constitutional niceties associated with fixing the scope of the EC's competence tended to fade from view, even though some of the measures within the legislative *acquis* look a great deal more like reflections of the favourable political attitude to an EC consumer policy that has its source in the 'Paris Summit' of 1972 than genuine bricks in the market-making programme. But – inevitably – these underlying questions of constitutional validity would regain prominence once a broad reading of the EC's competence was employed not by *all* the Member States in Council, but rather by *some* of them – enough to constitute a qualified majority. An outvoted minority would be sorely tempted to appeal to the limits on EC ambition imposed by Article 5(1)'s principle that the EC possesses no more than the defined competences and powers conferred on it by its Treaty.

Many harmonization measures were convincingly supported by explanations that legislative diversity among the Member States affected the free circulation of products and services. Damage to the process of economic integration explained the need to harmonize rules governing product safety (Chapter 9) and advertising (Chapter 8). But a batch of Directives were adopted pursuant to the Treaty-conferred competence to harmonize with no serious explanation or expectation that they would advance the process of market integration. This was especially conspicuous in the area of protection of the economic interests of consumers. One of the more egregious examples of this type of unconvincing harmonization was mentioned in Chapter 1: Directive 85/577 on doorstep selling.[18] It was based on Article 100 EC (now Article 94). The Preamble states that the practice of doorstep selling is the subject of different rules in different Member States. This is accurate. The Preamble then declares that 'any disparity between such legislation may directly affect the functioning of the common market'. No justification is offered for this claim. It is hard to believe it can be true. As will be explored in Chapter 4, the Directive then proceeds to establish a European-level regulation of the phenomenon of 'doorstep selling' by requiring *inter alia* that the consumer be permitted a minimum seven-day cooling-off period within which to withdraw from an agreed transaction. The use of the phrase 'any disparity between such legislation may directly affect the functioning of the common market' in the Directive's Preamble reflects the need to pay respect to the fundamental constitutional principle that the Community can act only where its Treaty equips it with competence. The language of (what was) Article 100 is borrowed to invest the 'doorstep selling' with constitutional respectability. But in fact the political environment demonstrates the ease with which the principle of attributed competence now found in Article 5(1) may be subverted. The Preamble also makes reference to Council Resolutions of 1975

[18]   *OJ* 1985 L372/31.

and 1981 on consumer protection and information policy (examined in Chapter 1) and observes that consumers may be 'unprepared' in negotiations for contracts away from business premises. In fact Directive 85/577 was a product of the political commitment to an EC consumer protection programme and not conceived as a necessary plank in promoting the common market. In the absence at the time of any formal Treaty revision giving effect to these wider aspirations by extending the list of available legislative competences to cover *inter alia* consumer protection, harmonization was used as the chosen route. At this time, before the entry into force of the Single European Act, the Member States were required to act unanimously to adopt such legislation. Given unanimity in Council, as was the case for measures such as that governing 'doorstep selling' which reflected the political consensus about the virtues of a consumer policy for the EC, constitutional sensitivity was kept on the sidelines and acted as no impediment to lawmaking in practice.[19]

This, as summarized in Chapter 1, is a form of 'competence creep' and it takes dangerously lightly the constitutional constraint of attributed competence found in Article 5(1) EC. After all, if the Council were to become able in practice to 'self-authorize' an extension in the scope of EC activity beyond the reach foreseen by the Treaty, then this would grievously undermine the process of ratification of the Treaty, conducted in each Member State according to local constitutional requirements but performed everywhere on the basis that only a limited grant of power was being made to European level.

The lurking anxiety that harmonization had, in short, gone too far – too far as a basis for an assertion of centralizing Community competence and too far as an incursion into national regulatory autonomy – was always likely to come to the fore once the voting rule in Council was altered from unanimity to 'QMV'. This occurred in 1987 on the entry into force of the Single European Act. Thereafter a Member State opposed to a proposed measure of harmonization could not simply veto it. It could vote against it but, if in a sufficiently small minority in Council, it could find itself outvoted and bound by legislation adopted pursuant to Article 95 (ex 100a) to which it was opposed. The temptation to proceed to the Court and argue that the legislation was anyway invalid as an improper exercise of the competence to harmonize laws is obvious. It took time for such litigation to occur, not least because it remains the case that most measures are supported by unanimity in Council even where this is not formally required. But in 2000 the Court was provided with the opportunity to clarify its view of the scope of legislative harmonization granted by the Treaty. It is the *Tobacco Advertising* judgment, and it is of the

---

[19] For concern at the time see House of Lords Select Committee on the European Communities (22nd Report, 1977–78); G. Close, 'The Legal Basis for the Consumer Protection Programme of the EEC and Priorities for Action' (1983) 8 *European Law Review* 221.

highest significance to understanding the permissible reach of Article 95 as a vehicle for advancing *inter alia* consumer protection at European level. It is of fundamental importance that the Court asserted a constitutional reading of the limits of the scope of the Treaty-conferred competence to harmonize laws, notwithstanding past practice that had placed the matter in the gift of the EC's political institutions.

TOBACCO ADVERTISING

In *Tobacco Advertising* – more properly, *Germany* v. *Parliament and Council*[20] – the Court was invited to annul Directive 98/43 on the advertising of tobacco products. The measure had been adopted as a measure of harmonization directed at integrating goods and services markets and was based on Articles 100a, 57(2) and 66 (now 95, 47(2) & 55). Germany had opposed the measure but had been outvoted in Council. Here, then, was the bite of qualified majority voting. But Germany persuaded the Court to annul the Directive. So Germany, having lost the political debate, was rescued by resort to arguments based on the constitutional limits imposed on the EC.[21]

The Court observed that

> the measures referred to in Article 100a(1) [now Art 95(1) EC] of the Treaty are intended to improve the conditions for the establishment and functioning of the internal market. To construe that article as meaning that it vests in the Community legislature a general power to regulate the internal market would not only be contrary to the express wording of the provisions cited above [Arts 3c & 7a EC, now 3(1)(c) & 14 respectively] but would also be incompatible with the principle embodied in Article 3b of the EC Treaty (now Art 5 EC) that the powers of the Community are limited to those specifically conferred on it.[22]

The Treaty confers no competence to harmonize *per se*. The competence is more limited than that and is, in short, tied to the process of market-building. This is not new, as a matter of principle. What is new is the opportunity taken by the Court to explore precisely where the limits of legislative harmonization might lie. The essence of the test established by the Court in this case and the small number that have followed in its wake[23] holds that a measure

---

20 Case C-376/98 [2000] ECR I-8419.
21 J. Usher, 'Annotation' (2001) 38 *Common Market Law Review* 1519; T. Hervey, 'Community and National Competence in Health after Tobacco Advertising' (2001) 38 *Common Market Law Review* 1421; D. Khanna, 'The Defeat of the European Tobacco Advertising Directive: a Blow for Health' (2001) 20 *Yearbook of European Law* 113.
22 Para. 83; see also paras 106–7.
23 Case C-377/98 *Netherlands* v. *Council* [2001] ECR I-7079; Case C-491/01 *R* v. *Secretary of State ex parte BAT and Imperial Tobacco* [2002] ECR I-11543; Cases C-465/00 et al., *Rechnungshof* v. *Osterrreichischer Rundfunk et al.* [2003] ECR I-4989.

of harmonization must actually contribute to eliminating obstacles to the free movement of goods or to the freedom to provide services, or to removing appreciable distortions of competition.

If a measure fails to cross this threshold, it must seek its legal basis elsewhere in the Treaty. The Tobacco Advertising Directive was not regarded as a valid exercise of the competence to harmonize laws because much of its content was directed at the suppression of advertising on products such as ashtrays, billboards and parasols for use in street cafés, where the contribution to the establishment and functioning of an internal market was minimal. The implication of the judgment was that the measure was in truth concerned with public health protection, and that even though the EC Treaty grants a competence in that field, the relevant provision, which is Article 152 EC, expressly excludes harmonization of laws. It would not have been constitutionally sturdy enough to support this Directive.

For consumer law, the same warning siren is sounded. National consumer laws may be the subject of a valid measure of harmonization, thereby generating a 're-regulatory' rule of EC consumer law, provided that the measure of harmonization actually contributes to eliminating obstacles to the free movement of goods or to the freedom to provide services, or to removing appreciable distortions of competition. But if that threshold is not crossed, the EC's competence to act in the field of consumer protection is supplied only by Article 153(3)(b), and, as explained more fully in Chapter 1, that stretches only to 'measures which support, supplement and monitor the policy pursued by the Member States'. This falls far short of a competence to set harmonized rules.

In pondering the new horizons of EC consumer policy advanced in the name of harmonization, it is fundamentally important to appreciate that the Court in *Tobacco Advertising* does not deny that public health policy and concern for consumer protection may legitimately inform the shaping of the harmonization programme. Quite the reverse. The Court insists that such concerns form a constituent part of the Community's other policies, including market-making pursued in the name of harmonization.[24] This follows from the directions in favour of policy integration found in Articles 95(3), 152(1) and 153(2) EC. This means *inter alia* that in principle the Community is able, by harmonization, to adopt a re-regulatory standard that restricts or even forbids particular forms of trading practice throughout the territory of the EU.[25] Were it otherwise, the validity of measures such as Directive 84/450 which forbids misleading advertising (Chapter 8) or even, at the extreme, Directive 2001/95 prohibiting the marketing of dangerous goods (Chapter 9) would be imperilled. The Court has not been lured down a path which envisages the internal

[24]   Cf. paras 78, 88 of *Tobacco Advertising*, para. 62 in *Ex parte BAT*, note 23 above.
[25]   Cf paras 98, 117 of *Tobacco Advertising*.

market being built by the EC only on the basis of market freedoms unfettered by regulatory prohibition. The Court's point is that the threshold of a required sufficient contribution to the improvement of the conditions for the establishment and functioning of the internal market must be crossed before the competence to harmonize exists and before the values of *inter alia* a high level of consumer protection may (and must) play their part in shaping the content of the harmonized regime.

As a general observation *Tobacco Advertising* injects a shadow of 'competence anxiety' into exploration of the scope of the harmonization programme. In strict legal terms this is not subsidiarity. The issue centres on Article 5(1) – is there an attributed competence to legislate? – whereas subsidiarity in Article 5(2), considered in Chapter 1, concerns the exercise of that competence. Since the challenged measure was not in compliance with Article 5(1) EC, subsidiarity in Article 5(2) EC was logically ignored by the Court in *Tobacco Advertising*. And, on the Court's current approach, subsidiarity has little vigour as a legal principle apt to form the basis for judicial review of EC legislative acts. In its ruling in *R* v. *Secretary of State ex parte BAT and Imperial Tobacco*[26] the Court concluded that the challenged Directive's objective was to eliminate the trade barriers raised by the differences between state laws by replacing them with common rules. This objective can be achieved only by action at Community level. Compliance with Article 5(2) is in principle vital, but by adopting this approach the Court seems highly unlikely to interfere with a legislative assertion that the subsidiarity principle is satisfied when it sets common rules. However, although *Tobacco Advertising* does not concern subsidiarity in its specific legal manifestation, in popular discourse what is at stake here has commonly been labelled 'subsidiarity'. It is subsidiarity in its general political sense, as an alarm bell sounding for fear of 'creeping' centralization. That central authorities may skate over a thin constitutionally approved mandate in a manner that disturbs local autonomy is familiar in many political systems founded on divided power.[27] The EC is grappling with this problem generally as it maps out its future, and its elaboration in the area of harmonization is just one example.

---

[26] Case C-491/01, note 23 above; see also Case C-103/01 *Commission* v. *Germany* judgment of 22 May 2003, esp. para. 47.

[27] Cf K. Nicolaidis and R. Howse (eds), *The Federal Vision: Legitimacy and Levels of Governance in the United States and the European Union* (Oxford: Oxford University Press, 2001) especially ch. 3, J. Donahue and M. Pollack, 'Centralization and its Discontents: The Rhythms of Federalism in the United States and the European Union', ch. 4, D. Lazer and V. Mayer-Schoenberger, 'Blueprints for Change: Devolution and Subsidiarity in the United States and the European Union'; E. Young, 'Protecting Member State Autonomy in the European Union: Some Cautionary Tales from American Federalism' (2002) 77 *New York University Law Review* 1612; L Catá Becker, 'Restraining Power from Below', *Federal Trust Paper* 15/04, July 2004, available via http://www.fedtrust.co.uk.

THE IMPACT OF *TOBACCO ADVERTISING* – PAST AND FUTURE

Do all the older measures of harmonization concerning consumer protection comply with the Court's test? Many were, remember, adopted at a time when sensitivity to the limits of the EC's attributed competence lay buried beneath the political force of unanimity in Council, and before the vocabulary which the Court now attaches to the definition of the limits of Article 95 had been concocted. Directive 85/577 on doorstep selling was mentioned above.[28] It is plain that the threshold for reliance on the Treaty as a basis for harmonization which is envisaged by the Court in *Tobacco Advertising* is a good deal higher than that with which compliance is asserted in that measure. The historical explanation for this lack of congruence is readily explained. The key to the functional expansion of the harmonization programme lies in the political willingness of the Member States acting unanimously in Council to treat the relevant Treaty provisions as little short of the *carte blanche* to harmonize which, as a matter of constitutional principle, the Treaty never declared them to be. This is not to say that because the reasons given for the older generation of consumer protection Directives do not reach the rigorous standards demanded by the Court in *Tobacco Advertising* no adequate reasons – by the standards of October 2000 – could be found. It is only to observe that previously no effort was made to provide a justification for compliance with the requirements of the Treaty provisions governing harmonization that was more sophisticated than mere repetition of the relevant words simply because there was no political or, in practice, legal need. If the Member States agreed, there was adopted legislation; if they did not, there was none. The task now is to rethink whether the older generation could satisfy the benchmark set by the Court in *Tobacco Advertising*, in part to determine whether the measures will stand if attacked, as may occur indirectly via proceedings before national courts even though direct actions before the European Court are of course time-barred. But the principal purpose of considering this issue lies in mapping the future.

What can we now expect of the European Community as a legislator in the field of consumer protection, given that harmonization has been exposed as subject to judicially defined constitutional limits? The debate is engaged. For example, in its 2003 report on the safety of services for consumers the Commission explicitly refers to the absence of evidence of barriers to trade or distortions deriving from different rules in different Member States and concedes that it is accordingly 'difficult to justify' harmonization.[29] The point

---

[28]   Note 18 above.
[29]   COM (2003) 313, 6 June 2003, p. 21. This is considered more fully in Chapter 9.

is political but also constitutional. Recent Commission documentation canvassing views on the appropriate direction for European Contract Law has also been issued in the shadow of awkward questions about the scope of available competence. The 2001 Communication on Contract Law[30] called explicitly for information on whether diversity between national contract laws 'directly or indirectly obstructs the functioning of the internal market, and if so to what extent', with a view to considering appropriate action by the EC. The follow-up action plan of February 2003 on 'A More Coherent European Contract Law'[31] refers to having unearthed 'implications for the internal market' arising from legal diversity. The Commission released 'European Contract Law and the revision of the *acquis*: the way forward'[32] in October 2004. It too nods to the need to connect proposed lawmaking with perceived inadequacies in the current state of the internal market project. *Tobacco Advertising* and the limits of the competence to act under Article 95 haunts the debate, but for the time being the Commission prefers to avoid aggressive engagement with the matter, sticking to the debate about substance. This highly topical dimension will be explored more fully in Chapter 7.

It is also significant, though of unclear constitutional status, that some measures harmonizing rules on consumer protection are explained not simply as contributions to the elimination of distortion caused by legislative diversity among the Member States. Some take a more active view of the consumer's role in market-making. Directive 99/44 on certain aspects of the sale of consumer goods and associated guarantees, based on (what is now) Article 95 EC and examined in Chapter 5, provides in its Preamble that 'Whereas the creation of a common set of minimum rules of consumer law, valid no matter where goods are purchased within the Community, will strengthen consumer confidence and enable consumers to make the most of the internal market . . .'. This 'confidence-building' rationale for harmonization was foreshadowed in the Preamble to Directive 93/13 on unfair terms in consumer contracts. It also connects with broader policy statements about the need to induce consumer confidence in order to bring about the integration of the market in reality and not simply on paper. For example the Report from the Commission on the *Action Plan for Consumer Policy 1999–2001* and on the *General Framework for Community activities in favour of consumers 1999–2003* asserts that 'Ensuring consumers are confident in shopping across borders is as important for making the internal market work as is making it easier for businesses to sell across borders.'[33] Underpinning the debate is the awkward question of whether a market for Europe can adequately be made by eliminating perceived

---

[30] COM (2001) 398, 11 July 2001.
[31] COM (2003) 68, 12 February 2003.
[32] COM (2004) 651.
[33] COM (2001) 486, 23 August 2001, p. 11.

trade barriers or whether a more aggressive commitment to centralized regulation designed to tackle the uncertainties in the market consequent on trade liberalization is required. It is an open question whether this confidence-building rationale for harmonization is valid. One plausible view is that these broader 'confidence-inducing' rationales for harmonizing laws represent a dimension to Article 95 that was simply not at stake in *Tobacco Advertising* and which is therefore not ruled out by that judgment.[34] This perspective holds that without a reliable pattern of legal rights 'on paper' the consumer will simply not treat the internal market as trustworthy or viable, and that market-making will be damaged thereby. An alternative – and no less plausible – view is that *Tobacco Advertising* is aimed precisely to suppress such vague claims to assert legislative competence pursuant to Article 95. This would locate more general regulatory ambitions to the textually limited provision found in Article 153(3)(b) (Chapter 1). A sub-theme in this debate asks whether it is in any event plausible to regard legislative harmonization as an effective method in boosting the consumer's confidence in crossing borders to shop. Linguistic variation and impeded access to justice may be much more serious hindrances than absence of minimum legal rights promised on paper.[35] Empirical evidence would be useful, though it is hard to gather.[36]

Questions about available competence remain open. The *Tobacco Advertising* litigation, which does not explicitly rest on any sensitivity to the rise of qualified majority voting rather than unanimity in Council but which would simply never even have arisen in a world of unanimity, is a strong indication of a changing mood. A (re-)constitutionalization of the previously political reading of the limits of competence is plain. Although it is not at all suggested that the presence of consensus in Council will never again generate harmonization measures that strain the bounds of EC competence, none the less it is the case that the context has altered. The question whether it is constitutionally valid for the EC to legislate has tended to stay hidden for much of the lifecycle of EC consumer protection law. It is now firmly on the political and legal agenda.

Moreover, as is explained in Chapter 1, the entry into force of the Treaty establishing a Constitution for Europe would not solve these questions. The Laeken Declaration of 2001 invited reconsideration of the role of just two explicitly listed Treaty provisions, Article 95 and 308. There were voices raised at the Convention on the Future of Europe in favour of the tighter draft-

---

[34] S. Weatherill, 'The Commission's Options for Developing EC Consumer Protection and Contract Law: Assessing the Constitutional Basis' (2002) 13 *European Business Law Review* 497.

[35] T. Wilhelmsson, 'The abuse of the confident consumer as a justification for EC consumer law' (2004) 27 *Journal of Consumer Policy* 317.

[36] Cf. in another sector N. Moloney, 'Confidence and Competence: the Conundrum of EC Capital Markets Law' (2004) 4(2) *Journal of Corporate Law Studies* 1.

ing or even elimination of these provisions as motors of 'competence creep'.[37] But the majority concluded that this would unduly harm the EU's capacity for effective problem-solving. Both were retained in the June 2003 draft agreed by the Convention and both are retained in the text signed in Rome in October 2004. The successor to Article 308 is Article I-18; the successor to Article 95 is Article III-172. No attempt has been made to alter the wording. The ambiguous status of the scope of the competence to harmonize will remain a hot topic for debate, unchanged by the entry into force of the Treaty establishing a Constitution for Europe (should that occur).[38] Even the Treaty's principal innovation relating to competence control, the monitoring role crafted for national parliaments, extends only to legislative proposals adopted under Article I-18 and not proposals for the harmonization of laws advanced under Article III-172. This is unfortunate, given the existing track record which suggest that the harmonization programme is a worrying source of 'competence creep'.[39] National parliaments are entitled to object to perceived violations of the subsidiarity principle in legislative proposals and will therefore have to try to 'work backwards' from subsidiarity to object to the claimed existence of a competence to harmonize in the first place.

'PRE-EMPTION' – THE EFFECT OF HARMONIZATION ON NATIONAL COMPETENCE

Article 5(1) governs the existence of competence, Article 5(2) – subsidiarity – conditions its exercise. But, assuming a valid Community legislative act, what is its effect on national competence in the field?

Article 153(5) is perfectly plain. EC measures which 'support, supplement and monitor the policy pursued by the Member States' – in the terms of Article 153(3)(b) – 'shall not prevent any Member State from maintaining or introducing more stringent protective measures'. The Community rules act as minimum standards. The same is true of other areas of Community regulatory policy, such as environmental protection (Article 176) and some aspects of social policy (Article 137). As Norbert Reich has observed, 'the more competences the Community is acquiring, the less exclusive will be its jurisdiction'.[40] In such fields the Community and the Member States share the

---

[37]   E.g. CONV 291/02 24 September 2002 (Heathcoat-Amory); WD 14–WG v. 7 August 2002 (Heathcoat-Amory, Working Group on Complementary Competencies).

[38]   Cf. H.-W. Micklitz, N. Reich and S. Weatherill, 'EU Treaty Revision and Consumer Protection' (2004) 27 *Journal of Consumer Policy* 367.

[39]   For criticism see S. Weatherill, 'Better Competence Monitoring' (2005) 30 *European Law Review* 23.

[40]   N. Reich, 'Competition Between Legal Orders: A New Paradigm of EC Law' (1992) 29 *Common Market Law Review* 861.

competence to act. Member States must implement the Community standard as a minimum. But they may do more, subject only to compliance with the Treaty, in particular the rules governing free movement of goods and services.

Article 95, the key legal base in the Treaty authorizing harmonization of laws, is rather different. It has no 'minimum' clause. It contains only the carefully limited possibility for a Member State to set stricter rules than the agreed harmonized standard found in Articles 95(4)–(9), set out above and subjected to Commission management.

One might assume that the objective of harmonization pursuant to Article 95, the promotion of an internal market, would dictate that there is no scope for Member States to choose to set stricter rules than the Community norm, other than via the exceptional Article 95(4)–(9) procedure. After all, 'minimum harmonisation' is arguably scarcely harmonization at all – it envisages a persistingly fragmented European market in so far as individual states choose to surpass the agreed Community regulatory standard.

In this vein it is perfectly common to discover instances of legislative harmonization that are interpreted to preclude any possibility of states choosing to set different rules.[41] Classic federalist jargon holds that the adoption of a Community rule 'pre-empts' national competence. The field is occupied by the Community, and barred to national lawmaking. It is a model that has a role in consumer protection. In *Pippig Augenoptik* v. *Hartlauer* the Court refused to allow scope for national suppression of comparative advertising that met the requirements of Directive 97/55.[42] The aim of Directive 97/55 is 'to establish conditions under which comparative advertising is to be permitted throughout the Community'. States could not act against comparative advertising that conformed to the standards required by the Directive (Chapter 8). Similarly a 'safe' product within the meaning of Directive 2001/95 is entitled to access to the markets of all the Member States and may not be excluded by stricter local rules. The slogan 'common rules for a common market' looms large. But for some aspects of consumer protection the matter is rather different. In the case of some of the batch of measures that harmonize laws protecting the economic interests of consumers one commonly finds a 'minimum clause' written into the Directive itself. For example, the Directive on unfair terms in consumer contracts[43] is minimum in character and therefore does not preclude the application of stricter control of unfair terms under national law. Another example is provided by the point that Member States must put in place the rules against misleading advertising that are found in Directive 84/450 but they may maintain or introduce stricter rules provided that such rules do not come into

---

[41]   E.g. Case 60/86 *Commission* v. *UK* [1988] ECR 3921; Case 150/88 *Parfümerie-Fabrik* v. *Provide* [1989] ECR 3891; Case C-83/92 *Pierrel* [1993] ECR I-6419
[42]   Case C-44/01 judgment of 8 April 2003.
[43]   Directive 93/13, *OJ* 1993 L95/29. See Chapter 5.

conflict with, *inter alia*, rules governing the free movement of goods in Article 28 or 49 EC (Chapter 8). Directive 85/577 governing 'doorstep selling' provides another example.[44] In *Buet*[45] a French decision to ban doorstep selling of certain materials was not treated as pre-empted by the existence of the Directive which governs exactly that marketing practice and which requires only that the consumer be given a seven-day cooling-off period after concluding such a contract. The Court took the view that because the Directive, though adopted under what was then Article 100 (and is now Article 94), provides explicitly in Article 8 that the Directive 'shall not prevent Member States from adopting or maintaining more favourable provisions to protect consumers in the field which it covers', stricter rules were allowed even where they obstructed imported goods, provided only that they were justified (which the Court thought they could be, given their function of protecting vulnerable consumers – see further Chapter 2). On this model, rather than setting a single Community rule as both floor and ceiling, the Community measure acts as a floor, but the ceiling is set only by primary Community law.

One might ask how market-building conducted in the name of harmonization could rationally permit such fragmentation. The correct answer at the political level would be that some of these measures – most strikingly Directive 85/577 on 'doorstep selling' – in fact had little to do with market-building and were instead, and as explained above, an instance of the Council borrowing the Treaty-conferred competence to harmonize laws in order to express a unanimous political preference for the development of a legislative programme of consumer protection at a time when the Treaty conferred no relevant competence in that field. And the inclusion of a 'minimum' clause was part of the political deal. But read formally, it seems that Directive 85/577 demonstrates that even harmonization under the core internal market provisions of Articles 94 and 95 (ex 100 and 100a) may incorporate scope for persisting market division, in so far as residual competence vested in a host state could be exercised in a manner that would restrict trade yet remain lawful according to the *Cassis de Dijon* formula. This practice seems to acknowledge the viability of a model of 'minimum harmonization'. The attraction of the minimum formula is strong in the area of consumer policy, not least because it avoids the risk that Community measures may suppress long-established and well-developed national initiatives. Minimum harmonization has the capacity to reflect the reality of legal and cultural heterogeneity between the Member States.[46]

---

[44] *OJ* 1985 L372/31. See Chapter 4.
[45] Case 382/87 [1989] ECR 1235.
[46] K. Mortelmans, 'Minimum Harmonisation and Consumer Law' [1988] *European Consumer Law Journal* 2; J. Stuyck, 'Patterns of Justice in the European Constitutional Charter:

However, this interpretation of the law has been thrown into doubt by the Court's ruling in *Tobacco Advertising*.[47] The Court criticized Directive 98/43 on the advertising of tobacco products because it 'contains no provision ensuring the free movement of products which conform to its provisions, in contrast to other Directives allowing Member States to adopt stricter measures for the protection of a general interest'.[48] This, among other unfavourable findings, deprived the Directive of a valid basis under Articles 57(2), 66 and 100a (now Articles 47(2), 55 & 95). In the subsequent ruling in *ex parte BAT* a plank in the Court's reasoning approving the validity of that measure of harmonization was the presence of a market access clause.[49] The implication is that it is a condition of the validity of a measure of harmonization that it excludes the possibility of states making stricter demands of imports than are envisaged by the EC act itself. 'Minimum harmonization' means only that the minimum can be surpassed in application to domestic products alone. For imports, only resort to the relatively narrow authorization procedure in Article 95(4) *et seq.* can secure a valid basis for applying rules above the harmonized norm.

What is as yet missing is any explanation from the Court of whether the acceptance in *Buet* of stricter rules above the harmonized norm is now discarded. If it is, then the common use of 'minimum' clauses in harmonization measures dealing with protection of the economic interests of consumers is vulnerable to the challenge that it is condemned as constitutionally invalid. But the fate of 'minimum harmonisation' is not yet sealed. There were other reasons in *Tobacco Advertising* for annulling the Directive, so it might be a mistake to read too much into the part of the judgment that dealt with the absence of a market access clause in favour of complying goods. In *María Victoria González Sánchez* v. *Medicina Asturiana*,[50] an important judgment dealing with the pre-emptive effect of the Product Liability Directive (85/374) considered in Chapter 6, the Court took the opportunity to include in its reasoning the observation that 'unlike, for example, Council Directive 93/13 . . . on unfair terms in consumer contracts . . . the Product Liability Directive contains no provision expressly authorising the Member States to adopt or to maintain more stringent provisions in matters in respect of which it makes provision, in order to secure a higher level of consumer protection'. In *DocMorris*[51] and in *Herbert Karner* v. *Troostwijk*[52] the Court seemed to revert

Minimum Harmonisation in the field of Consumer Law', in L. Krämer, H. Micklitz and K. Tonner (eds), *Law and Diffuse Interests in the European Legal Order* (Baden-Baden, Nomos, 1997).

47   Case C-376/98, note 2 above.
48   Para. 104 of the judgment.
49   Case C-491/01 note 23 above, paras 74–5 of the judgment.
50   Case C-183/00 [2002] ECR I-3901.
51   Case C-322/01 judgment of 11 December 2003.
52   Case C-71/02 judgment of 25 March 2004.

to the assumption already found in *Buet*[53] that states may be able to justify rules above the harmonized norm provided the Directive expressly authorizes this possibility, although it did not mention *Tobacco Advertising* at all.

It seems impossible to be confident about the Court's position until this case law develops further. At present one can only be placed on notice that the constitutional status of minimum clauses in measures of legislative harmonization remains ambiguous.[54] Moreover, as explained in Chapter 1, minimum harmonization is also out of favour with the Commission. As far as protection of consumers' economic interests is concerned, it considers that there is a need 'to review and reform existing EU consumer protection directives, to bring them up-to-date and progressively adapt them from minimum harmonization to full harmonisation measures'. A key priority in this move to full harmonization is 'to minimise variations in consumer protection rules across the EU that create fragmentation of the internal market to the detriment of consumers and business'.[55] This will be seen later in the book in connection with specific initiatives, such as consumer credit (Chapter 4) and in particular the proposed Directive on unfair commercial practices (Chapter 8).

---

[53] Case 382/87, note 45 above.
[54] P. Rott, 'Minimum Harmonization for the Completion of the Internal Market? The Example of Consumer Sales Law' (2003) 40 *Common Market Law Review* 1107; M. Dougan, 'Minimum Harmonisation and the Internal Market' (2000) 37 *Common Market Law Review* 853: M. Dougan, 'Vive La Différence? Exploring the Legal Framework for Reflexive Harmonisation within the Single European Market' (2002) 1 *Annual of German and European Law* 113.
[55] The Commission's Consumer Policy Programme for 2002–2006, COM (02) 208, *OJ* 2002 C137/2.

4. Market transparency and consumer protection

CHOICE OF REGULATORY TECHNIQUE

Requiring that the consumer be provided with specified information about a contemplated transaction is a regulatory technique that has enjoyed considerable popularity in the development of EC measures affecting protection of consumers' economic interests.[1] This approach to improving transparency in the pre-contractual phase has frequently been combined with protection in the post-contractual phase, most strikingly through the prescription of a 'cooling-off' period within which the consumer is entitled to exercise a right to withdraw from an agreed deal.

These techniques do not address directly the content of the bargain between trader and consumer. Contractual terms remain to be fixed by private negotiation. The assumption underlying the type of regulatory technique examined in this chapter is that an imbalance in economic power can be sufficiently corrected by adjusting the environment within which the bargain is struck by giving the consumer extra information in advance and extra time to consider the implications.

There is much to be said for these techniques as forms of regulation which minimize interference with private autonomy. Viewed in their most favourable light, they yield a more efficient market by promoting negotiation and informed consumer choice, without substituting public decision-making about the contents of contracts for private choice. More intrusive controls, such as a ban on particular types of contract, may unduly diminish consumer choice. To assert a power directly to check the validity of particular terms may distort the market, for example by dissuading traders from offering a wide choice. The aspiration to promote an 'informed consumer' is so appealing that mandatory information disclosure is occasionally employed as a technique to address

---

[1] S. Weatherill, 'The role of the informed consumer in EC Law and Policy' (1994) 2 *Consumer Law Journal* 49; S. Grundmann, W. Kerber and S. Weatherill (eds), *Party Autonomy and the Role of Information in the Internal Market* (Berlin: De Gruyter, 2002), especially Part 4. For discussion outside the EU context see G. Hadfield, R. Howse and M. Trebilcock, 'Information-Based Principles for Rethinking Consumer Protection Policy' (1998) 21 *Journal of Consumer Policy* 131.

health and safety issues too, as is illustrated by Directive 2001/37 on the labelling of tobacco products, considered in Chapter 8.[2]

Nevertheless these techniques may be vulnerable to criticism. Their efficacy depends on the capacity of the consumer to process the information that is supplied and to act rationally in response to it. In so far as consumers fail to behave in an alert and rational manner, regulatory intervention based on information disclosure may not yield the intended benefits. This criticism is especially pertinent if it is shown that a particular group of vulnerable consumers is to be ill equipped to meet the regulator's model of an attentive consumer. More fundamentally, regulatory adherence to the technique of mandatory information disclosure may be attacked for a failure to address substantive unfairness. Tinkering with the process of negotiation will be regarded as of peripheral importance if one holds the view that the consumer, however well supported by mandatory information disclosure, is unable to wrest a fair deal from the economically powerful supplier. Indeed, if a bargaining environment is fundamentally flawed by the imbalance between the parties, then to introduce disclosure requirements may even legitimate a pernicious practice. Better, from this standpoint, not to regulate at all than to regulate at the margins and to pretend a solution has been found.

Moreover, in the specific context of EC harmonization, there is a suspicion that harmonization at the level of information provision, rather than direct control of contract content, represents the line of least political resistance. An inability to agree contentious proposals to set basic minimum standards of fairness applicable to contract terms may cause agreement to be deflected to less controversial aspects of information disclosure. Aspects of EC consumer policy are, like many areas of any legislature's output, the result of political expediency rather than considered selection among available regulatory techniques.

These introductory observations are pitched at a rather broad level. Naturally, assessment of Community practice depends on awareness of the particular nature of consumer problems which arise in a range of sectors. In addition, underlying questions of political perception of the place of freedom and fairness in a market economy dictate one's attitude to the appropriate intensity of regulation of the contract. The remainder of this chapter examines the pattern of existing Community legislation in the field. This is chiefly comprised of Directives requiring the disclosure of information to the consumer, which are designed to promote a transparent bargaining environment in the market, and, in addition, securing a post-contractual 'cooling-off' period for the consumer. The chapter that follows then explores the cautious

---

[2]   Cf also the case of 'GMOs': C. MacMaoláin, 'The new genetically modified food labelling requirements: finally a lasting solution?' (2003) 28 *European Law Review* 865.

advances made by EC Directives towards direct intervention into the content of the contract.

CONSUMER CREDIT

Directive 87/102 was the Community's first venture into the legal regulation of the supply of consumer credit.[3] Directive 87/102 remains the key measure in the field, though it has been twice amended, first by Directive 90/88 and then by Directive 98/7.[4] The Directives harmonize national measures in the field. According to its Preamble each is based on the perception that differences between Member State laws governing the supply of consumer credit distort competition between grantors of credit and impede consumers from obtaining credit in other Member States. Harmonization is required in order to integrate the market for goods and services obtainable by consumers on credit. Accordingly Directive 87/102 is based on Article 100 EC, while amending Directives 90/88 and 98/7, which are both post-Single European Act initiatives, take Article 100a EC as their legal base. (As explained in Chapter 1, the Treaty of Amsterdam caused a renumbering of Articles of the EC Treaty on its entry into force in 1999. Articles 100 and 100a are today Articles 94 and 95 respectively.) However, in line with the thesis advanced in Chapters 1 and 3 of this book, the measure is not only designed to create an integrated market for credit but also to achieve protection of consumers of credit. It possesses a 'dual aim'.[5]

A central issue in any system of consumer credit regulation is the definition of the types of transaction which are subject to the rules in question. Article 1(1) provides simply that the Directive 'applies to credit agreements'. This is elaborated in Article 1(2), which offers amplification of the terms 'consumer', 'creditor', 'credit agreement', 'total cost of the credit to the consumer' and 'annual percentage rate of charge'. Article 2 provides exclusions for a variety of transactions. Article 2(1) covers deals to which the Directive is not applicable; Articles 2(2) and (4) permit Member States to opt to exempt further types of deal. Moreover, the European Court has concluded that the Directive cannot be interpreted to cover an agreement to act as guarantor for the repayment of credit.[6] That contract is distinct from the agreement to supply credit itself, and it lies beyond the reach of Directive 87/102.[7]

---

3   *OJ* 1987 L42/48.
4   *OJ* 1990 L61/14, *OJ* 1998 L101/17 respectively.
5   Case C-208/98 *Berliner Kindl Brauerei AG* v. *Andreas Siepert* [2000] ECR I-1741, para. 20; Case C-264/02 *Cofinoga Mérignan SA* judgment of 4 March 2004, para. 25.
6   Case C-208/98 *Berliner Kindl Brauerei AG* v. *Andreas Siepert* [2000] ECR I-1741.
7   The Court explicitly contrasted this finding with the wider scope of Directive 85/577 on 'doorstep selling', below.

Leaving aside such matters of detail, the key to understanding the approach favoured by these measures lies in their evident concern to improve transparency, so that the consumer is more fully aware of the costs of credit which he or she contemplates purchasing. The Recitals to the Directive assert that 'the consumer should receive adequate information on the conditions and cost of credit and on his obligations'. Article 3 of Directive 87/102 is central to the policy of information disclosure. It is aimed at ensuring that an advertisement or notice displayed at business premises involving an offer of credit and in which a rate of interest or figures relating to costs are indicated shall include 'a statement of the annual percentage rate of charge'. Article 4(1) provides that 'Credit agreements shall be made in writing. The consumer shall receive a copy of the written agreement.' That written agreement shall include matters listed in Article 4(2), which includes a statement of the annual percentage rate of charge. Supply of the agreement shall occur at the time the credit contract is concluded.[8] Article 1(4) of amending Directive 90/88 adds two further sub-paragraphs to Article 4(2). Article 4(3) of Directive 87/102 (as amended) provides that 'The written agreement shall further include the other essential terms of the contract'. This notion is not exhaustively defined. It is elaborated by an illustrative list of essential terms in an Annex to the Directive, which became Annex I as a result of amending Directive 90/88.

The scope of the requirement under Articles 3 and 4 to declare the annual percentage rate of charge was limited by Article 5 of Directive 87/102. Member States which, at the time of notification of the Directive, did not require the annual percentage rate of charge to be shown or which did not have an established method for its calculation 'shall at least require the total cost of the credit to the consumer to be indicated'. However, Article 5 declared that this was to apply 'pending a decision on the introduction of a Community method or methods of calculating the annual percentage rate of charge'. This matter was addressed in amending Directive 90/88, and Article 5 of Directive 87/102 was duly superseded by Directive 90/88. Directive 90/88 asserts the desirability of providing 'that one method of calculating the said annual percentage rate of charge should be used throughout the Community' and is directed to the creation of an appropriate mathematical formula which can be used for this purpose. The appropriate amendments to Directive 87/102 were made by Directive 90/88, including the insertion of a new Article 1a and two further annexes, Annexes II and III, which are directed to this end. Certain transitional periods were incorporated, stated to expire at the latest at the end of 1995, when a Council decision adopted on the basis of a Commission

---

[8] Case C-264/02 note 5 above: the Court there concluded that there was *no* requirement to supply information about the APR on *renewal* of the agreement on the existing terms and conditions.

proposal was to cause the introduction of a single Community mathematical formula for calculating the annual percentage rate of charge. This was delayed, according to the Commission, as a result of the 1995 enlargement of the Union and the slow transposition of Directives 87/102 and 90/88 by some Member States, and the interim pattern remained in place pending agreement in Council and Parliament.[9] But a breakthrough was eventually achieved, and the second amendment of Directive 87/102, made by Directive 98/7, established the foreseen permanent system for calculating the annual percentage rate of charge for consumer credit for the whole Community. Appropriate amendments were made to Article 1(a) and to Annexes II and III of the Directive. The aim of the system is to generate more informed consumer choice in the credit market by facilitating price comparison. The annual percentage rate of charge is defined as that rate which on an annual basis 'equalizes the present value of all commitments (loans, repayments and charges), future or existing, agreed by the creditor and the borrower' (Article 1a(1)(a) as amended). The Directive's Annexes contain the necessary mathematical formulae.

Article 15 of Directive 87/102 incorporates the 'minimum harmonization' formula. It states that 'This Directive shall not preclude member states from retaining or adopting more stringent provisions to protect consumers consistent with their obligations under the Treaty.' Existing techniques for protecting consumers, which may be more rigorous than those envisaged by these initiatives, need not be repealed. Nor are states impeded from innovating through new, more stringent regulatory techniques, provided that such intervention is compatible with primary Community law, in particular the Treaty provisions on free movement. The Commission has published information revealing that most Member States have gone far beyond the minimum protective standards required by the Directives.[10]

These measures leave largely unaffected the actual cost of credit. The substance of the bargain is in the main untouched, but the environment within which the bargain is made is adjusted by mandatory disclosure of particular types of information. The Directives' constitutional roots in the policy of market integration via Articles 94 and 95 (ex 100 and 100a) identify them as contributions to the process of integrating the market for financial services, but the terms on which such integration is to be achieved include mandatory transparency. So, subject to the existence of stricter national laws, credit may still be acquired by consumers on terms involving alarmingly high interest repayments, a notorious problem in this area. But, in theory, where high prices are payable under a contract, that will have occurred as a result of free and informed consumer choice between competing suppliers. The technique of

---

[9]   COM (96) 79.
[10] COM (95) 117, report on the operation of Directive 87/102.

information disclosure will, on a favourable interpretation, have improved the operation of the market without going so far as to rob the market of competition and consumer choice by, for example, fixing prices or limiting sources of supply by imposing a prior licensing system.

REFORM OF THE LAW GOVERNING CONSUMER CREDIT

It is probable that the legislative regime will be updated sooner rather than later. However, the thematically central focus on information disclosure established by Directive 87/102 will be largely retained. A 1997 Commission communication on the financial services sector set out the case that the legal rules had failed to keep pace with the changing structure of the market.[11] In 2001 the Commission initiated a further discussion[12] against a stated background assumption that the market for the supply of consumer credit remained disappointingly fragmented along national lines. It suggested three main factors contributing to this regrettable pattern: technical difficulties in penetrating a new market; insufficient harmonization of national laws; and the development of the commercial character of the sector since the existing Directives had been adopted. The Commission sounded an alert that it was favourably disposed to moving towards maximum in place of minimum harmonization, in order to eliminate the diversity in regulation consequent on Member State readiness to intervene in the market above the minimum standard required by Directive 87/102.

In September 2002 the Commission published a proposal for a new Directive which would replace Directive 87/102 as twice amended.[13] Neither Council nor Parliament welcomed the proposal with unqualified glee. A revised proposal was issued by the Commission in October 2004.[14] This takes account of many, though not all, amendments proposed by the Parliament. It is motivated by the concern to promote an intensification of cross-border competition in the market for the supply of credit to consumers, while also paying attention to the need to achieve a high standard of consumer protection. Article 95 EC is accordingly the chosen legal base. It is likely that a new Directive will be adopted in 2005.

Under the Commission's proposal core definitions – of creditor and of consumer – would be left untouched. The 2002 draft proposed to extend the

---

[11] COM (97) 309.
[12] http://europa.eu.int/comm/consumers/cons_int/fina_serv/cons_directive/cons_cred1a_en.pdf.
[13] COM (2002) 443, 11 September 2002.
[14] COM (2004) 747, 28 October 2004.

reach of the harmonized regime to cover all types of credit available to consumers. The exceptions found in the current regime (in particular in Article 2 of Directive 87/102) would be significantly curtailed. The 2004 draft backtracks to an extent from the 2002 draft. Some exclusions proposed by the Parliament are accepted and a 'light regime', involving reduced information requirements, is proposed for some types of credit, including overdraft facilities in bank accounts. None the less, even the 2004 version would bring some important areas of consumer borrowing which are not covered by Directive 87/102 within the scope of the regime. Home loans, for example, are currently covered only by a 'soft law' Resolution[15] which sets out good practice on transparency and provision of information to consumers.

Maximum harmonization is envisaged by the Commission. Member States would be prohibited from enacting or maintaining stricter rules in the area covered by the Directive. This would be a radical departure from the minimum formula preferred in Directive 87/102. The intention is to secure a more aggressive promotion of the integration of the market in the belief that intensified cross-border competition will serve the consumer interest. It is considered in Chapter 1 whether this is generally an appropriate model for EU consumer protection, but this instance provides a concrete manifestation of the Commission's strong current preference to move in the direction of maximum harmonization.

The central regulatory technique of the proposed new Directive would remain information disclosure. It would not seek to fix the cost of credit, and the Commission's stated view is that the rules would not reduce the availability of credit in the market. In the pre-contractual stage it would be mandatory to disclose stipulated information. The aim is to encourage informed 'shopping around'. The agreement itself would be required to include relevant detailed information and a copy must be supplied to the consumer. A 'cooling-off' period, absent from Directive 87/102, would be added. The consumer could withdraw within 14 days of the conclusion of the contract, a period that is consciously aligned with Directive 2002/65 on distant selling of financial services (below). The Commission's proposal is also designed to provide a more reliable method for calculating the annual percentage rate of charge according to a common standard. The 2002 proposal for a revised Directive admits that despite the efforts made in Directive 87/102 as twice amended there are still deficiencies in achieving a common approach across all the Member States.

[15] *OJ* 2001 L69/25, 1 March 2001.

CONSUMER CREDIT – 'OVER-INDEBTEDNESS'

The Commission's 1995 report on the operation of the regime initiated by Directive 87/102 floated ideas for intervention going beyond the emphasis on transparency and consumer information.[16] Although the Commission argued that a consumer who is aware of prices can spur the market to more efficient operation, it conceded that over-indebtedness, a problem which has stimulated responses at national level, may require action at Community level. The consumer aspect of financial services was one of ten priorities set out in the 1996–98 action plan and it has retained its place on the Commission's agenda in subsequently published policy documents and work programmes (Chapter 1). A statistical study of the phenomenon of consumer over-indebtedness was commissioned and published by the Commission in October 2001.[17] The next month the Council adopted a Resolution on consumer credit and indebtedness which noted variation in treatment of the phenomenon of consumer over-indebtedness at national level and called for the gathering of statistics on the levels of over-indebtedness and for exchange of information on best practice in tackling the problem.[18] Concrete legislative action to tackle over-indebtedness is missing from the current EC provisions, but the Commission's 2002 draft Directive would have attempted to move in the direction of preventive control.[19] It would have required the Member States to establish a central database containing data recording late payments, including identification of consumers and guarantors, and accessible by creditors. The idea was to establish a legal principle requiring 'responsible lending' which would involve *inter alia* checking the database before agreeing to supply credit. The 2004 draft is much less ambitious.[20] It relocates the principle of responsible lending to the provisions governing pre-contractual disclosure of information. Lenders would be required to assess the solvency of consumers on the basis of information provided by the consumer and, where appropriate, after consultation of the relevant database. Sanctions in the event of failure are left unspecified. The proposed mandatory creation of a database has been abandoned. Instead it would be stipulated that lenders throughout the EU should be entitled to non-discriminatory access to existing public and private databases. The risk of consumers incurring scarcely tolerable levels of debt would therefore be addressed by the supply of information in advance, coupled to the nebulous notion of 'responsible lending' and the opportunity to withdraw from a deal for a period of 14 days after its conclusion.

[16] Note 10 above.
[17] http://europa.eu.int/comm/consumers/cons_int/fina_serv/cons_directive/index_en.htm.
[18] *OJ* 2001 C364/1.
[19] Note 13 above.
[20] Note 14 above.

It is controversial whether this is a workable system of legal protection. It asks a great deal of effective data collection and dissemination. There may also be problems associated with lacking legal competence. The contribution made by the consumer credit Directives to the effective functioning of the common or internal market has never been convincingly demonstrated and they may be thought potentially vulnerable to challenge as improperly based on the Treaty provisions governing harmonization. This is the shadow of the Court's *Tobacco Advertising* ruling.[21] Legislative action aimed at tackling consumer over-indebtedness would be all the more vulnerable to, though (as elaborated in Chapter 3) not inevitably condemned by, the allegation that it does not fall within the scope of Article 95. Action could conceivably be taken by the EC pursuant to Article 153(3)(b) but the textual limits of that provision would restrict the permissible vigour of an EC intervention (Chapter 1).

CROSS-BORDER CREDIT TRANSFERS

The structure of the banking market in the Community has been dictated by the existence of different currencies in the Member States. The industry has largely been split along national lines. However, the level of cross-border financial activity has inevitably increased in accordance with the integration of the market for goods and services, and the creation of the euro, which became a common currency for the majority of the (then 15) Member States in 2002, has contributed a further impetus to the integration of the financial services sector. However, it has long been plain that the complexity of cross-border transactions, involving intermediary institutions and currency exchange, may cause extra cost and time in comparison with purely national deals. In 1990 the Commission issued a Recommendation on the transparency of banking conditions relating to cross-border financial transactions.[22] It is a further example of the thematic importance attributed by the Commission to consumer information. It is recommended that Member States 'ensure that institutions which undertake cross-border financial transactions within the meaning of the Recommendation apply the principles set out in the Annex'. The Annex declares that 'The aim of the principles set out in this Recommendation is to make more transparent the information supplied . . .'. Six principles are listed. The majority are directed at aspects of provision of information to the consumer of banking services.

At the time several Member States imposed binding rules in the area of transparency of banking conditions. The Preamble to the Recommendation

---

21   Case C-376/98 [2000] ECR I-8419. See Chapter 1.
22   Rec. 90/109 *OJ* 1990 L67/39.

stated that '[i]t does not appear expedient to ask those member states to amend their legislation by inserting rules relating solely to cross-border transactions'. It added that a number of Member States preferred to retain proven co-operation procedures in the field. Accordingly the 'soft law' approach, encouraging voluntary co-operation, was preferred. This lighter regulatory touch conforms to interpretations of the subsidiarity principle (Chapter 1).

It emerged that the Recommendation had negligible visible impact. Further study revealed that costs of transferring small sums between Member States remained high. A survey carried out in 1994 found that written information to customers was completely lacking in nearly half of 352 branches surveyed. Of a sample of over 1000 transfers, double charging occurred in 36 per cent of cases, and the average total cost of making a transfer of an amount equivalent to 100 euros was 25.4 euros.[23]

The Commission therefore concluded that the 'soft law' route was inadequate. It published a draft Directive,[24] which subsequently reappeared as the draft Directive on cross-border credit transfers.[25] The political environment was favourable and a Directive was duly adopted.

Directive 97/5 on cross-border credit transfers[26] was based on Article 100a EC. It lays down rules governing transparency and performance of cross-border payments. It applies to any credit transfer of an amount of less than 50 000 euros. Article 3 contains information on conditions for cross-border credit transfers that must be supplied to the consumer in advance. This includes an indication of the time needed for funds to be credited, the manner of calculation of any charges payable and details of complaint and redress procedures. After the cross-border credit transfer has occurred, Article 4 stipulates that suppliers shall provide consumers with clear information on the conditions and cost, unless the consumer has expressly accepted that this can be waived. Article 6 dictates that the cross-border credit transfer be executed within the agreed time limit. If this is violated, the consumer is to be compensated, which shall include interest. Compensation is also due in the absence of any agreed time limit where the transfer has not been executed at the end of the fifth banking business day following the date of acceptance of the order. The Directive contains further provisions directed at compensation in the event of non-performance. The system is subject to generally applicable rule of *force majeure* designed to protect financial institutions in exceptional circumstances. The measure also sets out rules governing the respective responsibilities of the institutions at

---

23 The evidence is summarized in J. Rinkes, 'EC Directive on cross-border credit transfers' (1998) 6 *Consumer Law Journal* 7.
24 *OJ* 1994 C360/13.
25 *OJ* 1995 C199/16.
26 *OJ* 1997 L43/25.

either end of the transaction, in an attempt to address the perceived problem of double-charging.

It is instructive to appreciate that the Commission's decision to shift away from issuing 'soft law' instruments to proposing formal legislation conforms fully to the principle of subsidiarity (Chapter 1). Although one might properly interpret subsidiarity as meaning that 'soft law' should be preferred over 'hard law' where both are equally effective in achieving the end in view, once the inadequacies of 'soft law' have been demonstrated, pursuit of the stipulated objective through binding legal instruments becomes appropriate. More generally, Directive 97/5 fits comfortably into the paradigm of consumer information as a dominant form of EC consumer information.[27] No attempt is made to dictate the cost of transfers. Instead the aim is to promote transparency in the market in order to generate a more informed, competitive bargaining process.

'DOORSTEP SELLING'

Directive 85/577 is concerned with the harmonization of laws concerning the protection of the consumer in respect of contracts negotiated away from business premises.[28] It is more commonly known as the 'Doorstep Selling' Directive. It is based on Article 100 EC, which is now Article 94, although its explanation of the need to achieve harmonization in the field in pursuit of the integration of the market is extraordinarily terse. Contracts between a trader and a consumer are commonly concluded away from the trader's business premises. Legislation governing such deals differs from state to state. In fact, states vary in their choice of public or private law to control such activities. The Recitals to the Directive proceed to declare that disparities may directly affect the functioning of the common market and accordingly claim a rationale for approximation of laws in the field. This is not convincing. More than most measures, this Directive demonstrates that under Treaty provisions such as Article 100 (now Article 94) which require unanimous agreement in Council, political consensus has on occasion been the key to the adoption of legislation. Explanation of economic rationales for action has tended to become little more than briefly asserted constitutional formality. In the wake of the Court's interpretation of the scope of the competence to harmonize laws in *Tobacco Advertising*[29] the Doorstep Selling Directive deserves to be rated as one of those most vulnerable to the allegation that it lacks constitutional validity (Chapter 1).

---

[27] Rinkes, note 23 above.
[28] *OJ* 1985 L372/31.
[29] Case C-376/98, note 21 above.

In line with the regulatory techniques used in the measures affecting the supply of credit, examined above, the Doorstep Selling Directive is concerned with harmonization of the rules governing the circumstances in which deals are made and not with the substance of the terms themselves. The Directive does not forbid sales away from business premises, nor does it directly address the content of concluded contracts. It requires that the consumer be allowed a 'cooling-off' period. The consumer has a minimum seven-day period in which to withdraw from a contract concluded in the circumstances defined by the Directive. The notions of trader and consumer are defined in Article 2. 'Doorstep selling' is a legally imprecise term and accordingly a fuller definition of the types of contract at issue is provided under Article 1, subject to a list of exceptions in Article 3(2). Article 3(2) excludes *inter alia* insurance contracts, contracts for securities and contracts for the construction, sale and rental of immovable property or contracts concerning other rights relating to immovable property.[30]

In *Heininger* the Court ruled that derogations from EC rules for the protection of consumers must be interpreted strictly.[31] The case concerned an agreement by a bank to lend money to Mr and Mrs Heininger, as consumers, to purchase a flat. The consumers subsequently brought an action revoking their declaration of intent to enter into the loan agreement, claiming that they had been induced to enter into it by an agent of the bank who had failed to inform them of their right to withdraw from the deal. The European Court accepted that the loan agreement was linked to a contract concerning a right relating to immovable property. A contract of the latter type is excluded from the scope of Directive 85/577 by Article 3(2). But the Court treated the loan agreement as a separate contract which fell within the scope of the protective regime when concluded 'on the doorstep'. The Court also rejected the submission that Directive 87/102 on consumer credit, adopted subsequently to Directive 85/577 on doorstep selling and containing no right of withdrawal, should be interpreted as having by implication set aside the consumer's right to withdraw in the case of contracts concluded on the doorstep but falling within Directive 87/102 by virtue of their subject matter. Nothing in Directive 87/102 supported such an interpretation. The Heiningers had not been given the required information on their right to withdraw. Therefore that right endured.

Legal certainty might appear to be compromised by the risk that consumers may be able to withdraw from deals a long time after their conclusion, but the Court pointed out a simple method for avoiding such uncertainty. Suppliers

---

30 The latter exclusion does not apply to a contract concerning the right to use immoveable property and also the associated provision of separate and more highly valued services: Case C-423/97 *Travel Vac SL* v. *Manuel José Antelm Sanchis* [1999] ECR I-2195.

31 Case C-481/99 [2001] ECR I-9945; see also Case C-203/99 *Veedfald* [2001] ECR I-3569, para. 15.

can comply with the obligations envisaged by the Directive and implemented into national law.[32]

That the doorstep selling regime may reach further in protecting consumers than that governing consumer credit is also confirmed by the Court's judgment in *Dietzinger*.[33] A contract of guarantee, concluded for the benefit of a third party, falls within the scope of Directive 85/577 where it is concluded on the doorstep (and where the other preconditions for application of Directive 85/577 are met).[34] By contrast, Directive 87/102 as amended governs credit agreements alone and not such third-party guarantee transactions.[35]

The control exercised over the defined transactions is contained in Article 4. Traders must give consumers written notice of their right of cancellation in accordance with the procedures in Article 4. Article 5 provides that the right to cancel may be exercised within a set period after the receipt of the Article 4 notice. The period must be not less than seven days from receipt of the notice. The precise method of renunciation which the consumer must adopt is to be determined by national law according to Article 5 and the European Court has shown no desire to interfere with the scope of that choice.[36] According to Article 7, the potentially complex issues of dealing with money or goods which may already have changed hands fall to be dealt with under national law. This is a readily comprehensible acknowledgement of the limits of the 'Europeanization' of private law. In *Heininger*[37] the Court similarly ruled that the effects of a cancellation of the loan agreement on the contract for the purchase of the immovable property fell to be governed by national law.

Directive 85/577 falls firmly within the category of those concerned to improve the consumer's information and bargaining position. The transaction may be concluded on the doorstep and enforced on whatever terms the parties may agree, but the consumer is to be supported in the pre- and post-bargaining phase by information provision and a right to withdraw. This secures consumer choice, but takes account of what the Recitals describe as the 'surprise element' that may taint negotiation away from business premises. So if a consumer enters into a deal covered by the Directive with a trader who has set up a stall in, say, a railway station, then the Directive, implemented into

---

[32] In the absence of national implementation the consumer's rights are much more precarious: on the absence of 'horizontal direct effect' of Directives before national courts, see Case C-91/92 *Faccini Paola Dori* v. *Recreb Srl* discussed in Chapter 10.

[33] Case C-45/96 [1998] ECR I-1199.

[34] Which in *Dietzinger* itself they were not since the guarantor was acting outside the scope of his trade while the party whose debt was guaranteed was not: this did not meet the requirements of Arts 1 & 2 Dir. 85/577. For criticism of this aspect of the judgment see N. Bamforth, 'The limits of European Union consumer contract law' (1999) 24 *European Law Review* 410.

[35] Case C-208/98, note 5 above.

[36] Case C-423/97 *Travel Vac SL* v. *Manuel José Antelm Sanchis* [1999] ECR I-2195.

[37] Case C-481/99, note 31 above.

national law, allows the consumer to rethink the deal and to withdraw within the defined period, which must not be shorter than seven days. The consumer will be able to defeat a breach of contract action brought before national courts by the supplier.[38] The Directive's perception of the need to protect the consumer leads to adjustment of national law of contract formation and, in an admittedly rather peripheral area, brings about a degree of harmonization of private law in Europe.

Article 8 of Directive 85/577 stipulates that it is a measure of minimum harmonization. Therefore, the Directive itself does not conclude debate on the regulatory choice that lies between, on the one hand, consumer protection achieved through information provision and, on the other hand, deeper inter-vention involving outright prohibition of particular practices. The Directive simply establishes a minimum level of protective regulation, which may be exceeded by states preferring to operate more stringent systems of protection entailing a consequential reduction in consumer choice. In *Buet* v. *Ministère Public*[39] the Court treated the minimum clause in the Directive to mean that stricter national measures are not pre-empted by the Directive but must conform to primary Community law. The case arose as a result of French rules forbidding doorstep selling of particular types of educational material. This plainly exceeded the restrictions on commercial activity imposed by Directive 85/577. However, the Directive's characterization as a measure of minimum harmonization led to the conclusion that the French rules were not pre-empted by Community intervention in the field. The Court then proceeded to rule that even though the ban exerted a restrictive effect on cross-border trade, it was compatible with Article 28 as a contribution to consumer protection justified under Community law (Chapter 2). So even though the Community legislature had not felt the need to introduce a prohibition in the field, it remained open to national authorities to maintain more extensive patterns of intervention in conformity with primary and secondary Community law. This tolerance of a model of 'minimum harmonisation' is arguably incompatible with the Court's insistence in *Tobacco Advertising* that a product that complies with a harmo-nized standard must be entitled to access to the markets of all the Member States. The very validity of a harmonization Directive would appear to be called into question in so far as a minimum clause envisages the possible continued application of barriers to cross-border trade. This clashes with the Court's assumption in *Buet* that a minimum clause lodged in a harmonization

---

[38]   The choice of the example of a railway station is deliberate; Italy's failure to implement this Directive combined with the Court's refusal to acknowledge the horizontal direct effect of Directives lay behind Ms Dori's inability simply to defeat a breach of contract action in the litigation that generated the ruling in Case C-91/92 *Faccini Paola Dori* v. *Recreb Srl*, mentioned in note 32 above and examined in Chapter 10.

[39]   Case 382/87 [1989] ECR 1235.

measure allows scope for persisting barriers to inter-state trade provided the stricter national measure is shown to be justified according to standards recognized by EC law governing free movement. As explained in Chapter 1, pending further judicial elaboration of the matter, the status of 'minimum harmonization' must be regarded as unsettled.

PACKAGE TRAVEL

Directive 90/314 deals with package travel, package holidays and package tours.[40] It is based on Article 100a EC. Member States have employed a range of techniques to regulate the package travel industry, including a civil law approach in Germany, administrative regulation in France and an essentially self-regulatory structure in the United Kingdom. This pattern of variation has served to prevent the integration of the market. The Directive's objective is the establishment of safeguards for those on package travel, package holidays and package tours. Its primary thrust is directed towards information disclosure, although to a limited extent it affects substance. It adopts the familiar (though today questioned) model of minimum harmonization (Article 8).

Not all travel is included. The Directive concerns only the 'package'. Article 2(1) defines the 'package' as a holiday lasting more than 24 hours or incorporating overnight accommodation and which includes a combination of at least two other components when sold or offered for sale at an inclusive price. The components are transport, accommodation, or other tourist services as defined. A simple house rental would not be covered. The consumer entitled to benefit from the Directive includes any person taking or agreeing to take a package, even as part of a business trip. Article 2(1) is perfectly capable of covering the case of a package holiday organized at the request of and according to the specifications of a consumer.[41] On the other hand, inter-state educational exchanges during which the student stays with a host family free of charge for several months do not fall within the protective scheme envisaged by the Directive.[42]

The Directive employs the technique of information disclosure to safeguard consumers of package holidays. Article 3(1) prohibits misleading information. Articles 3(2) and 4(1) address the process of supplying information. Article 3(2) provides that '[w]here a brochure is made available to the consumer, it shall indicate in a legible, comprehensible and accurate manner both the price and adequate information concerning' a list of matters including destination,

[40]   *OJ* 1990 L158/59.
[41]   Case C-400/00 *Club-Tour, Viagens e Turismo SA* [2002] ECR I-4051.
[42]   Case C-237/97 *AFS Intercultural Programs Finland* [1999] ECR I-825.

transport, type of accommodation and itinerary. Article 4(1) provides that the organizer and/or retailer shall provide the consumer before the conclusion of the contract with general information on passport and visa requirements and required health formalities and, in good time before the start of the journey, with information about, *inter alia*, details of the organizer and/or retailer's local representative or local agencies or, in any case, 'an emergency telephone number or any other information that will enable him to contract [*sic*] the organiser and/or the retailer'. Article 4(2) provides that Member States shall ensure that, *inter alia*, 'all the terms of the contract are set out in writing or such other form as is comprehensible and accessible to the consumer and must be communicated to him before the conclusion of the contract'. Moreover, states shall ensure that the consumer is given a copy of these terms.

The Directive makes a limited incursion into the substance of the bargain. It makes provision for transfer of bookings under Article 4(3), control of price variation under Article 4(4) and compensation for cancellation under Article 4(6). Article 5 provides that the package organizer may be made liable to compensate the consumer for damage suffered not only as a result of its own defective performance under the contract but also as a result of that of the retailer and the supplier. There is a presumption of fault against the operator, but liability is not strict.

Article 5 does not provide any detailed account of the damage for which the consumer is entitled to claim compensation. In particular, it does not spell out whether both personal injury and non-material loss, such as disappointed expectations of an enjoyable holiday, are covered by the Directive. It does, however, provide in Article 5(2) that Member States may allow compensation for damage other than personal injury to be limited under the contract provided that such limitation is not unreasonable. In *Simone Leitner* the Court ruled that this meant that the Directive implicitly recognizes the existence of a right to compensation for non-material damage.[43] It supplemented this interpretative stance by observing that the Directive's purpose of eliminating disparities between national laws in the area of package holidays pushed in favour of bringing rules governing compensation for non-material damage within its scope, for otherwise distortion caused by legal diversity would persist. It added that compensation for non-material damage arising from the loss of enjoyment of a holiday is of particular importance to consumers. In this fashion the 'dual purpose' of harmonization – economic integration and regulatory protection – was used to interpret the Directive on package travel to confer on consumers a right to compensation for non-material damage resulting from defective performance.[44]

---

[43]   Case C-168/00 [2002] ECR I-2631.
[44]   For a critical account of the Court's sense of adventure see annotation of the case by W.-H. Roth (2003) 40 *Common Market Law Review* 937.

Article 7 stipulates that the organizer and/or the retailer who is party to the contract shall provide sufficient evidence of security for the refund of money paid over and for the repatriation of the consumer in the event of insolvency. This is a potentially significant feature of the protective regime, although the advocate of effective consumer protection will frown at the complete lack of detail on how this shall be achieved within the Member States. Helpful interpretative guidance was supplied by the Court in the preliminary ruling in *Erich Dillenkofer et al.* v. *Germany*.[45] The applicants were consumers who had suffered loss when their package holiday organizers went insolvent. They did not recover their losses from the operators. German law had not yet been brought into line with the requirements of the Directive. The Court observed that 'the obligation to offer sufficient evidence of security necessarily implies that those having that obligation must actually take out such security'. Article 7 would otherwise be 'pointless'.[46] What is more, the Court added that Article 7 is sufficiently unconditional to rule out the possibility of allowing organizers to require travellers to pay a deposit in advance unless the deposit too is to be refunded in full in the event of the organizer's insolvency. The Court added that the Directive, though ostensibly a measure of market-making harmonization, was also properly interpreted as granting identifiable rights to consumers – namely, rights to the refund of money paid over and repatriation in the event of the insolvency of the organizer. This meant that Germany, having failed to implement the Directive so as to secure effective protection of such rights, was liable to compensate the affected consumers in accordance with the Court's established case law on the liability of a state that infringes its EC obligations.[47] The impression is that the Court is keen to interpret the obligations imposed by Article 7 in the light of the role of the Directive as an instrument of not only market integration but also consumer protection against all risks flowing from insolvency.[48]

In 1999 the Commission published a report into the application of the Directive.[49] This provides information on patterns of national implementation. It also tentatively airs ideas for reform of the law. For example, it is pointed out that Article 1 confines the 'package' to a holiday lasting more than 24 hours or incorporating overnight accommodation, comprising a combination of at least two other components. This would exclude a day trip to a major sporting event, including provision of a match ticket, although in such a case

---

[45]   Joined Cases C-178/94, C-179/94, C-188/94, C-189/94 & C-190/94 [1996] ECR I-4845.
[46]   Para. 41 of the judgment.
[47]   Most prominently Joined Cases C-6/90 & C-9/90 *Francovich and Others* v. *Italy* [1991] ECR I-5357; see further Chapter 10.
[48]   See also Case C-364/96 *VKI* [1998] ECR I-2949; Case C-140/97 *Rechberger* [1999] ECR I-3499.
[49]   SEC (1999) 1800.

the expense and disappointment of a failure to supply could frequently be a great deal more serious for the consumer than a typical week's package holiday. No specific proposal for extending the Directive has been forthcoming from the Commission. The 1999 report notes some unresolved questions of interpretation and in this vein pays particular attention to Article 7 of the Directive, which is identified as offering the widest scope for divergent interpretation among the provisions in Directive 90/314. It tracks the case law considered above and makes a firm case in favour of a strong pro-consumer reading of the obligations cast on Member States to ensure protection in the event of insolvency.

TIMESHARE

The phenomenon of 'timeshare' refers, loosely, to an agreement which allows a consumer use of property for a specified period in the year. The property is, in effect, rented out to a series of consumers, but the arrangement envisages a more long-term relationship than simple one-off holiday let. Marketing of timeshare has attracted criticism as a result of the perceived use of high-pressure selling tactics and failure on the part of consumers to grasp the nature of the deal on offer, and national controls have begun to develop. This yields the legislative diversity between states that has commonly been used as a rationale for the introduction of harmonization measures at EC level. It might be added that the sale of timeshare has typically, though not exclusively, involved consumers in one state acquiring an interest in property in another state, which is liable to give rise to serious difficulties in enforcement and complex questions of private international law. Harmonization of laws, especially at a minimum level, cannot fully resolve these problems, but the cross-border features of the timeshare sector make it a more plausible candidate for regulation at transnational level than some of the marketing practices considered in this chapter.

Directive 85/577 on doorstep selling may on occasion catch timeshare marketing,[50] but the EC entered the field in a sector-specific manner with the adoption of Directive 94/47 on 'protection of purchasers in respect of certain aspects of contracts relating to the purchase of the right to use immovable properties on a timeshare basis'.[51] The necessary detail governing the precise character of the timeshare contract is supplied by Article 2. The Directive covers a contract concluded for at least three years under which a real property right or any other right relating to the use of immovable property for a

---

[50] Case C-423/97 *Travel Vac SL* v. *Manuel José Antelm Sanchis* [1999] ECR I-2195.
[51] *OJ* 1994 L280/83.

specified or specifiable period of at least one week in the year is purchased. The legal base is Article 100a EC (which is now, after amendment, Article 95 EC) and, since it is a 'post-Maastricht' measure, it was made jointly by the Council and the Parliament in accordance with the co-decision legislative procedure set out in Article 189b, which is now Article 251.

The overall pattern of the harmonized system is largely comparable to that employed in relation to doorstep selling. The primary focus of the proposal is improvement in the transparency of the transaction, so that the consumer is aware of the nature of the deal that is being offered.[52] Article 1 of the Directive expressly limits its scope to information on the constituent parts of a contract and the arrangements for the communication of that information, and to the procedures and arrangements for cancellation and withdrawal. Other matters remain subject to regulation by the Member States.

Specified items must be included in the contract, which shall be in writing. An Annex to the Directive sets out the minimum requirements to be included in the contract. These cover matters such as the identities and domiciles of the parties, the exact nature of the right which is the subject of the contract, an accurate description of that property and its location, the state of completion of the property (where it is under construction) as well as supporting services such as gas, electricity, water and telephone connections plus a reasonable estimate of the deadline for completion. A useful insight into the type of information that consumers are thought typically to fail to acquire in the unregulated market for timeshare is provided by appreciation that the annexed list of information that must be supplied goes so far as to cover the services (lighting, water, maintenance, refuse collection) to which the purchaser has or will have access and on what conditions, and the common facilities, such as swimming pool and sauna, to which the purchaser has or may have access, and, where appropriate, on what conditions, as well as the arrangements for maintenance of and repair to the property. Moreover, Article 4 provides that the contract shall be drawn up either in the language of the Member State in which the purchaser is resident or in the language of the Member State of which he or she is a national (which shall be an official EC language), and it is the purchaser who chooses between these options.

The Directive also establishes the right of a consumer to withdraw from a contract for a period after its conclusion, at least ten calendar days in this instance. Member States remain free to impose extra requirements in respect of matters falling within the scope of the Directive in accordance with the 'minimum harmonization' formula (Article 11).

---

[52] For a comprehensive survey see F. Garron, 'La protection du consommateur sur le marché européen des droits de séjour à temps partagé' (2002) 38 *Revue Trimistrelle de Droit Européen* 223.

In 1999 the Commission published a report into the application of the Directive.[53] This surveyed patterns of transposition of the Directive among the Member States and includes information on the (relatively uncommon) circumstances in which Member States have chosen to take advantage of the minimum harmonization formula by setting rules stricter than the Directive. The Commission raised the possibility of extending the reach of the Directive to cover contracts and other practices currently outside its scope. It draws attention to information that in Spain timeshare property is offered for use over a period of 35 months. Article 2 places 36 months – three years – as the minimum period for invocation of the Directive's protection. It seems plain that suppliers are seeking to evade the regulatory regime. Accordingly the Commission airs the possibility of extending the reach of the Directive, although to do so might simply breed the relocation of such rather obvious commercial tactics to the new boundaries. Any system of legal control founded on detailed rules risks inadequate coverage of practices that may harm the consumer but slip outside the chosen precise definitions. No concrete proposal for reform of the Timeshare Directive has been forthcoming. A superior method for addressing such problems is to employ general clauses that forbid unfair practices, and this perception forms part of the background to the Commission's concern to secure the adoption of a Directive forbidding unfair commercial practices that would supplement sector-specific measures such as Directive 94/47 on timeshare. On the other hand the use of such generally expressed prohibitions instead of detailed rules brings costs in the shape of imprecision and unpredictability. The debate is tracked more fully in Chapter 8.

The Commission's 1999 report on the application of the Timeshare Directive also admits that failure by suppliers to perform agreed contractual obligations and associated difficulties for consumers in taking effective action when faced with such practices contaminates confidence in the sector. These matters lie beyond the formal reach of the Directive. More than most measures, the effective application of this Directive as an instrument of consumer protection against unscrupulous commercial tactics depends on ready access to justice. Problems will frequently arise in a cross-border context. The creation of a minimum level of consumer protection will of itself avail the consumer little, if the obstacles to vindication of legal rights are forbiddingly high. Moreover, in so far as such laws are designed to encourage the active consumer to treat the market as extending beyond his or her home state, such inhibition will harm the process of integration. These issues are considered further in Chapter 10.

---

[53]   SEC (1999) 1795.

DISTANCE SELLING

The notion of 'distance selling' embraces situations where the trader and the consumer are physically separated. Sale by fax, telephone or increasingly commonly available electronic media such as the Internet provide examples. Such techniques reflect technological innovation and they are particularly suited to cross-border trade. Where the subject of the transaction is itself intangible, the crossing of a national frontier becomes quite irrelevant and certainly no effective basis for regulating the conduct of the deal. To this extent, distance selling in the EC is not only a practical inevitability, it is also a desirable, pro-integrative development. Nevertheless, such trends may undermine the effective application of laws of market regulation. In response to the need for a common, cross-border pattern of control, reflecting the common, cross-border marketing strategies that are in many sectors firmly in place, the Community has secured agreement on rules regulating 'distance selling'.

However, as if to mock the stately pace of lawmaking compared with the rapid velocity of technological and commercial change, the EC's legislative intervention into 'distance selling' has developed at a slow pace and in a fragmented manner. The Commission first issued a proposal in 1992, taking Article 100a EC as the legal base.[54] This document is accompanied by an impressively full and helpful background explanation which identifies the need to cure the distortions caused by legislative diversity by adopting common rules which would address the concern that consumers may not be fully aware of the nature of the transaction. The Commission's proposal followed the well-established model of seeking to achieve transparency through mandatory information disclosure. Pending the adoption of binding rules the Commission in 1992 adopted a Recommendation on Codes of Practice for the protection of consumers in respect of distance selling.[55] It recommended that trade associations should adopt codes which include a list of points found in an Annex to the Recommendation and that they should secure compliance with the codes by members.

An adjusted Commission proposal appeared in 1993[56] and this eventually won the support of the Council and Parliament, though only after the conciliation procedure under (what was then) Article 189b (and is now Article 251) had been invoked. Directive 97/7 on the protection of consumers in respect of distance contracts[57] is based on Article 100a (which is now Article 95). Directive 97/7 conforms to the pattern of most of the measures considered in

---

[54]   COM (92) 11, *OJ* 1992 C156/14.
[55]   *OJ* 1992 L156/21.
[56]   *OJ* 1993 C308/18.
[57]   *OJ* 1997 L144/19.

this chapter in its emphasis on prior information disclosure and a post-contractual right to withdraw after 'cooling-off'.[58]

The Preamble to Directive 97/7 claims that cross-border distance selling could be one of the main tangible results of the completion of the internal market for consumers. It also cites the familiar explanation that divergent national regulation of the phenomenon of distance selling distorts competition between businesses in the internal market, providing an impetus for the adoption of harmonized Community rules. The Preamble also refers to the consistent theme in EC consumer protection policy, traced explicitly back to the first Council Resolution of 1975, of the need to protect the purchasers of goods or services from demands for payment for unsolicited goods and from high-pressure selling methods.

The broad notion of a 'distance contract' is obvious enough. It concerns a deal struck between two parties who are physically remote from each other. A more specific legal definition is supplied by Article 2. A 'distance contract' is one that concerns goods or services concluded between a supplier and a consumer under an organized distance sales or service provision scheme run by the supplier, who, for the purpose of the contract, makes exclusive use of one or more means of distance communication. A 'means of distance communication' is one which, without the simultaneous physical presence of the supplier and the consumer, may be used for the conclusion of a contract between those parties. Annex I to the Directive helpfully provides an indicative list which covers media such as letters, telephones, videophone, e-mail, fax and teleshopping.

Article 3 contains two sets of exclusions. Some contracts are excluded entirely, while others are excluded only in part from the regime established by the Directive. The contracts excluded entirely are those made in circumstances where the definition of a distance contract is met but where the nature of the transaction makes it unnecessary, even absurd, to introduce requirements to disclose information and to permit a 'cooling-off' period. These are contracts concluded by means of automatic vending machines and contracts concluded with telecommunications operators through the use of public payphones, as well as contracts concluded at an auction. Other contracts are excluded entirely less because of their peculiar character and more because of successful lobbying for exclusion by the sector concerned. Contracts for the construction and sale of immovable property or relating to other immovable property rights, except for rental, are excluded; so too are those relating to financial services (though this sector has been the subject of subsequent intervention, see Directive 2002/65, below).

---

[58]   Cf J. Dickie, 'Consumer Confidence and the EC Directive on Distance Contracts' (1998) 21 *Journal of Consumer Policy* 217.

A second group of contracts is not entirely excluded, but is excluded from the Directive's provisions requiring information disclosure (Articles 4 and 5), providing for a cooling-off period (Article 6) and stipulating that an order be executed by a supplier within 30 days unless contrary provision is made (Article 7(1)). The contracts are those for the supply of foodstuffs, beverages or other goods intended for everyday consumption supplied to the home of the consumer, to his residence or to his workplace by regular roundsmen ('the milkman's exception'); and contracts for the provision of accommodation, transport, catering or leisure services, where the supplier undertakes, when the contract is concluded, to provide these services on a specific date or within a specific period. Residual provisions of the Directive – such as the ban on inertia selling (Article 9, below) – apply to these partially excluded contracts.

Article 4 contains key requirements of prior information. The consumer must be provided with a number of pieces of information in good time before the conclusion of any distance contract. The list includes the identity of the supplier and, in the case of contracts requiring payment in advance, the supplier's address; the main characteristics of the goods or services; the price of the goods or services including all taxes; delivery costs, where appropriate; and the arrangements for payment, delivery or performance. The minimum duration of the contract shall be revealed where appropriate in the case of contracts for the supply of products or services to be performed permanently or recurrently.

Article 4(2) provides that the commercial purpose of the information supplied must be made clear, and that it shall be provided in a clear and comprehensible manner in any way appropriate to the means of distance communication used. Due regard shall be had to the principles of good faith in commercial transactions, and to the principles governing the protection of those who are unable under national law to give their consent, 'such as minors'. Article 4(3) adds that in the case of telephone communications, the identity of the supplier and the commercial purpose of the call shall be made explicitly clear at the beginning of any conversation with the consumer. The intention is that the consumer be given the opportunity to slam the phone down without further ado, though the reader doubtless is able to draw on personal experience in wondering how faithfully this requirement is observed.

Article 5 provides that the information covered by Article 4 shall be confirmed to the consumer either in writing or 'in another durable medium available and accessible' to the consumer in good time during the performance of the contract, and at the latest at the time of delivery. This obligation is lifted only where the information has already been given to the consumer before conclusion of the contract in writing or in another durable medium. In any event it is required that written information be supplied to the consumer on the conditions and procedures for exercising the right of withdrawal, the supplier's address to which the consumer may address complaints and any after-sales services and guarantees which exist. An exception is foreseen for services performed through the use of a means of distance communication, supplied on only one occasion and invoiced by the operator of that means (Article 5(2)). But even here the consumer must be able to obtain the supplier's address to which complaints may be addressed. 'Getting it in writing' is evidently the leitmotif. This general pattern of mandatory information disclosure conforms to the long-standing predilections of the EC legislature visible in this chapter, although the detailed provision made by Directive 97/7 is relatively elaborate.

In the case of supply of goods the right of withdrawal provided for in Article 6 endures for a period of at least seven working days beginning on the day of receipt by the consumer of the information foreseen by Article 5. In the case of supply of services, the seven-day period runs from the day of conclusion of the contract or from the day on which the obligations to provide the information foreseen by Article 5 were fulfilled if they are fulfilled after conclusion of the contract, provided that this period does not exceed a special three-month period included in Article 6(1). This provides that if the supplier has failed to fulfil the obligations of information provision laid down in Article 5, the maximum length of the period within which a consumer may withdraw from the contract shall be capped at three months.

Article 6(2) insists that the only charge that may be made to the consumer because of the exercise of the right of withdrawal is the direct cost of returning the goods. Article 6(3) sets some limited restrictions on the exercise of the right to withdraw, perhaps most significantly in relation to contracts for or the supply of goods or services the price of which is dependent on fluctuations in the financial market which cannot be controlled by the supplier.

Article 7 is unusual in that it delves into the content of the bargain struck between supplier and consumer. It concerns performance. Article 7(1) dictates that the supplier must execute the order within a maximum of 30 days from the day following that on which the consumer forwarded his order to the supplier. This is striking, surprising and apparently heavily pro-consumer in intent. However, the parties are free to provide that this requirement be set aside and it is likely that alert suppliers will take care to make such provision in their contracts and even more likely that consumers will in any event be blissfully unaware of the point.

Article 7(2) provides that where a supplier fails to perform on the grounds that the goods or services ordered are unavailable, the consumer must be informed of this situation and must be able to obtain a refund of any sums paid within 30 days at most. This consumer-friendly proviso is also qualified. Member States may lay down that the supplier must provide the consumer with goods or services of equivalent quality and price provided that this possibility was provided for before the conclusion of the contract or in the contract.

'Inertia selling' is prohibited by Article 9 of the Directive. Member States shall prohibit the supply of goods or services to a consumer where such supply involves a demand for payment where they the goods and services have not been ordered by the consumer. An absence of a response by a consumer to unsolicited supply shall not constitute consent to enter into a contract.

Article 10 adds restrictions on the use of certain means of distance communication. A supplier using an automatic calling machine or a fax must obtain the consent of the consumer in advance. Other means of distance communication which permit individual communications are to be used only where there is no clear objection from the consumer.

Article 14 contains the 'minimum' clause. Member States may apply more stringent provisions of consumer protection. These must be compatible with the Treaty, most conspicuously with the rules governing free movement. Article 14 makes explicit the legislature's view that stricter intervention may permissibly include a ban on the marketing of certain goods or services, particularly medicinal products, by means of distance contracts. This would in principle require checking against the requirements of Articles 28 and 49, for the EC legislature is not competent to set aside the application of the rules of the Treaty. It is however probable that such intervention inspired by concern for public health would be treated as justified notwithstanding its impact on cross-border trade (Chapter 2). It is also relevant, though not in law decisive, that, as the Preamble points out, the Community itself forbids some aspects of trade in medicinal products (through Directive 89/552 on television broadcasting and Directive 92/28 on the advertising of medicinal products for human use).

DISTANCE SELLING OF FINANCIAL SERVICES

Supply of financial services is peculiarly well suited to use of technological methods in which consumer and supplier are physically distant. The exclusion of financial services from the scope of Directive 97/7 on distance selling was therefore a regrettable testimony to the effective lobbying of the EC's political institutions by commercial operators in the financial services sector. This was not new. Insurance contracts and contracts for securities had already been excluded from the scope of the Doorstep Selling Directive. The Commission added a statement to Directive 97/7. This declared 'the importance of protecting consumers in respect of distance contracts concerning financial services' and referred to its Green Paper entitled *Financial Services – Meeting*

Consumers' Expectations.[59] Moreover, the Commission's 1996–98 action plan placed the consumer dimension of financial services among ten priorities, and the sector has thereafter remained high on the policy agenda (Chapter 1). The advent of a single currency for most of the European Union has sharpened awareness of the potential advantages to the consumer of tackling remaining obstacles to an integrated market for financial services. The Commission decided to press ahead with a legislative proposal designed to bring to an end the immunity of the financial services sector from the rules governing distance selling.

The Commission issued a proposal for a Directive, which was subsequently revised,[60] and eventually adopted by the Parliament and Council. This is Directive 2002/65 concerning the distance marketing of consumer financial services.[61] It amends Directive 97/7. Its legal base is provided by Articles 47(2), 55 and 95 EC, revealing that this is a measure dedicated to the integration of markets for both goods and services. The Preamble declares the familiar dual concern to promote market integration through the adoption of common rules and also to achieve a high level of consumer protection. The Directive is not identical to its thematically connected predecessor, Directive 97/7, but they have a great many features in common, and the two now form the core of the EC's harmonized treatment of distance contracts. The key definitions largely apply in common. So does the emphasis on promoting transparency as the key technique for securing the protection of the consumer bold enough to participate in 'faceless trade' in the financial services sector.

Article 3 covers information which must be supplied to the consumer before the conclusion of the distance contract. This is close to the model foreseen by Directive 97/7 and covers matters such as the identity and address of the supplier, a description of the main characteristics of the financial service and information regarding the price, including the arrangements for payment and for performance, and the minimum duration of the distance contract in the case of financial services to be performed permanently or recurrently. Matters of redress and available compensation schemes are also covered.

The requirements found in Directive 97/7 governing provision of this information in a clear and comprehensible manner with due regard *inter alia* to the principles of good faith in commercial transactions and the protection of those who are unable under national law to give their consent, such as minors, are transplanted to Directive 2002/65. The same is true of the requirement to disclose the identity of the supplier and the commercial purpose of the call at the beginning of any telephone conversation with the consumer.

---

[59]　COM (96) 209.
[60]　*OJ* 1998 C385/10, *OJ* 2000 C177/21.
[61]　*OJ* 2002 L271/16.

Article 5 of Directive 2002/65 concerns the communication of contractual terms and conditions and the information referred to in Article 3(1) and Article 4 to the consumer 'on paper or on another durable medium available and accessible to the consumer in good time before the consumer is bound by any distance contract or offer'. Special provision is made for the case of the contract concluded at the consumer's request using a means of distance communication which does not enable the due provision of the contractual terms and conditions and the stipulated information. In such circumstances the supplier shall provide the necessary details immediately after the conclusion of the contract.

Article 6 lays down a right of withdrawal. The consumer shall have a period of 14 calendar days to exercise this right. This period is longer, extending to 30 calendar days, in the case of distance contracts relating to life insurance. The Directive includes necessary detail concerning how to fix the start of this period. The right of withdrawal shall not apply to financial services whose price depends on fluctuations in the financial market outside the supplier's control, which may occur during the withdrawal period.

The Directive's provisions on withdrawal are stipulated not to apply to credit agreements cancelled under the conditions of Article 6(4) of Directive 97/7 or Article 7 of Directive 94/47 on timeshare. Keeping the package of EC legislation concerning consumer contracts neat demands careful demarcations.

Unsolicited services are forbidden, though the possibility of 'tacit' renewal of contracts is acknowledged (Article 9). Unsolicited communications by automatic calling machines and fax shall require prior consent given by the consumer (Article 10). Other means of distance communication which allow individual communications shall be either forbidden by Member States unless the consent of the consumers concerned has been obtained, or shall be open to use only if the consumer has not expressed a manifest objection.

IMPROVING THE QUALITY OF THE *ACQUIS COMMUNAUTAIRE*

The collection of measures considered in this chapter makes up a species of European contract law. It is consumer contract law that is at stake, and, although this chapter has aimed to show how techniques of pre-contractual information disclosure and a post-agreement cooling-off period provide thematic connections between the measures under inspection, it is evident that this is far from a systematic body of law of the type which one would expect to see in an orthodox national legal order. The EC rules supplement national contract law, which continues to evolve formally unaffected by the EC in the areas untouched by the programme of harmonization of laws and which is allowed space to develop even in the areas subjected to the discipline of harmonization by virtue of the minimum formula that is common to these Directives.

The Commission has lately initiated a process designed to generate a debate on the proper role of the EU in crafting a European contract law. It was initiated by a Communication on European Contract Law in 2001,[62] advanced in February 2003 by the Action Plan on a More Coherent European Contract Law[63] and then put on to a more concrete footing in October 2004 by the communication 'European Contract Law and the revision of the *acquis*: the way forward'.[64] That debate is surveyed in Chapter 7. It is of the highest significance to charting the future trajectory of the EU's involvement in contract law, which could range from a low-profile commitment to simply filling gaps in the legal infrastructure required for a unified economic space to much more ambitious notions of a (more or less) comprehensive pattern of 'Europeanized' principles. It is the Commission's proposed 'Common Frame of Reference' that has generated the most interest. Moreover, the Commission's current preoccupation to shift the norm for EC lawmaking away from a minimum model to a 'maximum' model which instead assumes that EC intervention terminates the possibility of Member States setting stricter rules in the sector in question would, if carried through systematically, change the face of the pattern of regulation surveyed in this chapter. To be specific, it would flatten the regulatory playing field but, in doing so, it would eliminate the scope for local innovation.

Of more direct detailed relevance to the material considered in this chapter, an aspect of the current debate concerns the unsatisfactory absence of internal conformity in the legislative *acquis*. As is perfectly evident, the areas in which the EC has chosen to invest effort in the production of binding rules represent a rather peculiar mix of those visibly tied to transnational commercial practice (timeshare, package holidays, distance selling) and those with no conspicuous cross-border dimension (doorstep selling, credit). But even within this patchwork model of lawmaking there are eccentric variations of detail which mar the coherence and intelligibility of the EC's contribution to consumer protection. There is, for example, no uniform length fixed for the 'cooling-off' periods in the Directives examined in this chapter. The Doorstep Selling Directive allows seven days as a minimum time for post-agreement reflection by the consumer; for timeshare the period is fixed at ten calendar days. The case of distance selling is more complicated again, for a basic period of seven working days is supplemented by a special three-month cap on the consumer's right

---

[62] COM (2001) 398.
[63] COM (2003) 68.
[64] COM (2004) 651.

to withdraw where the supplier has failed to fulfil the stipulated obligations of information provision. A statement annexed to Directive 97/7 on distance selling noted that the Commission plans to examine the possibility and desirability of harmonizing the method of calculating the cooling-off period under existing consumer protection legislation. The Commission's Consumer Policy Strategy for 2002–2006 also refers to the desirability of cleaning up these oddities,[65] and the Commission's three documents on European contract law, mentioned above,[66] are similarly disposed to such reform. It is pertinent to recall that neatness is not a virtue in its own right. There are circumstances in which different cooling-off periods for different transactions may make sense. Such sophisticated analysis is missing from the track record of EC lawmaking but one could, for example, make a case for a relatively long cooling-off period where the consumer cannot be expected quickly to identify any possible flaw in the transaction.[67] So, as the Commission proposes, the law can usefully be made tidier and more coherent, but it is not necessarily rational for EC law to promote a uniform period of 'cooling-off' applicable to all transactions.

---

[65] *OJ* 2002 C137/2. See Chapter 1 for further discussion of the Strategy.
[66] Notes 62–4 above.
[67] P. Rekaiti and R. Van den Bergh, 'Cooling-off periods in the Consumer Laws of the EC Member States: a Comparative Law and Economics Approach' (2001) 23 *Journal of Consumer Policy* 371.

5. Regulating the substance of consumer transactions

CHOICE OF REGULATORY TECHNIQUE

Techniques such as information disclosure and 'cooling-off' periods, examined in the last chapter, can be summarized as attempts to use the law to support the consumer in the pre- and post-contractual phase. They aim to make the consumer more fully aware of the nature of the transaction under contemplation; and to provide an opportunity for withdrawal even after the deal has been agreed. So, to the extent provided by the Directives, the consumer is encouraged to think again before contracting and allowed to change his or her mind even after contracting. But the terms of the bargain themselves are unaffected by these measures. The assumption of the technique of information disclosure is that the consumer, armed with a clearer appreciation of what is on offer, will be able to negotiate a deal closer to his or her real preferences. In consequence, the market system will work more efficiently. 'Cooling-off' periods offer a fall-back protection.

Such legal intervention designed to improve the conduct of the bargaining process attracts the criticism that it may simply not go far enough to achieve effective protection of the consumer. The technique of informing the consumer assumes, among other things, that the consumer is capable of grasping the nature of the information provided. The more complex the product or service and/or the more complex the nature of the information, the less likely that the consumer will be able to respond intelligently to such information. In certain circumstances it may be true that some, perhaps most, consumers will be capable of making the necessary informed decisions, but a group of less skilled consumers may be unable to do so. The risk then is that vulnerable consumers will be exposed to a market in which expectations of self-awareness among some consumers are pitched at too high a level. Information disclosure as a regulatory technique assumes the generation of a competitive market in which traders are induced to offer better terms as a result of the consumer's capacity to perceive what is on offer and to shop around. In some markets, at least, this will not correspond to the true operation of the market. Legal regulation accordingly needs to be shaped in a way that is sensitive to these concerns.[1] 'Cooling-off' periods may end too early to give the consumer a genuine chance to reassess a purchasing decision, and in any event, even if a right of withdrawal is invoked, in practice it may not help the consumer to renegotiate a better deal. Worse still, if one perceives an endemic likelihood of exploitation as a result of the differential between the economic power of the trader and that of the consumer, then tinkering with the negotiating process may be regarded as worse than doing nothing, for it will disguise and thus legitimate the fundamental unfairness of the outcome of a system based on contractual freedom, even where spuriously 'informed'. This combination of reasons may lead one to suppose that in some degree the law needs to move beyond adjustment of the bargaining environment towards regulation of the terms of the bargain themselves.

However, the extra step of using the law directly to address the 'fairness' of a contract is controversial on several levels. Most of all, it represents an assault on the notion of freedom of contract – that parties have autonomy to enter into bargains as they see fit, to fix terms as they choose and to expect the law to protect and enforce agreements that have been freely entered into. To use the law to alter bargains struck by private parties may, on some accounts, damage commercial confidence in the reliability of the law and thus hamper the operation of a market economy. More politically, such intervention attracts criticism for its challenge to individual freedom. However, in the consumer sphere in particular, it has been recognized in recent decades that notions of the purity of contractual freedom are not necessarily consistent with the reality of modern market conditions. In a world of mass production of technologically advanced products and services, provided through extended distribution chains which leave the consumer remote from the producer and, typically, subject to contractual terms contained in the small print of standard-form contracts, the idea of free negotiation is a myth. The bargain has lost its sanctity as an expression of individual will. Contracts, indeed, may be mass-produced, just as goods are. There remain widely divergent views on the appropriate legal responses to such commercial development, but there is a general acceptance that contractual freedom cannot be viewed in the same

---

[1] For a comparative inquiry see G. Howells and T. Wilhelmsson, 'EC and US Approaches to Consumer Protection – should the gap be bridged?' (1997) 17 *Yearbook of European Law* 207. For more general inquiry into the proper impact on policy-making of appreciation of the limits of consumer ability to process information see J. Hanson and D. Kysar, 'Taking Behavioralism Seriously' (1999) 112 *Harvard Law Review* 1420; C. Sunstein (ed.), *Behavioral law and economics* (Cambridge: Cambridge University Press, 2000); R. Korobkin and T. Ulen. 'Law and Behavioural Science: Removing the Rationality Assumption from Law and Economics' (2000) 88 *California Law Review* 1051.

light today as it was 50 or more years ago.[2] As a general observation, a willingness to use the law to check some aspects of the content of a contract, rather than simply the process of its formation, has evolved.

DIRECTIVE 93/13 ON UNFAIR TERMS IN CONSUMER CONTRACTS

These are policy debates that have been played out in many national systems in recent years. Community law too has broken through the barrier separating regulation designed to achieve 'mere' procedural fairness from regulation addressing substantive fairness. Directive 93/13 on unfair terms in consumer contracts[3] is applicable to all contracts concluded after 31 December 1994. This remarkable Directive has a scope that is, admittedly, limited in some detailed respects. However, its general impact is highly significant. Sweeping beyond the relatively minor tinkering with the fundamentals of the law of contract formation resulting from the measures covered in the last chapter, Directive 93/13 is properly regarded as the first incursion of Community law into the heartland of national contract law thinking. This makes it a challenge for national private lawyers, expected to adapt to Community law method after decades of perceiving Community law as, more or less, an enterprise engaged in creating new or extended patterns of public law. But Directive 93/13 is a challenge for Community lawyers too, for under the camouflage of the harmonization programme the Directive takes the EC system deep into largely uncharted private law territory.

The Directive was almost 20 years in the making.[4] The Consumers' Consultative Committee expressed a desire for Community action against unfair contract terms in 1977.[5] The Parliament called for a Directive in 1980.[6] Within the Commission, work in the field began in the late 1970s, although it was not until 1984 that its first official document, a discussion paper, was published.[7] Revised proposals based on what was then Article 100a EC, and is now (after amendment) Article 95, emerged thereafter in 1990 and 1992.[8] The proposals, in

---

[2] T. Wilhelmsson, *Social Contract Law and European Integration* (Aldershot: Dartmouth, 1994); M. Trebilcock, *The Limits of Freedom of Contract* (Cambridge, MA: Harvard University Press, 1993); H. Collins, *Regulating Contracts* (Oxford: Oxford University Press, 1999).

[3] *OJ* 1993 L95/29.

[4] See L. Niglia, *The Transformation of Contract in Europe* (The Hague: Kluwer Law International, 2003).

[5] CCC 48/77.

[6] *OJ* 1980 C291/35.

[7] COM (84) 55, Unfair Terms in Contracts concluded with Consumers.

[8] *OJ* 1990 C243/2, *OJ* 1992 C73/7.

their several different forms, provoked often heated debate both about the competence of the Community to legislate in the field and the desirability of the details of particular proposals.[9] A number of the Member States possess legislation in the field of unfair contract terms, but the control techniques employed are diverse. Some legal systems control certain types of clause in certain types of contract directly, either by directing that courts should not apply them or by directing that judges should assess whether or not to enforce them in the circumstances of the particular case. Other systems prefer administrative procedures, involving the adoption of orders forbidding the use of particular terms.

The significant variation in legal technique between the Member States has been conventionally used to make the case for harmonization under the Treaty. The Directive's Preamble supplements this with the claim that creating minimum legal rights that consumers can enjoy throughout the territory of the EU will promote confidence in the viability of the internal market. Whether this truly suffices to provide a constitutional justification for Directive 93/13 is not certain in the wake of the Court's *Tobacco Advertising* ruling, and is discussed in that context in Chapter 3. This chapter examines the substance of Directive 93/13. Against the background of regulatory diversity among the Member States, the attempt in practice to find common principles in order to put in place a measure of harmonization at EC level was predictably problematic. That the Directive as finally agreed operates as a minimum measure, allowing states flexibility to apply or maintain more stringent measures of consumer protection, will be no surprise to the observer of the pattern of legal harmonization in this area. Naturally and perhaps gratifyingly the use of the minimum formula places limits on the extent to which the Directive undermines existing national contract law tradition. However, the compromises required to secure agreement in Council involved more than the mere inclusion of the minimum harmonization clause. It also proved necessary to abandon some aspects of the early proposals in the field before agreement was finally secured in March 1993 and the Directive was adopted. In many respects it is an extraordinarily ambitious measure, albeit less ambitious than some might have hoped. Most of all, it opened up a new potential 'growth area' – European (or at least EC) private law. This field of inquiry has developed with such remarkable pace that whereas the first edition of this book was content to use a subsection of this chapter to trace progress, this second edition devotes a separate chapter, Chapter 7, to the controversial phenomenon of European private law.

---

[9]   An especially illuminating contribution is that of H. Brandner and P. Ulmer, 'The Community Directive on Unfair Terms in Consumer Contracts' (1991) 28 *Common Market Law Review* 615, which severely criticizes an earlier draft from a German perspective. On subsequent developments in Germany see H.-W. Micklitz, 'German Unfair Contract Terms Act and the EC Directive 93/13', in J. Lonbay (ed.), *Enhancing the Legal Position of the European Consumer* (London: BIICL, 1996).

Contracts Falling within the Scope of Application of the Directive

A definitional issue of major importance lies in the identification of the types of contract which are subjected to the controls envisaged by the Directive. The Directive covers contracts concluded between a seller or supplier and a consumer (Article 1). These terms are defined in Article 2 with reference to acting outside his trade, business or profession (consumer) and acting for purposes relating to his trade, business or profession whether privately or publicly owned (seller or supplier). The consumer must be a natural person,[10] whereas the seller or supplier may be a natural or legal person.

The Recitals to the Directive clarify that this definition excludes, *inter alia*, employment contracts, contracts relating to succession rights, contracts relating to rights under family law and contracts relating to the incorporation and organization of companies or partnership agreements. However, it includes insurance contracts, although, as a result of the application of Article 4, the price of insurance as such does not fall to be checked against the required standard of fairness. It also includes oral contracts. Contracts for the sale of land are also capable of falling within the scope of the Directive.[11]

In so far as the Directive is based on an expectation that a risk of exploitation is inherent in contracts concluded between economically imbalanced parties, it can be criticized for an irrational limitation to contracts between consumers and traders. After all, similar problems may infect the relationship between large and small businesses. Indeed the power differential between such parties may be a good deal wider than between small trader and consumer. Some national systems accordingly govern business contracts, not simply consumer contracts, although typically through an appropriately modified regime. The EC Directive is, admittedly, limited in its focus (although it does not preclude wider coverage under national law). At this stage of the development of 'European private law', where its very existence is neither universally accepted nor desired, it is perhaps necessary simply to acknowledge this restricted coverage, which cannot readily be defended on policy grounds. It should also not be neglected that the Directive's limitation to consumer contracts is explicable in the light of its roots in EC Consumer Protection Programme (Chapter 1).

Terms Falling within the Scope of Application of the Directive

The terms which are to be controlled require identification. Article 3 controls

---

10 This was applied by the Court in Joined Cases C-541/99 & C-542/99 *Cape Snc* v. *Idealservice Srl* [2001] ECR I-9049.

11 Cf. S. Bright and C. Bright, 'Unfair Terms in Land Contracts: Copy Out or Cop Out?' (1995) 111 *Law Quarterley Review* 655.

only contractual terms which have not been individually negotiated (although national law may go further in the scope of its coverage). This notion is explained further in Article 3(2). A term shall always be regarded as not individually negotiated (and therefore within the scope of the Directive) 'where it has been drafted in advance and the consumer has therefore not been able to influence the substance of the term, particularly in the context of a pre-formulated standard contract'. It rests with the seller or supplier who claims that a standard term has been individually negotiated to prove this.

The limitation to terms which have not been individually negotiated is more than simply a practical method of fixing the outer limit of potential legal intervention into the parties' bargain. It is of significance in an assessment of the underlying purpose of the Directive. Where the consumer has actually engaged in negotiation with the trader, it seems to be assumed that that process of negotiation acts as adequate protection from the risk of the imposition of unfair terms; or at least that the justification for legal intervention is lost. Only where negotiation is absent is intervention in the substance of the deal admitted. This is by no means uncontroversial. One might go so far as to adopt precisely the opposite perspective and argue that face-to-face discussion deepens the risk that the economically powerful trader will exploit the consumer. However, the Directive's limitation to terms that have not been individually negotiated demonstrates a suspicion of 'mass-produced' contracts, at least at the threshold of jurisdiction to check enforceability.

'Unfairness' under Directive 93/13

Proceeding from an assumption of imbalance in the supplier/consumer relationship, the Directive requires the Member States to provide that unfair terms shall not bind the consumer. This is a direct check on the enforceability of contractual terms and not simply a method of encouraging the consumer to bargain for a better deal and/or to reject an unacceptable deal of the type surveyed in the previous chapter.

The key to the Directive is its approach to the identification of unfairness. According to Article 3 a term covered by the Directive shall be regarded as unfair if, 'contrary to the requirement of good faith, it causes a significant imbalance in the parties' rights and obligations arising under the contract, to the detriment of the consumer'. An Annex to the Directive provides an indicative and non-exhaustive list of the terms which may be regarded as unfair. This, then, is neither a black nor white, but a grey list. National courts and tribunals may use it as an interpretative aid. This is an aspect of the measure which altered as negotiation progressed. Earlier drafts of what ultimately became Directive 93/13 proposed a black list, but in the face of disagreement this was abandoned.

In *Commission* v. *Sweden*[12] the Commission sought the Court's confirmation of its view that the Swedish failure to reproduce the Annex in the text of its implementing laws was inadequate. Sweden had instead reproduced the Annex, with a commentary, in the statement of reasons for the laws. The Court refused to uphold the Commission's complaint. It pointed out that a term appearing in the Annex's list is not necessarily unfair and, conversely, a term that does not appear in the list is not necessarily fair. It is a grey list. So achieving the full effect of the Directive in the national legal order is not dependent on embedding the Annex's list into implementing measures. EC law governing the implementation of Directives requires only that the legal situation resulting from national measures be sufficiently precise and clear and that individuals be made fully aware of their rights. The Commission had failed to defeat the Swedish government's claim that according to Nordic legal tradition the preparatory material in which the Annex could be found might easily be consulted and that this was sufficient to guarantee public awareness. One may note that implementation according to this method is unlikely to suffice in a legal tradition marked by a lesser expectation that citizens will look beyond the formal text. The Nordic countries may be a special case, and one would normally expect to see Directive 93/13's Annex attached to national implementing measures. Indeed the Court's rather generous treatment of Sweden's implementation of Article 3 may be contrasted with the approach taken to Dutch implementation of Articles 4(2) and 5. In *Commission* v. *Netherlands*[13] the Court held it essential that the legal position under national law be sufficiently precise and clear and that individuals be made fully aware of their rights. The Netherlands had not implemented the Directive by adopting specific provisions but rather relied on achieving its aims through schematic interpretation of existing Dutch law, backed up by judicial readiness to ensure conformity with the Directive. This did not achieve the requirements of legal certainty, which are of particular importance in the field of consumer protection. The Dutch judgment is not incompatible with that in the Swedish case, where the Court concluded that the demands of legal certainty were satisfied. However, the further a Member State chooses to diverge from explicit use of the text of the Directive in its implementing measures, the harder will be its task in meeting the EC law requirements that national law be clear and precise and that individuals be fully aware of their rights.

It is plain that the elaboration provided by the grey list in the Annex will be of great significance in the practical application of the system by national courts. The list includes 17 terms. They are a mixed bag but not a random

---

[12]   Case C-478/99 [2002] ECR I-4147.
[13]   Case C-144/99 [2001] ECR I-3541.

collection. There are linking themes.[14] By implication, targets at which the system is aimed seem to include unilateral decision-making power claimed by a supplier, a lack of proportionality in the nature of the obligations and an absence of information provided to the consumer. Where a term imports such deficiencies into the bargain, then it is ripe for characterization as 'unfair' within the meaning of the Directive, which will cause it to be regarded as unenforceable. Terms which illustrate the notion of unilateral decision making include '(f): authorizing the seller or supplier to dissolve the contract on a discretionary basis where the same facility is not granted to the consumer, or permitting the seller or supplier to retain the sums paid for services not yet supplied by him where it is the seller or supplier himself who dissolves the contract'; or '(j): enabling the seller or supplier to alter the terms of the contract unilaterally without a valid reason which is specified in the contract'. Terms suggesting lack of proportionality include '(e): requiring any consumer who fails to fulfil his obligation to pay a disproportionately high sum in compensation'. Threads which provide an incentive to improve transparency and consumer information on pain of holding terms unfair and unenforceable may be traced in '(i): irrevocably binding the consumer to terms with which he had no real opportunity of becoming acquainted before the conclusion of the contract'.

To repeat, the appearance in a contract of a term included in the Annex does not automatically mean it is an unfair term; the particular circumstances must always be examined. Article 4 of the Directive provides that unfairness shall be assessed 'taking into account the nature of the goods or services for which the contract was concluded and by referring, at the time of conclusion of the contract, to all the circumstances attending the conclusion of the contract . . .'. Underpinning the Court's ruling in *Commission* v. *Sweden* is the point that it would be to misapprehend the illustrative nature of a grey list to treat its contents as a group of inevitably indefensible terms. Nevertheless, it is probable that in practice those seeking to defend terms falling within the grey list before national courts and tribunals will find that they face a difficult task. At the same time, reference to notions such as 'disproportionately' high sums in term (e) and 'undue' restriction in term (q) in the grey list make plain the discretion vested in judges asked to examine particular terms in their context. More generally, in so far as the Directive is correctly analysed as having as its theoretical base a suspicion about matters such as unilateral decision-making power, lack of proportionality and lack of information, it creates an instrument for strengthening the consumer's contractual position by offering protection against the enforcement of unfairly prejudicial terms.

---

[14] T. Wilhelmsson, 'Control of Unfair Contract Terms and Social Values: EC and Nordic Approaches' (1993) 16 *Journal of Consumer Policy* 435; C. Willett, 'Directive on Unfair Terms in Consumer Contracts' [1994] *Consumer Law Journal* 114.

Unfairness and Price

The most fundamental unfairness faced by a contracting consumer might be thought to be the risk that he or she will find that the price is too high. But the Directive does not permit a consumer to argue that this central term of the contract is unfair. According to Article 4,

> assessment of the unfair nature of the terms shall relate neither to the definition of the main subject matter of the contract nor to the adequacy of the price and remuneration, on the one hand, as against the services or goods supplies [*sic*] in exchange, on the other, in so far as these terms are in plain intelligible language.

This is a rather obscure formulation. Rather more helpfully, it is explained in the Recitals to the Directive that

> assessment of unfair character shall not be made of terms which describe the main subject matter of the contract nor the quality/price ratio of the goods or services supplied; . . . the main subject matter of the contract and the price/quality ratio may nevertheless be taken into account in assessing the fairness of other terms.

It seems, then, that unfairness does not arise simply where goods or services are overpriced, provided the relevant terms are in plain, intelligible language. This limitation to the scope of application of the Directive acts as an important constraint on the power of a judge to assess unfairness in a consumer contract.

The Use of Plain, Intelligible Language

Article 5 provides that in the case of contracts where all or certain terms offered to the consumer are in writing, these terms must always be drafted in plain, intelligible language. Where there is doubt about the meaning of a term, the interpretation most favourable to the consumer shall prevail. This fits comfortably with the policy objective of securing transparency.

As mentioned above, Article 4 of the Directive provides that 'assessment of the unfair nature of the terms shall relate neither to the definition of the main subject matter of the contract nor to the adequacy of the price and renumeration, on the one hand, as against the services or goods supplies [*sic*] in exchange, on the other', but adds that this applies only 'in so far as these terms are in plain intelligible language.' Therefore where the requirement of plain intelligible language has not been met, the (in short) 'core terms' of the contract lose their immunity from review. This does not undermine the principle that supervising the fairness of the price normally lies beyond the judicial function. It is instead an assertion of the powerful concern to promote transparency.

Unfairness and Good Faith

At an early stage in the Directive's lifecycle Article 3's linkage of unfairness
to the concept of an outcome 'contrary to the requirement of good faith' was
identified as likely to prove difficult to handle.[15] Its content depends on the
nature of the bargain. The Preamble to the Directive invites consideration of
the strength of the bargaining power of the parties and of whether the
consumer was induced to agree to the term. The notion of good faith is familiar in German civil law. Aspects of English law may conceivably perform
similar functions but by contrast they are not recognizably packaged as a law
of good faith. In fact English law may be more persuasively analysed as
concerned to suppress bad faith rather than promote good faith.[16] In any event
it is plain that 'good faith' has a much more developed (albeit far from
uniform) meaning in continental legal systems than in the common law.[17] This
seems likely to impede the development of a common approach to the Article
3 test. Yet unfairness and good faith are prime candidates for
'Europeanization' via the use of the Article 234 (ex 177) preliminary reference
procedure.[18] In so far as the European Court is offered and accepts invitations
to supply a common interpretation of such phrases within the Directive,
Europeanized notions will be digested by judges in all 25 Member States in
the application of provisions derived from the Directive. In theory at least,
Article 234 (ex 177) cuts a direct channel of communication between national
courts and the European Court and an indirect channel between national courts
in different states, and through those channels flows a stream of developing
European private law.[19] The theory is beginning to be supplemented by judicial practice.

'Europeanization' through Case Law

One might readily assume that it will be relatively rare for cases concerning
Directive 93/13 to be the subject of preliminary references by national courts
to the European Court. The Directive concerns only consumer contracts. Most
such contracts concern matters that are relatively small-scale. Rarely will the

---

[15]   H. Collins, 'Good Faith in European Contract Law' 1(1994) 4 *Oxford Journal of Legal
       Studies* 229; M. Tenreiro, 'The Community Directive on Unfair Terms and National Legal
       Systems' (1995) 3 *European Review of Private Law* 273.
[16]   E. McKendrick, *Contract Law* (Basingstoke: Macmillan, 2003), chs 12, 17.
[17]   R. Brownsword, N. Hird and G. Howells (eds), *Good Faith in Contract: Concept and Context*
       (Aldershot: Ashgate, 1999); R. Zimmermann and S. Whittaker, *Good Faith in European
       Contract Law* (Cambridge: Cambridge University Press, 2000).
[18]   S. Weatherill, 'Prospects for the Development of European Private Law through Europeanization
       in the European Court of Justice' (1995) 3 *European Review of Private Law* 307.
[19]   Niglia, *The Transformation of Contract in Europe*, note 4 above.

pattern of litigation be apt for the delay and expense caused to the parties by a preliminary reference to Luxembourg. Moreover, even where litigation reaches the higher courts there is some indication of judicial unwillingness to refer questions to Luxembourg. In *Director General of Fair Trading* v. *First National Bank plc*,[20] the first case to reach the House of Lords concerning the UK's measures introduced to implement Directive 93/13, their Lordships were correctly anxious to interpret the UK regulations to conform to the Directive. However, they declined to make use of the preliminary reference procedure. This was surprising. It was hard to regard the matter as free from interpretative doubt since the House of Lords was taking a view different from the Court of Appeal in the same case.[21] The reluctance to refer regrettably robbed the European Court of an opportunity to provide authoritative interpretation of the meaning and scope of the 'good faith' principle in Directive 93/13.[22]

None the less a trickle of case law is reaching the European Court. This offers it the opportunity to provide a common 'Europeanized' interpretation of terms found in Directive 93/13. *Oceano Grupo Editorial SA* v. *Rocio Murciano Quintero*[23] concerned a contract for the supply of an encyclopaedia. The contract contained a term conferring jurisdiction on the courts in Barcelona, the seller's home city but not the home city of the consumer. Was this unfair? The Spanish court referred a logically preliminary question. It asked whether a national court is empowered to consider of its own motion whether a term is unfair within the meaning of Directive 93/13 on unfair terms in consumer contracts. The Directive is silent on the matter. It is arguable that the Court could have perfectly coherently ruled that this is a procedural matter falling for determination according to national law, but it did not do so. In pursuit of the achievement of the objectives of the Directive, it was more ambitious. It stated that 'the system of protection introduced by the Directive is based on the idea that the consumer is in a weak position vis-a-vis the seller or supplier, as regards both his bargaining power and his level of knowledge'. A consumer may be ignorant of available legal protection and this prompted the conclusion that 'effective protection of the consumer may be attained only if the national court acknowledges that it has power to evaluate terms of this

---

20   [2001] 3 WLR 1297, [2002] 1 All ER 97.
21   P. Nebbia, 'Annotation' (2003) 40 *Common Market Law Review* 983.
22   E. Macdonald, 'Scope and Fairness of the Unfair Terms in Consumer Contracts Regulations' (2002) 65 *Modern Law Review* 763; S. Whittaker, 'Assessing the Fairness of Contract Terms: The Parties' Essential Bargain, its Regulatory Context and the Significance of the Requirement of Good Faith' [2004] *Zeitschrift für Europäisches Privatrecht* 75.
23   Cases C-240/98 to C-244/98 [2000] ECR I-4941. See S. Whittaker, 'Judicial Interventionism and Consumer Contracts' (2001) 117 *Law Quarterly Review* 215; J. Stuyck, 'Annotation' (2001) 38 *Common Market Law Review* 719; S. Weatherill, 'Can there be common interpretation of European Private Law?' (2002) 31/1 *Georgia Journal of International and Comparative Law* 139.

kind of its own motion'. It seems logical to go further and to conclude from this reasoning that the Directive requires, rather than simply empowers, judges to scrutinize the fairness of terms of their own motion.[24] As for the impugned contract term itself, the European Court was decisive. It hindered the consumer's right to take legal action, a type of term mentioned in the Directive's Annex's grey list. It advantaged the seller. It was condemned by the Court as unfair within the meaning of Article 3 of the Directive.

The Court similarly used the harmonization Directive as a springboard to interpret rules of civil procedure relevant to the vindication of consumer rights in *Cofidis SA*.[25] The preliminary reference concerned a procedural rule prohibiting the national court, on expiry of a limitation period, from finding a term to be unfair. Here too the Court could conceivably have left this within the autonomy of the legal order of the Member States; but here too it judged that the Directive demanded more. In proceedings in which consumers are defendants, it ruled that the imposition of such a limitation period was incompatible with the protection intended to be conferred on them by the Directive.

These rulings suggest that the Court, provided with an appropriate opportunity, is eager to interpret relevant notions in harmonization Directives in a 'Europeanized' manner, rather than leaving matters to be settled according to local procedures. And the Court's 'Europeanized' slant is heavily influenced by the concern to find an interpretation that secures effective consumer protection. The Court is not, however, inclined to convert itself into a forum for judging whether any contract term is fair or not. In *Freiburger Kommunalbauten* v. *Hofstetter*,[26] the Court refused to provide a judgment on the fairness of an impugned term. A construction company (FK) sold a parking space in a multi-storey car park it was building for a consumer, Hofstetter. The contract stated that the consumer should pay the whole price in advance once FK had provided security. FK did this by providing a bank guarantee, under which the bank agreed to meet claims which the consumer might have against FK, for example for defective performance. The consumer refused to pay until the work was complete. FK claimed interest due for late payment under the contract. The consumer claimed the term was unfair. The Bundesgerichtshof, the highest civil court in Germany, referred the question of unfairness to the European Court under the Article 234 procedure. The European Court pointed out that Article 4 of the Directive requires that the consequences of a term must be taken into account, which will involve reference to national law. The Court would interpret the 'general criteria' in the Directive but assessment of the fairness of a particular term belongs with the

---

[24] S. Whittaker, 'Judicial Interventionism and Consumer Contracts (2001) 117 *Law Quarterly Review* 215.

[25] Case C-473/00 [2002] ECR I-10875.

[26] Case C-237/02 judgment of 1 April 2004.

national court, which is able to consider the circumstances of the particular contractual relationship at stake and the costs and benefits to the consumer of the clause.

The Court will not normally judge the fairness of a particular term. *Oceano Grupo* was explained in *Freiburger Kommunalbauten* v. *Hofstetter* as a case where the term offered no possible benefit to the consumer, only to the seller, and where accordingly assessment of the wider circumstances could not disturb a finding of unfairness. In *Freiburger Kommunalbauten* v. *Hofstetter* the situation was more nuanced. A contractual requirement of payment in advance might appear harsh from the consumer's perspective, but security was provided and, in addition, advance payment might permit the builder to reduce its borrowings and thereby reduce the price. The European Court would not displace the national court's job of deciding whether the term was fair in the circumstances. The Court is however willing to interpret 'general criteria'. There are many such general phrases and concepts in Directive 93/13 and in other relevant harmonization Directives which are potential contenders for a 'Europeanized' interpretation which will serve to push the bounds of the practical impact of harmonization further outwards. 'Good faith' remains a candidate. So too does the definition of a contract. This is a fundamental issue, yet it too is a potential focus for a harmonized European approach which may jolt existing national assumptions.[27]

Case law emerging through the Article 234 preliminary reference procedure is based on a relationship of collaboration between the European Court and the referring national court. Preliminary rulings are not limited in effect to the case at hand and the principles of law should be applied by all courts in the EU.[28] So a bilateral judicial relationship becomes multilateral. There is also intriguing scope for a greater degree of horizontal cross-fertilization of judicial thinking. A ruling in one Member State that a term in a consumer contract is unfair cannot be binding on a court dealing with a similar issue in another Member State. But both courts would be applying rules sourced from Directive 93/13. There is scope for advocates, judges and jurists more generally to learn and to draw inspiration from what is happening in courts across the territory of the 25 Member States. This is plainly dependent on such information on judicial practice being readily available. To this end the Commission has created 'CLAB', a database on national case law concerning unfair contract terms. This is electronically accessible[29] and is designed to provide a systematic

[27] S. Whittaker, 'Unfair Contract Terms, Public Services and the Construction of a European Conception of Contract' (2000) 116 *Law Quarterly Review* 95; M. Van Hoecke, 'Deep Level Comparative Law', *EUI Working Paper Law No. 2002/13* (Florence, 2002).
[28] Case 283/81 *CILFIT* [1982] ECR 3415.
[29] http://europa.eu.int/comm/consumers/cons_int/safe_shop/unf_cont_terms/clab/index_en.htm.

guide to the treatment of unfair terms in national practice. It is, of course, only as good as the information that is fed into it, and in this respect the Commission is heavily dependent for the success of CLAB on participation and input from national level. If successfully managed, CLAB raises the intriguing prospect of a rich comparison between approaches to unfairness in different jurisdictions under the same umbrella, Directive 93/13.

Enforcement

Article 6 of the Directive requires Member States to provide that unfair terms shall not bind the consumer. The contract shall continue to bind the parties if capable of remaining in existence without the unfair terms.

Article 7 provides that 'member states shall ensure that, in the interests of consumers and of competitors adequate and effective means exist to prevent the continued use of unfair terms in contracts concluded with consumers by sellers or suppliers'. It is further provided in Article 7(2) that the 'means' referred to shall include

> provisions whereby persons or organisations, having a legitimate interest under national law in protecting consumers, may take action according to the national law concerned before the courts or before competent administrative bodies for a decision as to whether contractual terms drawn up for general use are unfair, so that they can apply appropriate and effective means to prevent the continued use of such terms.

The enforcement procedures foreseen by Article 7(2) do not attract the rule of interpretation contained in Article 5, which provides that in the case of contracts where terms offered to the consumer are in writing, doubt about the meaning of a term shall be resolved in the manner most favourable to the consumer. As the Court explained in *Commission* v. *Spain*,[30] were such a pro-consumer rule to prevail, the effectiveness of the enforcement procedures would be reduced. An ambiguous term might escape prohibition because it is capable of being interpreted in a fair manner, even though in practice it may be applied in an unfair manner. So in enforcement actions foreseen by Article 7(2), as distinct from individual consumer disputes, objective interpretation is the rule.

Article 7 is significant in its extension of enforcement mechanisms beyond litigation involving private parties (Article 6) into the realms of public enforcement. However, it is far from clear precisely what is required by Article 7(2). Its rather unclear phrases may require subsequent elucidation of the nature of the enforcement obligation which is placed on Member States. It is

---

[30]   Case C-70/03 judgment of 9 September 2004.

especially obscure whether Member States are obliged to empower consumers' representative organizations to bring such proceedings as part of the general quest to secure the effective enforcement of EC law at national level, or whether such an obligation arises only where such organizations already enjoy privileged status under comparable national laws. The matter might have been settled as a result of litigation initiated in the UK by the Consumers' Association, which was at first excluded from the enforcement structure in the UK's regulations designed to implement Directive 93/13. A preliminary reference was made asking whether this complied with the Directive[31] but the case was withdrawn before the European Court had the opportunity to address the point. A Labour government took office in 1997 and promised to amend the regulations in order to confer a recognized status on the Consumers' Association as an enforcement agency. This promise was kept in implementing regulations introduced in 1999,[32] eliminating the need for litigation.

The pattern of enforcement has been supplemented by Directive 98/27 on injunctions for the protection of consumers' interests.[33] This measure is examined at more length in Chapter 10, which deals with general problems of securing effective law enforcement. Directive 98/27 is particularly significant in a cross-border context. It puts in place a type of 'mutual recognition' of enforcement agencies.

Minimum Harmonization

As already mentioned, Directive 93/13 adheres to the technique of minimum harmonization in Article 8. This seems both desirable and necessary in the light of the prevailing diversity between national systems. It would be extremely difficult to establish a common Community rule apt to replace national rules both for technical reasons of drafting and because of the risk that existing stricter national rules may be undermined. Although this diminishes the capacity of the Directive to create a level playing field for commercial actors, a Community minimum seems appropriate.

The choice of the minimum harmonization model demands that care be taken in implementation. Measures implementing the Directive will not simply pre-empt national law and become the sole source of legal control. The Member States will be obliged to consider how best to incorporate the rules drawn from the Directive into their (in many cases) existing sophisticated

---

31 Case C–82/96 *R* v. *Secretary of State for Trade and Industry, ex parte Consumers' Association*, withdrawn in 1997.
32 G. Howells and S. Weatherill, *Consumer Protection Law* (Aldershot: Dartmouth Publishing Company, 2005), Ch. 5.
33 *OJ* 1998 L166/51.

regimes. It is already apparent that the desirable route of consolidation, yielding a single legal regime, has not been universally followed. This results in a fragmentation of consumer protection law within the national system.[34] Consumer protection law needs to be clear and simple if it is to be widely understood and used. Those states which have simply 'bolted on' measures implementing Directive 93/13 to their existing legal regimes diminish the practical utility of the whole system. It may be that the intransparency that results from taking the easy, 'bolt-on' option is a reason for doubting whether the obligation to implement the Directive in accordance with Articles 10 and 249 EC has been met.[35]

DIRECTIVE 99/44 ON CONSUMER SALES AND GUARANTEES

The adoption of Directive 93/13 on unfair terms did not bring to an end the Commission's ambitions to assert an EC law intervention into national consumer contract law. In November 1993 it published a Green Paper on 'Guarantees for Consumer Goods and After-Sales Service'.[36] Benefiting the consumer through improved transparency was a major stated objective underpinning the Green Paper, but, like the Directive on unfair terms in consumer contracts, it also envisaged regulation of the substance of the transaction. Whereas Directive 93/13 envisages a 'negative' control in the sense that it renders unfair terms unenforceable, the Green Paper on guarantees tended towards a positive intervention by inserting a basic protective term governing product quality into consumer contracts. This theme has been maintained. Debate was sharpened and a more precise shape for the harmonized system emerged. Further Commission proposals for legislation were advanced in 1996 and 1998.[37] Eventually Directive 99/44 on certain aspects of the sale of consumer goods and associated guarantees was adopted by the Council and Parliament.[38]

Directive 99/44 takes Article 95 EC as its legal base. In constitutional terms this is harmonization of laws designed to promote the establishment and functioning of the internal market. The Preamble to the Directive draws on the

---

[34] On the UK position see Howells and Weatherill, note 32 above, ch. 5, and, on motivations for reform, see H. Beale, 'Unfair terms in contracts: proposals for reform in the UK' (2004) 27 *Journal of Consumer Policy* 289. More generally see E. Hondius, 'The Reception of the Directive on Unfair Contract Terms by the Member States' (1995) 3 *European Review of Private Law* 241.
[35] F. Reynolds, 'Annotation' (1994) 110 *Law Quarterly Review* 1.
[36] COM (93) 509.
[37] *OJ* 1996 C307/8, *OJ* 1998 C148/12.
[38] *OJ* 1999 L171/12.

familiar insistence that Member States' laws in the area vary, causing market fragmentation and distortion of competition between sellers. It also contends that 'the creation of a common set of minimum rules of consumer law, valid no matter where goods are purchased within the Community, will strengthen consumer confidence and enable consumers to make the most of the internal market'. This follows thematically from the 1993 Green Paper, which asserted that 'Cross-border shopping can only flourish if the consumer knows he will enjoy the same guarantee and after-sales service conditions no matter where the supplier is located'.[39] Community intervention is portrayed as a means to induce consumers to treat the market as integrated. This is similar to the reasoning that informs Directive 93/13 on unfair terms in consumer contracts. It is of equally constitutionally ambiguous pedigree (Chapter 3).

The Preamble to Directive 99/44 also draws on Articles 153(1) and (3) EC to insist on the salience of the quality of the chosen harmonized regulatory environment. The Community should contribute to the achievement of a high level of consumer protection. In this vein the core of Directive 99/44 is found in Article 2(1). It provides that the seller must deliver goods to the consumer which are in conformity with the contract of sale. Article 3(1) provides that the seller shall be liable to the consumer for any lack of conformity which exists at the time the goods were delivered. This is a form of legal guarantee of the minimum level of contractually warranted quality standards. It offers the consumer a basic legal protection which is independent of any negotiation with the seller.

Like Directive 93/13, Directive 99/44 goes beyond the EC's thematic concern for transparency and consumer information to deal instead with the content of the bargain struck between the parties.[40]

Conformity with the Contract of Sale

Article 2(1)'s guiding notion that goods shall be in conformity with the contract of sale is amplified by Article 2(2) of the Directive. A presumption of the necessary conformity applies if the goods comply with the description given by the seller and possess the qualities of the goods which the seller has held out to the consumer as a sample or model; if they are fit for any particular purpose for which the consumer requires them and which he made known to the seller at the time of conclusion of the contract and which the seller has

---

[39] Note 36 above, p. 5.
[40] For a survey of its effects see D. Oughton and C. Willett, 'Quality Regulation in European Private Law' (2002) 25 *Journal of Consumer Policy* 299; T. Krümmel and R. D'Sa, 'Sale of consumer goods and associated guarantees: a minimalist approach to harmonized European Union consumer protection' (2001) 26 *European Law Review* 312; M. Bianca and S. Grundmann, *EU Sales Directive: Commentary* (Antwerp: Intersentia, 2002).

accepted; if they are fit for the purposes for which goods of the same type are normally used; and if they show the quality and performance which are normal in goods of the same type and which the consumer can reasonably expect, given the nature of the goods and taking into account any public statements on the specific characteristics of the goods made about them by the seller, the producer or his representative, particularly in advertising or on labelling. Article 2(5) supplements this by providing that any lack of conformity resulting from incorrect installation of the consumer goods shall be deemed to be equivalent to lack of conformity of the goods if installation forms part of the contract of sale of the goods and the goods were installed by the seller or under his responsibility.

Article 2(3) offers a degree of reassurance to a seller. There shall be deemed not to be a lack of conformity if, at the time the contract was concluded, the consumer was aware, or could not reasonably be unaware of, the lack of conformity. In this context the assumption of a self-aware consumer serves to limit potential seller liability. The same protection is available to the seller if the lack of conformity has its origin in materials supplied by the consumer.

Remedies Available to the Consumer

Article 3 governs the rights of the consumer in the event that a lack of conformity exists at the time the goods were delivered.

A framework of remedies is carefully constructed. Article 3(2) establishes the basic pattern. It provides that the consumer shall be entitled to have the goods brought into conformity free of charge by repair or replacement *or* to have an appropriate reduction made in the price or the contract rescinded with regard to those goods.

It is stipulated that repair or replacement shall be completed within a reasonable time and without any significant inconvenience to the consumer, taking account of the nature of the goods and the purpose for which the consumer required them. However, the consumer's ability to insist on free repair or replacement is lost where this becomes impossible or disproportionate. Article 3(3) defines a 'disproportionate' remedy as one which imposes costs on the seller which, in comparison with the alternative remedy, are unreasonable, taking into account the value the goods, the significance of the lack of conformity, and whether the alternative remedy could be completed without significant inconvenience to the consumer. In principle the assertion of the relevance of a principle of proportionality appears sensible. It will avoid waste. But effective consumer protection law is sharp-edged and precisely worded. One must express concern that these vague phrases will allow some sellers to use the language of disproportionality to obstruct consumers seeking to secure the remedies of repair or replacement foreseen under the Directive.

The remedies other than repair or replacement involve an appropriate reduction of the price or rescission of the contract. These arise if the consumer is entitled to neither repair nor replacement, or if the seller has not completed the remedy within a reasonable time, or if the seller has not completed the remedy without significant inconvenience to the consumer. Article 3(6) maintains the concern to apply a principle of proportionality. It declares that the consumer is not entitled to have the contract rescinded if the lack of conformity is minor. Price reduction is then the norm.

Time Limits

Article 5 governs time limits. The seller is liable where the lack of conformity becomes apparent within two years of the delivery of the goods. National legislation governing limitation periods must not rule out an action within this period.

Article 5(3) offers a special form of protection for the consumer where lack of conformity becomes apparent within six months of delivery of the goods. Such lack of conformity is presumed to have existed at the time of delivery unless this presumption is incompatible with the nature of the goods or the nature of the lack of conformity. Otherwise it falls to the seller wishing to escape liability to prove the goods were in conformity at the time of delivery.

Guarantees

Article 6 establishes a special regime for guarantees.

The background to the concern of Directive 99/44 with guarantees can be traced back to the 1993 Green Paper.[41] That document distinguished between the so-called 'legal guarantee' and the 'commercial guarantee'. The terminology has been abandoned, but the distinction remains. The 'legal guarantee' refers to the minimum level of contractual warranty of quality set by law. Its content varies state by state, and it is now the subject of the basic requirement of conformity with the contract of sale stipulated by Article 2(1) of Directive 99/44 – though it is no longer labelled the 'legal guarantee'. The 'commercial guarantee' is distinct in law. It exists not by operation of law but rather as a result of negotiation between the parties. It typically covers a promise that the product will be repaired if it breaks within a certain period. This is the target of Article 6 of Directive 99/44 – though the label 'commercial guarantee' has been abandoned. The guarantee is the subject of definition in Article 1. It means 'any undertaking by a seller or producer to the consumer, given without extra

---

[41] Note 36 above.

charge, to reimburse the price paid or to replace, repair or handle consumer goods in any way if they do not meet the specifications set out in the guarantee statement or in the relevant advertising'.

A perennial problem in consumer protection is that guarantees of this type are often very tempting and may form an important inducement to the consumer pondering a possible purchase. But the legal status of such guarantees is sometimes ambiguous. In particular, in so far as the guarantee has been promised by a party (such as a manufacturer) with whom the consumer otherwise has no direct commercial or contractual link, it could in some legal systems prove to be unenforceable – to the consumer's considerable surprise and dismay. The issue is addressed by Article 6 of Directive 99/44.

Article 6(1) provides that a guarantee shall be legally binding on the offeror under the conditions laid down in the guarantee statement and the associated advertising. The guarantee shall state that the consumer has legal rights under applicable national legislation governing the sale of consumer goods and make clear that those rights are not affected by the guarantee. It shall set out in plain intelligible language the contents of the guarantee and the essential particulars necessary for making claims under the guarantee, notably the duration and territorial scope of the guarantee as well as the name and address of the guarantor.

This is a helpful provision from the perspective of the consumer. It is none the less not the most ambitious version that could be imagined. In particular Article 6 of Directive 99/44 does not determine in the abstract when and how a guarantee of this nature shall be legally binding. Instead it leaves it to the offeror to set the conditions according to which the guarantee shall bind, albeit that Article 6 also includes some requirements as to content and transparency. And the trader could clearly choose to offer no such guarantee.

The Commission's preferred solution in the 1993 Green Paper was to propose a mandatory legal framework applicable to all 'commercial guarantees', which would be enforceable up and down the distribution chain. This would co-exist with a 'European Guarantee' which traders could choose to use. This would include the application of standard guarantee conditions in all the Member States for the same type of goods of the same brand. This approach finds only a weaker echo in the finally adopted version of Article 6 of Directive 99/44.

Producer Liability

Article 2(1)'s rule of conformity with the contract binds the seller alone. The producer is not subject to this obligation. Article 6 does not require that a guarantee bind the producer, though arrangements made by the parties may accommodate this. One may question whether this absence of recognition of producer liability is consistent with the reality in modern manufacturing conditions that it is the producer, rather than the seller, who carries primary responsibility for the condition of the product that will be purchased by the consumer. The Directive's limitations have been criticized in this vein,[42] and the matter may yet return to the legislative agenda. Article 12 of the Directive instructs the Commission to review the application of the Directive and report to the Parliament and the Council not later than 7 July 2006. One issue alone is explicitly picked out as appropriate for examination by the Commission: the case for introducing the direct liability of the producer.

Waiver of Rights

Article 7 seeks to ensure that the ill-informed or unsuspecting consumer does not give away rights. It provides that any contractual terms concluded with the seller before the lack of conformity is brought to the seller's attention which directly or indirectly waive or restrict the rights resulting from this Directive shall, as provided for by national law, not be binding on the consumer. This is subject to the proviso that Member States may provide that, in the case of second-hand goods, the seller and consumer may agree contractual terms with a time period for the liability of the seller which is shorter than the two years stipulated by Article 5(1). Moreover, Member States shall take the necessary measures to ensure that consumers are not deprived of the protection afforded by this Directive as a result of opting for the law of a non-Member State as the law applicable to the contract where the contract has a close connection with the territory of the Member States.

Minimum Harmonization

Article 8 asserts the familiar 'minimum' proviso. Other rights which the consumer may invoke under national rules governing contractual or non-contractual liability are not set aside by the Directive. And Member States may adopt stricter measures designed to ensure a higher level of consumer protection.

The minimum formula contained in Directive 99/44 offers an illuminating insight into why the Commission has become mistrustful of the inclusion of such clauses in harmonization measures. A UNICE survey published in 2004 identified a vast array of transposition techniques adopted in the Member States, including many instances of readiness to set stricter rules than foreseen

---

[42] R. Bradgate and C. Twigg-Flesner, 'Expanding the Boundaries of Liability for Quality Defects' (2002) 25 *JCP* 345. Cf. H. Beale and G. Howells, 'EC Harmonisation of Consumer Sales Law – a Missed Opportunity?' (1997) 12/1 *Journal of Contract Law* 21.

by the Directive.[43] This lends weight to the Commission's case that minimum rule-making is not capable of providing the basis for a transparent, unfragmented pattern of regulation – that is, in short, incompatible with a common market. That case is not unanswerable: one might object that the benefits of maximum harmonization, counted in improved coherence in the legal framework, are outweighed by the costs of suppression of opportunity to select patterns of consumer protection that are appropriate for local needs. That is a key current debate in EC consumer policy, tracked in Chapter 1.

Implementation of the Directive has presented different challenges in different Member States.[44] It has generated some important reforms of national law going beyond what is mandated by the Directive. In Germany a broader reform of sales law was triggered by an appreciation that a narrow implementation of the Directive alone, alongside existing sales law, would generate an uncomfortable and incoherent pattern. [45] This trend may also be identified in the field of unfair terms in the wake of Directive 93/13. [46] It offers a reminder that the ripples of harmonization may extend beyond the formal reach of a Directive.

---

[43]   Available via http://www.unice.org.

[44]   See Special Issue of the *European Review of Private Law*, vol. 9, issues 2 & 3 (2001).

[45]   M. Krajewski, 'The new German Law of Obligations' [2003] *European Business Law Review* 201; H.-W. Micklitz, 'The New German Sales Law: Changing Patterns in the Regulation of Product Quality' (2002) 25 *Journal of Consumer Policy* 379.

[46]   Cf. Beale, note 34 above.

6. Product liability

THE PRODUCT LIABILITY DIRECTIVE

Directive 85/374 (as amended) harmonizes laws concerning liability for defective products.[1] It is commonly referred to as the 'Product Liability Directive'. Strictly, it is a measure adopted in order to advance the integration of the market. Its Treaty base is Article 100 (which is now Article 94). Harmonization of national provisions concerning the liability of the producer for damage caused by defectiveness of products is required in the light of the distortions in competition in the Community and the impact on the movement of goods which are caused by divergences between the laws of the different Member States. However, the harmonization of laws governing liability for defective products has a profound impact on the position of the consumer. Accordingly Directive 85/374 is a major measure of Community consumer protection policy, albeit, in strict constitutional terms, as an incidental consequence of its principal objective.

The first Commission proposal in the field of product liability appeared in 1976.[2] The fact that it took nine years thereafter to achieve agreement on the Directive indicates the depth of controversy which surrounded this initiative. National systems of tort law vary, especially in their choice of the criteria according to which shall be judged the liability of the supplier to an injured consumer.[3] Aspects of the debate are reflected in the text of the Directive that was finally adopted. In several areas the mark of uncomfortable compromise is unmistakeable. In particular, a small number of options is permitted to Member States, which detracts from the uniformity of the rules which are to be implemented. In fact, this Directive is a perfect case study of the problems which confront the Community legislature when it attempts to drive the policy of internal market-building deep into the heartland of national private law.

Given the precarious sensitivity of the negotiations that led to the adoption of Directive 85/374 it is no surprise that the bargain reached in 1985 has been

---

[1]   *OJ* 1985 L210/29, as amended by Dir. 1999/34 *OJ* 1999 L141/20.
[2]   *OJ* 1976 C241/9.
[3]   G. Howells, *Comparative Product Liability* (Aldershot: Dartmouth Publishing Company, 1992).

left largely untouched. Two Commission reports into the operation of the Directive have been published,[4] but neither recommended any significant change. The sole amendment to Directive 85/374 was effected by Directive 1999/34.[5] This achieved an extension in the scope of the regime to cover primary agricultural products. As the Commission has observed, it took the alarm about such products felt 'in the aftermath of the mad cow crisis' to provide the political impetus to reform.[6] Directive 1999/34 is based on Article 95.

The Harmonized Liability Regime under the Directive

If one begins with an appreciation that divergence between national rules governing liability for the supply of defective products hinders market integration, then one's concern focuses on the need to establish a common rule and not on the content of that rule. Theoretically, the objective of harmonization will be achieved by setting the liability threshold at any level, provided only that it operates at a uniform level throughout the Community. The Product Liability Directive was adopted under Article 100. This was before the Single European Act inserted, *inter alia*, what is now Article 95(3) into the Treaty and almost a decade before the entry into force of what is now Article 153(2), a creature of the Maastricht Treaty, which for all their imperfections at least ensure an association of sorts between internal market policy and the quest to achieve high levels of consumer protection (Chapter 1). However, the basis of the harmonized regime established by the Directive is liability without fault on the part of the producer of a defective product. Such a system of 'strict' liability, in contrast to fault-based liability, is considerably to the advantage of a consumer who has suffered loss. The Recitals to the Directive justify the choice of a harmonized system founded on liability without fault with reference to 'the fair apportionment of the risks inherent in modern technological production'. More fully, one would explain the allocation to the producer of the risk of defectiveness as efficient and fair in the light of the producer's capacity to buy insurance against loss and thereby to spread the costs of compensating a small number of injured consumers among all purchasers by reflecting insurance costs in a slightly higher price. Fault-based liability systems typically leave the consumer injured in the absence of fault without redress, which attracts criticism for its inequitable allocation of risk. Moreover, the difficulty and cost of showing fault in private litigation often deters a consumer from pursuing a claim even where there are chances of

---

[4]   COM (95) 617, COM (2000) 893.
[5]   Note 1 above.
[6]   COM (2000) 893, p. 6.

success. Accordingly, the influence of consumer protection is felt in the structure of this Directive. It has been drafted in part with reference to the need to secure effective consumer protection, despite its formal legal basis under Article 100 as a measure of market integration.

The core of the Directive is found in Article 1, which declares that 'The producer shall be liable for damage caused by a defect in his product.' This is a dramatically strong pro-consumer statement of risk allocation. On its face, the Directive is a remarkable piece of legislation, which seems to cut deep into national private law. Article 1 raises several definitional issues which are addressed in the succeeding Articles of the Directive.

Products Covered by the Directive

By virtue of Article 2, those products covered by the Directive comprise all moveables even if incorporated into another moveable or into an immoveable. It is explicitly stated that electricity is included in the notion of a product.

The sole amendment to the original Directive 85/374 was made by Directive 1999/34, and it addressed only the issue of how to define a product. In its original version Directive 85/374 excluded primary agricultural products and game from its scope, although it was explicitly provided that Member States could opt to bring such products within the scope of their implementing measures. The initial exclusion of these products, which may certainly cause harm to the consumer, is readily attributable to the power of the farming lobby in Europe. But both the exclusion and, as a logical supplement, the 'opt-in' provision were eliminated by Directive 1999/34. The Preamble to that Directive states that bringing primary agricultural products within the scope of the Product Liability Directive would 'help restore consumer confidence in the safety of agricultural products'. That confidence had been battered by, in particular, the mad cow crisis to which the Commission referred in explaining the impetus that propelled Directive 1999/34 through the legislative process.[7] The Preamble also observes that the requirements of a high level of consumer protection are served by facilitating claims for compensation for damage caused by defective agricultural products.

Persons Liable under the Directive

The liability of a 'producer' covers the manufacturer of a finished product, the

[7] Ibid. On this see U. Pachl, 'Product liability: is it strict enough?' (1998) 8 *Consumer Policy Review* 176. The more general law and policy of the 'mad cow crisis' is examined by E. Vos, 'EU Food safety Regulation in the aftermath of the BSE crisis' (2000) 23 *Journal of Consumer Policy* 227; K. Vincent, 'Mad Cows and Eurocrats – Community responses to the BSE Crisis' (2004) 10 *European Law Journal* 499.

producer of any raw material or the manufacturer of a component part (Article 3). This embraces a wide range of actors, from the single craftsman or -woman to the large multinational enterprise. Moreover, it extends to persons presenting themselves as producers, by, for example, affixing their name or trade mark to the item. This would catch the supermarket which chooses to apply its own brand name to a product. Such a marketing strategy converts the supermarket into a producer for the purposes of the Directive. Article 3(2) brings the importer of a product into the Community within the scope of liability as a producer for these purposes.

A supplier may incur liability for the supply of a defective product, although under Article 3(3) the supplier is able to escape liability by identifying the producer or his or her own supplier. In the light of this provision, commercial prudence dictates that suppliers of products should maintain careful records of the source of goods which they supply. Without such records, the buck will stop with them. From the perspective of the consumer, this system ensures that a claim for compensation cannot be defeated by an initial inability to identify the original producer, provided a supplier can be identified. The claim can be pursued against the supplier or against a party further up the chain identified by the supplier.[8] However, contributory neglience by the consumer may operate to reduce an award in accordance with Article 8(2) of the Directive.

Article 7(c) provides that a producer is not liable as a result of the Directive where it is proved that 'the product was neither manufactured by him for sale or any form of distribution for economic purpose nor manufactured or distributed by him in the course of his business'. This frees the person who cooks for guests at a private dinner party from liability should the food prepared be defective. A charity might similarly be able to enjoy the benefit of this exclusion. Article 7(c) does not, however, exclude the supply of a kidney in the course of medical treatment from the reach of the Directive, even where the treatment is financed by public funds and no direct charge is made of the patient. In *Henning Veedfald*[9] the Court insisted that such circumstances maintain an economic character and the exclusion of liability offered by Article 7(c) does not apply.

The Notion of 'Defectiveness'

The key notion of 'defectiveness', which is a condition of liability in Article 1, is elaborated in Article 6, which states that a product is defective where it

---

[8] On how this might be done see C. Hodges, 'Product liability of suppliers: the notification trap' (2002) 27 *European Law Review* 758.

[9] Case C-203/99 [2001] ECR I-3569.

does not provide the safety which a person is entitled to expect. Expectation is to be judged with reference to all the circumstances; a non-exhaustive list is supplied in Article 6(1). The list includes reference to '[t]he use to which it could reasonably be expected that the product would be put', which indicates that a product may be defective where it causes damage as a result of foreseeable misuse. Article 6(2)'s insistence that a product is not to be considered defective solely because a better product is subsequently put into circulation demonstrates that the product must achieve a relative level of safety, not an absolute level. The fundamental issue arising under Article 6 of the Directive is that it ensures that the focus is on the condition of the product, whereas by contrast a fault-based system looks to the conduct of the producer.

The 'Development Risk' Defence

The system of strict liability on which the Directive appears to be based is diluted by the inclusion of a so-called 'development risk' defence in Article 7(e). A producer of a defective product is able to escape liability by proving 'that the state of scientific and technical knowledge at the time when he put the product into circulation was not such as to enable the existence of the defect to be discovered'.

The producer of a product which is, with hindsight, indubitably defective does not incur liability if he/she is able to show the flaw to be, loosely interpreted, unknown and unknowable. In such circumstances the allocation of risk is shifted back on to the shoulders of the unlucky consumer.

The precise nature of this defence was controversial at the time of the adoption of Directive 85/374 and it still awaits helpful judicial elaboration. It is unclear how heavy the burden of proof on the producer is designed to be – what of a defect suspected but not strictly 'discovered'? or the defect in, for example, a drug which has been publicized by one scientist only in an obscure journal in a minor language? or even identified by one scientist but not publicized at all?[10] One can cogently argue that Articles 1 and 7(e) of the Directive are irreconcilable, in that the apparent focus on the defective condition of the product within Article 1 is at odds with the reassertion of patterns of producer knowledge in Article 7(e). It may even emerge that the combination of Articles 1 and 7(e) of the Directive does little more than assert an essentially fault-based liability regime, albeit with a burden cast on the producer to show the absence of fault rather than on the consumer to show its presence.[11]

[10] C. Newdick, 'The Development Risk Defence of the Consumer Protection Act 1987' (1988) 47 *Cambridge Law Journal* 455.
[11] C. Newdick, 'Risk, Uncertainty and Knowledge in the Development Risks Defence' (1991) 20 *Anglo-American Law Review* 309.

The matter was aired before the European Court in infringement proceedings initiated by the Commission against the United Kingdom. In *Commission v. United Kingdom*, the Court provided a ruling which resolved the complaint in the United Kingdom's favour but which did not fully address the wider issues.[12] The United Kingdom implemented Article 7(e) of the Directive in such a way that it is a defence for the producer to show 'that the state of scientific and technical knowledge at the relevant time was not such that a producer of products of the same description as the product in question might be expected to have discovered the defect if it had existed in his products while they were under his control'.[13] This reworking of Article 7(e) of the Directive is based on a belief that the defence is properly interpreted to act as a potentially significant protection for the (loosely stated) 'non-negligent' producer. The Commission took the view that this was an incorrect implementation of the Directive. However, the United Kingdom's implementing measures include an explicit statement that their purpose is to make such provision as is necessary to comply with the Product Liability Directive and a direction to the courts to construe them accordingly.[14] In view of the presence of that linkage between the UK measure and Directive 85/374, coupled with the absence of any evidence that the Directive had been misapplied by courts in the UK, the European Court refused to accept that the Commission had proven that the UK was in breach of its Treaty obligations. This leaves open some awkward questions of interpretation. The Court made clear that the defence is available only where the objective state of scientific and technical knowledge, including the most advanced level of such knowledge, was not such as to enable the existence of the defect to be discovered. The defence is emphatically not based on the subjective state of the producer's knowledge. According to the Court the defence is lost where that knowledge was 'accessible'[15] at the time when the product in question was put into circulation. Quite how one judges accessibility in this context matters enormously to the allocation of risk between producer and consumer, but it remains unclear.[16] The Court rather gnomically added that this point raises difficulties of interpretation which, in the event of litigation, the national courts will have to resolve, having recourse, if necessary, to Article 234 EC. But although in finding implementing measures to be inadequate it is not necessary to establish their actual effects where the wording of the legislation itself 'harbours the insufficiencies or defects of transpo-

---

[12]   Case C-300/95 [1997] ECR I-2649.
[13]   Section 4(1)(e) Consumer Protection Act 1987. See G. Howells and S. Weatherill, *Consumer Protection Law* (Aldershot: Ashgate, 2nd edn, 2005), ch. 4.
[14]   Section 1(1) Consumer Protection Act 1987.
[15]   Para. 29 of the judgment.
[16]   For divergent views on these 'Unanswered questions' see C. Hodges (1998) 61 *Modern Law Review* 560, M. Mildred and G. Howells (1998) 61 *Modern Law Review* 570.

sition',[17] the Court on the facts of the case did not consider that the Commission had shown such blemishes.

Given these complexities, one may naturally wonder why the development risk defence was included in the Directive at all. A rationale for this producer-friendly defence lies in the perception that, in the absence of such a defence, producers would have had a greatly diminished incentive to invest in new products, not least because of problems in securing insurance cover under a system of 'pure' strict liability. Accordingly, during the negotiation of the Directive, proponents of the development risk defence, most prominently the government of the United Kingdom, emphasized its role in sustaining incentives to pursue technological innovation, which is in the long run to the advantage of the consumer and of society generally. North American evidence of the damage done by rising awards, leading to an upwards spiral in insurance costs, was commonly cited. None the less this view was unacceptable to several Member States, who regarded such protection for the producer as incompatible with a vigorous consumer policy. North American evidence was, for many observers, at best equivocal and at worst irrelevant to the very different legal and commercial conditions prevailing in Europe.[18] The disagreement was resolvable only through a compromise which wrecked the uniformity of application of the Directive on this particular point. Article 15(1)(b) permits Member States the option of extending liability even to defects of this type. So in some states the development risk defence will be available to traders faced with claims by consumers harmed by the supply of defective products, but in other states, where different choices have been made, no such protection can be relied on. One may readily have predicted that relatively few states would choose to exercise the option foreseen by Article 15(1)(b) and thereby to deny their traders the protection of the defence, for this would impose costs on them from which their competitors elsewhere in the EU would be immune. So it has proved. The Commission reported in 2000 that among the (then) 15 Member States the defence had been set aside only by Luxembourg and Finland, and in part by Spain, France and Germany.[19]

The compromise solution which the development risk defence represents

---

[17] Case C-392/96 *Commission* v. *Ireland* [1999] ECR I-5901, para. 60 of the judgment.

[18] For comparative discussion see M. Shapo, 'Comparing Products Liability: Concepts in European and American Law' (1993) 26 *Cornell International Law Journal* 279; G. Howells and T. Wilhelmsson, 'EC and US Approaches to Consumer Protection – should the gap be bridged?' (1997) 17 *Yearbook of European Law* 207; G. Howells and M. Mildred, 'Is European Product Liability more Protective than the Restatement (Third) of Torts: Product Liability?' (1998) 65 *Tennessee Law Review* 985; M. Reimann, 'Liability for Defective Products at the Beginning of the Twenty-First Century: Emergence of a Worldwide Standard?' (2003) 51 *American Journal of Comparative Law* 751; J. Stapleton, 'Bugs in Anglo-American Products Liability' (2002) 53 *South Carolina Law Review* 1225.

[19] COM (2000) 893.

has always been ripe for reconsideration. This was fully recognized in Directive 85/374 itself. As part of the political deal struck, it was provided in Article 15(3) that in 1995 the Commission should report on the operation of the development risk defence and the optional exclusion of it. The Council was invited by Article 15(3) to consider whether to repeal Article 7(e), which would strip producers of protection from liability for loss caused by unknown and unknowable defects. Most proponents of effective consumer protection would favour this deletion and would portray it as apt to deliver a more coherently structured system of liability for the supply of defective products.[20] However, the balance struck in the original Directive remains undisturbed. The Commission report on the application of the Directive, which was published in late 1995, is a profoundly uninspiring document.[21] It contains just one page of comment. The Commission observes that the Directive has eased the burden on the plaintiff, but that it does not appear to have caused an increase in the number of claims brought, nor in the level of insurance premiums payable. The Commission confesses that 'experience is still limited' and that accordingly it does not intend to submit proposals for amendment of the Directive. It will continue to monitor developments. This does not refute the notion that harmonization is a gradual process, based on experience accumulated over time, but it serves as a reminder that the process may be extremely slow.

In 1999 the Commission issued a Green Paper designed to promote debate on the future shaping of the legal regime.[22] This was followed by a second Commission report into the operation of the Directive, published in January 2001.[23] This concluded blandly that on the basis of the limited information available it would be premature to propose any changes to the existing regime, other than that already achieved by Directive 1999/34. In support of this cautious stance, one may note that such empirical evidence as exists concerning the effect of differently structured liability regimes remains equivocal.[24]

In June 2004 the Commission published a report into the economic impact of the development risk defence.[25] This had been commissioned from Fondazione Rosselli, private consultants based in Turin. This concedes that the

---

[20]   See, e.g., M. Goyens (ed.), *Directive 85/374/EEC on product liability: ten years after* (Louvain-la-Neuve: Centre de Droit de la Consommation 31, 1996).

[21]   COM (95) 617.

[22]   COM (99) 396. See J.J. Izquierdo Peris, 'Liability for defective products in the European Union: Developments since 1995 – the European Commission's Green Paper' (1999) 7 *Consumer Law Journal* 331; M. Mildred, 'A Response to the European Commission Green Paper on Liability for Defective Products' (2000) 9 *Nottingham Law Journal* 104.

[23]   COM (2000) 893.

[24]   See, e.g., D. Dewees, D. Duff and M. Trebilcock, *Exploring the Domain of Accident Law: Taking the Facts Seriously* (Oxford: Oxford University Press, 1996); M. Galanter, 'Real World Torts: an Antidote to Anecdotes' (1996) 55 *Maryland Law Review* 1093; G.T. Schwartz, 'Empiricism and Tort Law' (2002) *University of Illinois Law Review* 1067.

[25]   Available via http://europa.eu.int/comm/internal_market/en/goods/prodliability.htm.

defence has been little used in litigation but asserts that this is only one measure of its impact. It concludes that elimination of the defence might plausibly deter innovation by producers, but concedes that it is very difficult to collect sound empirical data on the effect of the defence. It also takes the view that insurance costs would rise were the defence to be removed, and that some risks would be uninsurable. It finds the defence to have helped in stabilizing the cost of insurance in the EU. To this extent the report is favourably disposed to what is describes as the 'balance' achieved by the inclusion of the defence. It also raises the possible value of schemes that would offer consumers the protection that they would enjoy were the defence to be eliminated though without actually eliminating the defence – such as compensation funds, perhaps industry-specific in nature and composed of a mix of contributions from public and private sources. The report also refers to the political nature of the deal struck that allows Member States to choose whether or not to apply the defence. It advocates a move to a common EU-wide approach.

The Commission has for some time appeared unpersuaded that proposing any significant alteration of the bargain governing the liability system struck in 1985 is justified or politically worthwhile. This reticence seems likely to endure.

Limiting the Producer's Total Liability

Article 16 of the Directive permits Member States to choose to place a limit of not less than 70 million euros on the total liability of a producer for damage resulting from a death or personal injury and caused by identical items with the same defect.

This option was also the subject of an explicit invitation in Directive 85/374 to the Commission to submit a report to the Council on its effect with a view to possible repeal of the optional ceiling on liability. No proposal of this nature has been advanced by the Commission.

Article 12 controls a distinct aspect of the possible sheltering of a producer from liability. It stipulates that liability towards the injured party may not be limited or excluded.

'Pre-emptive' Effect

In contrast to the majority of the measures harmonizing laws governing the protection of economic interests of consumers which are examined in Chapters 4 and 5, the Product Liability Directive contains no 'minimum' formula. And, since the legal base of the Directive is Article 100, now Article 94, the 'minimum' clause in Article 153(5), governing consumer protection, is irrelevant (Chapter 1). The only provision in Directive 85/374 which addresses its relationship with national law in the relevant field is Article 13. It stipulates that the Directive 'shall not affect any rights which an injured person may have according to the rules of the law of contractual or non-contractual liability or a special liability system existing at the moment when this Directive is notified'.

The Court took the opportunity to address the meaning of this provision in a trio of cases decided in 2002.

In *María Victoria González Sánchez* v. *Medicina Asturiana*[26] Ms González Sánchez sued Medicina Asturiana for compensation for injury allegedly caused on their premises in the course of a blood transfusion. She claimed to have been infected by the Hepatitis C virus. The Spanish court concluded that the rights afforded to consumers under pre-existing Spanish law were more extensive than those available under the rules introduced to transpose Directive 85/374 into domestic law. The European Court was asked for a preliminary ruling on the question whether Article 13 of the Directive should be interpreted as precluding the restriction or limitation, as a result of transposition of the Directive, of rights granted to consumers under the legislation of the Member State.

The Court identified the purpose of the Directive in establishing a harmonized system of product liability as 'to ensure undistorted competition between traders, to facilitate the free movement of goods and to avoid differences in levels of consumer protection'.[27] It determined that accordingly within its field of application harmonization is complete. Article 13 did not permit the Member States the possibility of maintaining a general system of product liability different from that provided for in the Directive.

The same identification of a 'complete' system of harmonization emerges from the Court's two other rulings of the same day dealing with Directive 85/374: *Commission* v. *France*[28] and *Commission* v. *Greece*.[29] The Court's stance heavily emphasizes the function of the Directive in levelling the commercial playing field. It conforms to the slogan 'common rules for a common market'. However, this approach is hostile to local diversity and to scope for Member States that may wish to upgrade consumer protection. Legislative reform will be required if the pre-emptive effect of Directive 85/374 is to be loosened.[30] Thematically these judgments are connected to *Tobacco Advertising* as part of a trend of making more clear-cut the differ-

---

26 Case C-183/00 [2002] ECR I-3901.
27 Para. 26 of the judgment.
28 Case C-52/00 [2002] ECR I-3827.
29 Case C-154/00 [2002] ECR I-3879.
30 The judgments provoked a rather alarmed Council Resolution of 19 December 2002 on amendment of the liability for defective products Directive, *OJ* 2003 C26/02, considering 'that against this background there is a need to assess whether Directive 85/374/EEC, as amended by Directive 1999/34/EC, should be modified in such a way as to allow for national rules on liability of suppliers based on the same ground as the liability system in the Directive concerning liability of producers'.

ences in pre-emptive effect between Articles 94 and 95 on the one hand and other more recently introduced provisions of the Treaty such as Article 153 that are not tied explicitly to the internal market programme and which are more generous to the preservation of state regulatory autonomy, on the other (see more fully Chapter 3).

THE DIRECTIVE AND A EUROPEAN TORT LAW

The sceptical observer may readily be forgiven for doubting the value of EC intervention. The Directive offers scope for an enhanced level of consumer protection in the Community, especially in those countries, such as the United Kingdom, previously wedded to a fault-based liability system. Yet the development risk defence undermines even this advance. In circumstances which are ill defined, though admittedly unusual, it allows the producer of an unarguably defective product to escape liability, so that the consumer will have to bear the loss suffered. The inclusion of the defence in national implementing measures is not mandatory, but, as one would have readily anticipated, few states have chosen to reject it given that such a step would place 'their' firms at a competitive disadvantage in comparison with firms in neighbouring states. So in most Member States consumer protection is diluted by the availability to producers of the defence. It is also pertinent to note that the optional nature of the defence taints the clarity of the regime established by the Directive. What price effective harmonization? The optional nature of the development risk defence has attracted criticism for its capacity to induce forum shopping by consumers (who will prefer to sue in the few states that have opted to exclude the defence); and to distort business choices about where to locate (there may even be a preference to 'test' products in states that maintain the defence). Empirical evidence of such trends is admittedly scarce, but the anxiety about the peculiar shape of the liability system agreed by compromise in Directive 85/374 persists.

Choice of liability rules engages a host of distinct, often competing, conceptions about the function of the private law in regulating the economy in particular and society generally.[31] Community intervention in the field is driven explicitly by the process of market integration. It becomes difficult for the Community to reflect the range of interests underpinning national systems in a harmonized rule. This in turn sometimes causes the harmonization measure to burst. In order to secure political agreement, a common rule must be adjusted to include options which contradict the notion of a common pattern. This is visible in the Product Liability Directive.

---

[31] J. Stapleton, *Product Liability* (London: Butterworths, 1994); A. Grubb, *The Law of Product Liability* (London: Butterworths, 2000).

It remains contentious how far options granted in Directives constitute an acceptable recognition of national peculiarities and how far they undermine the whole notion of the level playing field within the Community. It is politically realistic to suppose that complete unanimity is frequently neither feasible nor, perhaps, desirable, but a Directive which is pitted with options may simply conceal fundamental disagreement which it was judged politically expedient to conceal with a well-nigh worthless legislative product. The Product Liability Directive does not deserve such vicious condemnation. The amendment effected by Directive 1999/34 has eliminated one of the optional oddities of the original text by providing that primary agricultural products are covered by the Directive, not simply an optional extra as Member States choose, and, more generally, it cannot be dismissed as worthless either as a means of securing an undistorted market or of improving consumer protection. But the optional development risk defence in particular undermines the coherence of the EC's common regime governing product liability.

The Directive was hailed at the time of its adoption as a step towards the Europeanization of private law. Article 1 in particular seems to involve an ambitious assertion of a European standard for product liability, and invites the European Court, fed by Article 234 (ex 177) references, to shape European notions of defectiveness. Yet only a trickle of cases has been referred to the European Court under Article 234 in connection with the interpretation of the Directive, and none has provided the springboard to a profound judicial inquiry into what is meant by 'defectiveness' or by the development risk defence. In fact, there have been relatively few reported decisions before national courts, although the numbers have begun to increase in recent years.[32] This relative paucity of reported litigation by no means constitutes conclusive proof that the Directive's impact has been slight, for it is conceivable that, for example, the existence of the Directive may have prompted informal settlements (typically by insurance companies) in favour of the consumer in circumstances which previously would have left the consumer without a remedy in law or practice.[33] Moreover, cases involving personal injury, complicated by issues of causation mixed with assessment of defectiveness, typically take several years to reach full trial. However, while there is evidence that the EC's approach to product liability has acquired adherents among lawmakers elsewhere in the world, the dearth of litigation stands as a rebuke

---

[32]   A. Schuster, 'Review of case law under Directive 85/374/EEC on liability for defective products' (1998) 6 *Consumer Law Journal* 195; E. Deards and C. Twigg-Flesner, 'The Consumer Protection Act 1987: Proof at last that it is protecting consumers?' (2001) 10 *Nottingham Law Journal* 1. In an English case an unusually thorough examination of the issues is provided by J. Burton in *A and others* v. *National Blood Authority* [2001] 3 All ER 289, noted by G. Howells and M. Mildred (2002) 65 *Modern Law Review* 95.

[33]   M. Mildred, 'The Impact of the Directive in the United Kingdom', in Goyens (ed.), *Directive 85/374/EEC on product liability: ten years after*, as note 20.

to its influence in practice.[34] In sum, two decades after its adoption the impact of the Product Liability Directive remains difficult to measure. In 2003 the Commission published a study on 'Product Liability in the European Union', prepared by Lovells (Solicitors).[35] This revealed a general perception that there has been a rise in the number of product liability cases brought in Europe in recent years and in the degree of success met in such cases, but the Directive was identified as only one factor driving these trends. Enhanced consumer awareness of rights and improved access to legal assistance were also cited. In general, practical experience remains relatively thin and no consensus about pressing need for reform could be detected.

LIABILITY FOR THE SUPPLY OF DEFECTIVE SERVICES

It is natural to speculate whether the liability system for supply of defective goods introduced in 1985 by the Product Liability Directive could profitably be extended into the field of liability for the supply of defective services. The Commission decided to test the water in 1990 by publishing a draft Directive on the liability of suppliers of services.[36]

In some respects the draft was designed to complement the Product Liability Directive, although there were differences between the two regimes. The core of the draft Directive's proposal for a common regime was contained in Article 1:

> The supplier of a service shall be liable for damage to the health and physical integrity of persons or the physical integrity of movable or immovable property, including the persons or property which were the object of the service, caused by a fault committed by him in the performance of the service.

This appears to impose fault-based liability, and is thus quite distinct from the approach taken in Article 1 of the Product Liability Directive. However, the proposal qualified this position significantly by providing that the supplier must prove the absence of fault. This would offer practical advantages to the consumer claimant. However, the nature of the proposed regime would be affected by the requirement that 'In assessing the fault, account shall be taken of the behaviour of the supplier of the service, who, in normal and reasonably foreseeable conditions, shall ensure the safety which may reasonably be expected.'

---

[34] Cf. M. Reimann, 'Product Liability in a Global Context: the Hollow Victory of the European Model' (2003) 11 *European Review Private Law* 128.

[35] Available via http://europa.eu.int/comm/internal_market/en/goods/prodliability.htm.

[36] COM (90) 482.

In accordance with the use of Article 100a (which is now Article 95) as the proposed legal base, the Commission presented the proposal with scrupulous care as an attempt not merely to protect the consumer, but primarily as an instrument designed to liberate trade by reducing uncertainty about insurance costs borne by suppliers operating in different states with different legal regimes. It was, however, plain even in 1990 that the draft Directive on liability of suppliers of services was released into a harsh, unyielding political environment. The draft was subjected to sustained criticism. The services industry, especially in its influential professional sector, lobbied hard against the initiative and little support was forthcoming among the Member States. The draft appeared in the Commission's report submitted to the Edinburgh European Council in December 1992 in which the Commission reviewed existing and proposed legislation in the light of the subsidiarity principle (Chapter 1). The draft Directive on services liability featured in the list of measures which contained excessive detail and which were to be revised and drafted in a more general style.

It became plain that there was an absence of political will behind the proposed Directive. Eventually, a Communication from the Commission on new directions on the liability of suppliers of services was published in 1994.[37] The Commission concluded that its 'proposal stands no chance of being adopted without sweeping changes which would risk voiding it of much of its substance'. It therefore withdrew it. In the Communication on new directions, the Commission comments further that the specific circumstances of different services deserve greater consideration. The Commission 'will if necessary prepare draft texts concerning sectors in respect of which particular needs are established'.

It is not necessary simply to conclude that a political climate of suspicion about new Community initiatives of market regulation is solely to blame for this episode of thwarted ambition. Services are, after all, materially distinct in some respects from goods, particularly where they are intangible. The structure of a liability regime governing the supply of services may coherently differ from one affecting the supply of goods, as was indeed already envisaged in the Commission's original 1990 draft based on a type of fault-based liability regime. However, it is hard to avoid the conclusion that the political climate of subsidiarity was in this instance fatal to the Commission's attempt to persuade a sufficient number of Member States of the advisability of Community action in the field. A new pathway to the growth of a European tort law was therefore blocked. A defective product used in the course of providing a service falls within Directive 85/374 but there is no EC Directive covering supply of defective services.

---

[37] COM (94) 260.

7. European private law

A 'EUROPEAN PRIVATE LAW'

It seems a big jump from the subject matter of the previous three chapters to the dauntingly grand topic of European private law. But the debate is moving inexorably in this direction. In the early years of the EC's intervention into private law one could readily treat Directives on topics such as doorstep selling and timeshare as oddities which contributed to the creation of a special set of rules governing the formation of particular consumer contracts but which had little impact on the general structure of national law. But more recent measures such as Directive 93/13 on unfair terms in consumer contracts and Directive 99/44 on consumer sales and guarantees are much more ambitious. They challenge the very notion of contractual autonomy. And although the majority of the relevant EC harmonization measures concern consumer law, there is also a group of Directives touching commercial contract law. Measures such as Directive 2000/35 on late payments in commercial transactions[1] and Directive 86/653 on commercial agents[2] fall outside the scope of this book, but they add to the dimensions of an EC private law shaped by the harmonization programme. Principles have emerged – most prominently, information provision but, for some commentators, building towards a broader basis of promoting fairness in the market – that provide a thematic pattern to the apparent patchwork of the EC's legislative *acquis*. And so, *via* an emphasis on consumer contract law, has developed the increasingly vigorous sub-discipline of 'European contract law'.[3] Moreover, the implementation of these

---

[1] *OJ* 2000 L200/35.
[2] *OJ* 1986 L382/17.
[3] See, e.g., but by no means taking the same view, H-W. Micklitz, 'Principles of Social Justice in European Private Law' (2000) 19 *Yearbook of European Law* 167; J. Stuyck, 'European Consumer Law after the Treaty of Amsterdam: Consumer Policy in or beyond the Internal Market?' (2000) 37 *Common Market Law Review* 367; G. Howells and T. Wilhelmsson, 'EC Consumer Law: has it come of age?' (2003) 28 *European Law Review* 370; R. Schulze and G. Ajani (eds), *Gemeinsame Prinzipen des Europäischen Privatrechts* (Baden-Baden: Nomos, 2003); H. Rösler, *Europäisches Konsumentenvertragsrecht* (Munich: C.H. Beck, 2004); K. Riesenhuber, *Europäisches Vertragsrecht* (Berlin: De Gruyter, 2003); Sixto A. Sánchez Lorenzo, *Derecho Privado Europeo* (Granada: Editorial Comares, 2002); T. Wilhelmsson, 'Varieties of Welfarism in European Contract Law' (2004) 10 *European Law Review* 712; S. Grundmann, W. Kerber and S. Weatherill, *Party Autonomy and the Role of*

measures has – in different ways in different jurisdictions – caused perturbations in the national legal orders of the Member States of the EU. The European Court's interpretative role blends in a further source of dynamic change. The incremental growth of the programme of legislative harmonization affecting private law provides a springboard to exploration of where this process of legal 'Europeanization' might and should lead.

It is a rich debate, which is also periodically fierce and controversial. For some, the lesson of the rising tide of the EC's influence on national private law is that it is time to pursue the creation of a much more systematic structure within which to house European private law. The most vivid – and inflammatory – version of this perspective holds that a European civil code should be elaborated. Others draw a quite opposite conclusion, preferring to regard the fragmentary input of the EC's Directives as potentially harmful to the long-cherished shape of national legal orders and, worse still, as an exercise conducted under the label of harmonization which is ignorant of and hostile to Europe's deep cultural diversity. Such critics contend for fewer, not more, harmonization initiatives at European level, while also maintaining that the degree of commonality that has been achieved so far is in any event grossly exaggerated because of failure to appreciate that law in practice is remote from law on paper.

In between these poles there is plenty of room for more nuanced versions of these radically divergent descriptions and prescriptions.[4] The Commission has lately attempted to adopt an ostentatiously open-minded stance in its view on the future shaping of European contract law. It has insisted that it wants neither to fuel a reckless drive towards wholesale harmonization of private law nor simply to abandon as futile the quest to achieve a degree of worthwhile harmonization. In particular, the Commission has set itself the task of identifying just what is currently missing from the state of contract law in the EU which is required in order to make real the Treaty commitment to the establishment and maintenance of an internal market. This chapter describes the Commission's initiatives, beginning with its Communication issued in 2001, and assesses where its thinking is likely to lead in the shaping of private law by both national and European-level lawmakers. The concern is not only with the substance of any EC initiatives but also with the scope of available compe-

---

Information in the Internal Market (Berlin: De Gruyter, 2001); S. Grundmann, 'The Structure of European Contract Law' (2001) 9 *European Review of Private Law* 505; S. Grundmann, 'The Optional European Code on the Basis of the *Acquis Communautaire* – Starting Point and Trends' (2004) 10 *European Law Journal* 698.

4   For a survey of some of the copious literature see G. Alpa, 'European Private Law: Results, Projects and Hopes' (2003) 14 *European Business Law Review* 379; H. MacQueen, 'Reviews' (2004) 8 *Edinburgh Law Review* 133. For a collection of essays see S. Grundmann and J. Stuyck (eds), *An Academic Green Paper on European Contract Law* (The Hague: Kluwer, 2002).

tence to legislate in the private law field. Then the chapter (necessarily briefly) surveys the lively academic debate that has been conducted both for and against the several possible models of 'European private law' that one could envisage.

This is a long journey for a mere consumer lawyer. But it is where the programme of legislative harmonization affecting private law has led.

THE COMMISSION'S PROCESS OF CONSULTATION ON EUROPEAN CONTRACT LAW

In 2000 the Commission published a report on the implementation of Directive 93/13 on unfair terms in consumer contracts.[5] It claimed that '[d]espite the misgivings of the proponents of a certain legal doctrine who feared that unity of contract law would be rent asunder, the Member States were able to integrate the Directive into their legal orders without major problems . . .' (p. 30). Such a bland, even complacent, observation was hardly likely to mollify critics who treat the EC's intervention into private law in the name of harmonization as disruptive of local systems of legal classification and apt to usurp culturally deep local preferences in the name of economic growth. Nor was this satisfactory as a contribution to the debate about just what should be the scope of legislative harmonization affecting private law.

Happily the Commission soon adopted a more sophisticated approach. In the background was a political readiness on the part of the Member States to address the possibility of greater convergence in this area. The European Council held under the Finnish Presidency in Tampere in October 1999 requested in its conclusions 'an overall study on the need to approximate Member State's legislation in civil matters'.[6]

In July 2001 the Commission issued a Communication on European Contract Law.[7] This was designed to generate a debate about the proper shape of an EC supplement to existing long-established systems of contract law in the Member States. Most of all, the 2001 Communication promised a willingness on the part of the Commission to reflect critically on the desirability of maintaining the hitherto fragmented, patchwork model of lawmaking in the field at EC level. In its 2001 Communication the Commission floated four options for future EC action in the field of contract law (though they are not mutually exclusive).

The first option was no EC action. This was based on the perception that

---

[5] COM (2000) 248.
[6] Presidency conclusions, Tampere European Council 15 and 16 October 1999, para. 39.
[7] COM (2001) 398.

markets have a capacity to achieve self-correction without legal intervention that should not be underestimated. The second option centred on the promotion of the development of common contract law principles leading to greater convergence of national laws. There would be Commission support for research into comparative law. The third option was to improve the quality of legislation already in place. The current legislative *acquis* is marked by odd inconsistencies, such as the lack of uniform length fixed for 'cooling-off' periods in the consumer Directives considered in Chapter 4 of this book, and by a general absence of common definitions for key phrases. The fourth and most ambitious option was the adoption of new comprehensive legislation at EC level, taking the form of a European code that could either replace national law or co-exist with it as an optional instrument. This fourth option was advanced with great caution.

The 2001 Communication attracted a great deal of attention.[8] This was hardly surprising. The Commission's Communication signalled a clear readiness to engage with the question of how far the EC should reach into the field of private law. It served as a focus for a debate that had been brewing for most of the decade since Directive 93/13 on unfair terms in consumer contracts ignited a general concern among private lawyers about the impact of the EC.

The reaction was varied. However, few voices were raised in favour of the fourth and most ambitious of the options, the elaboration of a comprehensive system of European contract law, and indeed many urgently sought to decry such perceived excessive intervention into national autonomy. The main themes of the debate surrounded the key questions that the Commission had astutely placed on the agenda – most of all, why might an EC contribution to contract law be required, and what form might it take? The search was for the benefits and also the costs of EC intervention.

In February 2003 a follow-up emerged from the Commission. This was the Action Plan on a More Coherent European Contract Law.[9] This revealed the outcome of the process of consultation and the fate of the four options put forward in the 2001 Communication. The Commission, having digested the feedback received from the 2001 Communication, had moved towards a preference for solutions that fall between the extremes of inaction and comprehensive intervention. So the planned way forward was located in a combination of options 2 and 3 from the 2001 menu. The sector-specific

---

[8]   E.g. Grundmann and Stuyck, *An Academic Green Paper*; D. Staudenmayer, 'The Commission Communication on European Contract law and the Future Prospects' (2002) 51 *International and Comparative Law Quarterly* 673; Special Issue of *European Review of Private Law* (2002) vol. 10/1; W. Van Gerven, 'Codifying European private law? Yes, if . . .!' (2002) 27 *European Law Review* 156; S. Weatherill, 'The European Commission's Green Paper on European Contract Law: Context, Content and Constitutionality' (2001) 24 *Journal of Consumer Policy* 339.

[9]   COM (2003) 68, 12 February 2003.

approach to legislation will be maintained, with additions proposed only where a need is convincingly demonstrated. In addition a mix of regulatory and non-regulatory measures will be used to increase the coherence of the EC contract law *acquis*. The action plan refers to problems associated with the current absence of comprehensive definitions of abstract notions such as 'damage', which may lead to inconsistencies in application at national level. The Commission airs the idea of developing a 'common frame of reference' for European contract law principles. This would provide a pool of expertise on which jurists could draw in seeking to resolve difficulties and ambiguities in the interpretation of EC measures relevant to contract law. The Commission also proposes that the elaboration of EU-wide general contract law terms should be encouraged. A further (tentatively expressed) idea involves the drawing up of an optional instrument which parties may choose to use in order to facilitate the process of cross-border contracting. It would exist in parallel to national contract law systems. In the 2003 action plan the Commission is non-committal on a number of aspects of its optional instrument, including the type of legal instrument that would be used. The Commission invited further comment.

Like its 2001 predecessor, the 2003 action plan attracted a torrent of comment.[10] Again, this was scarcely surprising – the debate about the future of European Contract law was intensifying. There was general satisfaction that the Commission had set aside any overt intention to move towards anything akin to a European civil code (although some suspicion was voiced that this reticence was only a tactical holding measure). On the other aspects of the action plan there was some lack of certainty about what the Commission had in mind. This was perhaps understandable, since the 2003 action plan had been designed more to promote further debate than to offer immutable solutions.

In October 2004 the Commission, having absorbed feedback on the 2003 action plan, issued a third document in the series. This was 'European Contract Law and the revision of the *acquis*: the way forward'.[11] It builds on the three measures suggested by the 2003 action plan and uses them to map the 'way forward' for European contract law. In the matter of the first measure, improving the quality of the EC contract law *acquis*, the central role of the proposed common frame of reference (CFR) is confirmed. This is to be the subject of elaboration, with 2009 foreseen as a target date for its adoption. By providing clear definitions of legal terms and principles and drawing on EC and Member

10 E.g. J. Karsten and A. Sinai, 'The Action Plan on European Contract Law: Perspectives for the Future' (2003) 26 *Journal of Consumer Policy* 159; C. von Bar and S. Swann, 'Response to the Action Plan on European Contract Law' (2003) 11 *European Review of Private Law* 595; D. Staudenmayer, 'The Commission Action Plan on European Contract Law' (2003) 11 *European Review of Private Law* 11; W. Blair and R. Brent, 'A Single European Law of Contract?' (2004) 15 *European Business Law Review* 5.
11 COM (2004) 651. It is available via http://europa.eu.int/comm/consumers/cons_int/safe_shop/fair_bus_pract/cont_law/communication2004_en.htm.

State practice, the 'CFR' will provide a basis for seeking to improve the exist-ing and future and legislative *acquis*. Although it is envisaged as a non-binding instrument, the 'CFR' is plainly intended to become influential in the drafting and interpretation of legislative measures relevant to (*inter alia*) consumer contract law.

As a second measure the promotion of the use of EU-wide standard terms and conditions is also promised, in line with the idea floated in the 2003 Action Plan. This would be driven by private parties. The Commission would not prepare the standard terms, but rather would merely seek to act as facilita-tor, for example by hosting a website on which information could be shared. The focus here is on business-to-business and business-to-government contracts, not the consumer sector. The third measure, concerning the viabil-ity of an optional instrument in European contract law, co-existing with national law, is again the subject of discussion in the 2004 Communication, albeit of a brief and inconclusive nature. The Commission promises to continue to reflect on 'the opportuneness of such an instrument' (p. 8). Its planned impact on the consumer sphere remains undecided.[12]

The intended nature of the CFR has generated the most interest, combined with a degree of mistrust. In July 2004 a Call for Expression of Interest was published by the Commission. Expert researchers will be funded by the Commission and a supporting network of stakeholder experts on the CFR is to be assembled.[13] A first meeting of Member State experts was held in early December 2004.[14] Stakeholders – drawn from among business, professional and consumer interests – had their first meeting two weeks later.[15] The aim is to sustain an intensive dialogue about the shape of the CFR, involving close atten-tion to the practical value of the instrument, although those whose input is encouraged doubtless possess their own particular aims[16] and it is therefore ulti-mately the Commission itself that will be responsible, following a further round of consultation, for choosing the eventual shape and content of the CFR. The Commission's stated perception in the October 2004 Communication is that the aim will be to identify 'best solutions', and account will be taken of national practice, the EC *acquis* and relevant international instruments, albeit that the

[12]   Cf. D. Staudenmayer, 'The Place of Consumer Contract Law within the Process on European Contract Law' (2004) 27 *Journal of Consumer Policy* 269, 280–84.
[13]   31 July 2004, available *via* http://europa.eu.int/comm/consumers/cons_int/safe_shop/ fair_bus_pract/cont_law/callinterest_en.htm.
[14]   http://europa.eu.int/comm/consumers/cons_int/safe_shop/fair_bus_pract/cont_law/wshop 122004_en.htm.
[15]   http://europa.eu.int/comm/consumers/cons_int/safe_shop/fair_bus_pract/cont_law/cfr_ 15122004_en.htm.
[16]   Cf. M. Hesselink, 'The Politics of European Contract Law: Who has an interest in what kind of contract law for Europe?', ch. 12 in Grundmann and Stuyck, *An Academic Green Paper*; M. Hesselink, 'The Politics of a European Civil Code' (2004) 10 *European Law Journal* 675.

CFR is to be fit for the EC's specific requirements (p. 11). It would set out common fundamental principles of contract law, including guidance on where exceptions could be required. The principles would be supported by definitions of key concepts and the whole would be supported by model rules which would form the bulk of the CFR. The primary criterion to be used in deciding which areas should be covered is 'the usefulness in terms of increasing the coherence of the *acquis*' (p. 11). The CFR would then be available to the Commission as a 'toolbox' on which it could draw in preparing proposals for legislative improvement to the existing body of EC contract law or for new instruments.

The CFR could be seen as an exercise in applied comparative law, designed to nourish a dynamic process of co-ordinated learning in Europe. The appealing promise is of 'a significantly higher degree of coherence in European contract law'.[17] The Commission's concern is conspicuously to move away from orthodox notions of legislative harmonization. Moreover the 2004 Communication asserts explicitly that the Commission does not intend to propose a European civil code (p. 8), although this assertion is made in the context of the 'optional instrument', not the 'common frame of reference'. For all the Commission's evident concern to persuade that the CFR is simply a device for improving the quality of the regulatory environment others have been more sceptical of the mild presentation of what is at stake. For some critics it is the common frame of reference which may sow the seeds of a code and, moreover, some among that body of sceptics identify a risk that the emphasis may be on the contribution of the CFR to economic growth in preference to wider distributional concerns.[18]

The evolution of the CFR will be fascinating to watch. However one judges its perceived virtues and vices, it is plain that if the Commission's intentions are fulfilled it will become very important in the shaping of European contract law in general and consumer contract law in particular.

The October 2004 document also refers to perceived failings of a minimum model of rule-making (p. 3). This conforms to the general concerns currently expressed by the Commission about the fragmenting effect of a model of minimum rule-making and its intention to press for maximum harmonization in order to drive forward market integration more vigorously. Recent consumer policy documents have identified this switch to be in both the commercial and the consumer interest (Chapter 1). The 2004 Communication reveals that this policy preference is to be used in the rethinking European contract law.[19]

---

17 Staudenmayer, 'The Place of Consumer Contract Law within the Process on European Contract Law', 277. See also J. Karsten and G. Petri, 'Towards a Handbook on European Contract Law and Beyond' (2005) 28 *Journal of Consumer Policy* 31.
18 Cf. Study Group on Social Justice in European Private Law, 'Social Justice in European Contract Law: a Manifesto' (2004) 10 *European Law Journal* 653.
19 Karsten and Petri, 'Towards a Handbook on European Contract Law and Beyond', note 17 above.

REFLECTIONS ON THE ISSUE OF COMPETENCE

Article 5(1) EC asserts the constitutionally fundamental principle that the EC can do no more than its Treaty permits. It has only the competence conferred on it by its Member States. It enjoys no explicit competence to legislate in the field of contract law. It is the harmonization programme that supplies the key to understanding the basis for EC legislative intervention into contract law. This pattern has been tracked in Chapters 1 and 3. In so far as national laws vary, the argument has typically proceeded that the construction of a unified trading space within the EU was hindered. Therefore harmonization of laws at EC level was required. So the strict constitutional purpose of harmonization was rule-making designed to make an integrated market, but its effect was to allocate to Community level (albeit, by virtue of the minimum formula, typically not exclusively) the competence to decide on the substance of the rules in question. So choices about the nature and purpose of consumer protection inform the level at which harmonized rules governing contract law shall be pitched.

It is one thing for the Community legislature to harmonize laws in order to integrate markets while also taking account of concern to secure a high standard of consumer protection. It is quite another to pursue an active policy of consumer protection under the camouflage of the harmonization programme. But the allegation is that the presence of unanimous support among the Member States for measures promoting consumer policy at European level constitutes part of the explanation for the advance of legislative consumer policy affecting contract law in the 1970s and 1980s, which in some cases appeared to have little connection with the process of market-building in pursuit of which it was ostensibly designed. Directive 85/577 on doorstep selling was considered in this light in Chapter 1 and, more fully, in Chapter 3, though it is not the only suspect. That was a harmonization measure affecting contract law lacking any carefully explained connection with the process of European market-making.

An improperly generous reading of the scope of the EC's competence by the political institutions cannot withstand the scrutiny of the Court. The key ruling in *Tobacco Advertising, Germany* v. *Parliament and Council*,[20] confirms that harmonization is connected with choices about the proper level of public health or consumer protection.[21] This association is openly recognized, indeed required, by the EC Treaty itself in Articles 95(3) and 153(2) EC. However – and contrary to some previous legislative practice – the judgment

---

[20]   Case C-376/98 *Germany* v. *Parliament and Council* [2000] ECR I-8419.
[21]   See, e.g., paras 78, 88 of the judgment. See also Case C-491/01 *R* v. *Secretary of State, ex parte BAT* [2002] ECR I-11543, paras 62, 79.

insists that a defined threshold of a sufficient contribution to market-making must be crossed. It is a condition of the validity of an act of legislative harmonization that it actually contribute to eliminating obstacles to the free movement of goods or to the freedom to provide services or to removing appreciable distortions of competition. Only then does the requirement of taking appropriate account of a protective dimension come into play.

'Curing' legal diversity *per se* will evidently not do as an adequate basis for intervention founded on Article 95 EC. The EC measure must work harder in the service of market integration. This raises questions about the legal validity of some already adopted Directives that affect contract law but assert their contribution to market-making in a laconic fashion which reveals that in pre-*Tobacco Advertising* days, when unanimity in Council was the key to legislative advance, consitutional sensitivity was not on the EC legislature's agenda. 'Competence sensitivity' now pervades the Commission's thinking about the future of European contract law. In the documents issued in 2001, 2003 and 2004 the debate is not simply about what should be done by the EC in the field of contract law. It is also about what – constitutionally – can be done.

In the 2001 Communication both the fourth and final option and, less obviously but unarguably, the third option raised questions as to whether the EC was truly competent to adopt the envisaged binding measures. The constitutional dimension was addressed only briefly in the Communication. But it is plain that the shadow of the *Tobacco Advertising* ruling has been cast over the Commission's thinking. The Communication calls explicitly for information on whether diversity between national contract laws 'directly or indirectly obstructs the functioning of the internal market, and if so to what extent', with a view to considering appropriate action by the EC's institutions.[22] The Commission is actively seeking to uncover areas in which the internal market is malfunctioning because of deficiencies in the existing bloc of harmonized contract law. The Commission wants hard – Court-proof – data to underpin any claim to competence under the Treaty to shape an EC contract law. The Communication addresses these issues predominantly in the language of subsidiarity (Article 5(2) EC) rather than attributed competence (Article 5(1) EC), which is constitutionally a mistake,[23] but the general perception that justification for EC intervention must be found and carefully explained holds good. The mood is different from the relatively carefree attitude to competence taken in the consumer contract law Directives adopted in the 1980s.

The 2003 action plan[24] sets aside option four on the 2001 menu but its intention to improve the quality of the *acquis* ensures that the scope of the

---

[22] Paras 23–33, 72 of the 2001 Communication, note 7 above.
[23] Weatherill, note 8 above.
[24] COM (2003) 68, note 9 above.

competence to harmonize laws pursuant to Article 95 remains a live issue.[25] Once again the constitutional dimension is not explored in depth in the Commission's Communication, but once again it is undoubtedly relevant and once again the Commission nods in its direction. The action plan insists on having unearthed 'implications for the internal market' arising from legal diversity, drawing a distinction for these purposes between the impact of mandatory and non-mandatory rules of national law.[26]

The October 2004 publication, 'European Contract Law and the revision of the *acquis*: the way forward',[27] maintains the trend. The awkward questions of competence lurk beneath the discussion and are visible to the trained eye. But the Commission studiously avoids aggressive engagement with the matter. Issues of competence are merely glimpsed. The goal of eliminating internal market barriers is explicitly associated with review of the consumer-related harmonization *acquis* (p. 3). The question is asked: 'Is the level of harmonization sufficient to eliminate internal market barriers and distortions of competition for business and consumers?' (p. 4). The debate is therefore to be conducted with respect for the 'problem of competence' but the Commission has the question 'should we do this?' much higher up the agenda than the question 'are we competent to do this?' Similarly the Communication prefers to avoid any concluded view on the legal base of an 'optional instrument'. Articles 308, 95 and 65 EC are cited, but the Commission observes (pp. 21–2) that the question of legal base is tied to those concerning legal form, content and scope. Accordingly reflection on the question of legal base can be left to addressed 'within a larger debate on the parameters of an optional instrument'.[28]

Why does the Commission prefer to set aside detailed inquiry into matters of competence? One answer is that they involve close analysis of the scope of Article 95 (in particular) in the wake of the *Tobacco Advertising* judgment and that they are accordingly fiendishly complicated. In particular, the status of the 'confidence-building' rationale for harmonization, examined in Chapter 3, is highly ambiguous. Entry into this esoteric debate would probably distract attention from the mainstream of the Commission's purpose in its Communications, which is to solicit views on what is really needed and wanted of the EC as a contract lawmaker. This reason for reticence on the constitutional dimension is supplemented by a serious strategic point. Had the

[25] M. Kenny, 'The 2003 Action Plan on European Contract Law: is the Commission running wild?' (2003) 28 *European Law Review* 538; S. Weatherill, 'European Contract Law: Taking The Heat out of Questions of Competence' (2004) 15 *European Business Law Review* 23.
[26] Part 3.2, paras 25–51; also para. 14. The Annex to the Communication provides detailed account of responses to the 2001 Communication received by the Commission.
[27] COM (2004) 651, note 11 above.
[28] Cf Karsten and Petri, 'Towards a Handbook', note 17 above.

Commission include an extended treatment of available legal competence in its 2001 Communication it would doubtless have faced the protest that it was revealing a predilection for those options which most seriously engage the issue of competence, namely option 3 and, most provocatively, option 4. In order to avoid an imbalanced debate the Commission may have acted wisely in striving to maintain an open-minded focus on what is normatively desirable in the field of EC contract law. Only later will it address questions of competence in detail. It is also pertinent to note that the increased attention given to 'softer' forms of activity in the 2003 and 2004 documents – such as the non-binding common frame of reference – has also served to take some of the heat out of the debate about available competence.[29] This has close associations with the much broader agenda for change in how the EU operates mapped out by the Commission in its 2001 White Paper on Governance.[30]

Another point in favour of allowing the competence question to keep a low profile pending attention to substantive concerns arises because of the possibility of Treaty revision. When the Commission launched its inquiry into contract law in 2001 it was perfectly possible that Treaty revision would change the constitutional ground rules. There is a good case to be made in favour of setting to one side concern about constitutional hurdles that might in any event prove temporary. However, it is now apparent that Treaty revision will not change the rules, at least in the medium term. As explained in Chapter 1, the successor to Article 95 in the Treaty establishing a Constitution for Europe is Article III-172. No attempt has been made to alter the wording. The ambiguous status of the scope of the competence to harmonize will remain a hot topic for debate, unchanged by the entry into force of the Treaty establishing a Constitution for Europe (should that occur). Even the Treaty's principal innovation relating to competence control, the monitoring role crafted for national parliaments, extends only to legislative proposals adopted under Article I-18 and not proposals for the harmonization of laws advanced under Article III-172.

THE BROADER DEBATE ABOUT THE DESIRABILITY OF A EUROPEAN CONTRACT LAW

The constitutional discussion, portrayed in its narrowest context, asks whether the EC can act to harmonize contract law. Broader questions ask whether it should. It is on this point that a vigorously constructive debate is much needed.

The very notion of European private law has attracted criticism on several

---

[29] Weatherill, note 25 above.
[30] *European Governance: a White Paper*, COM (2001) 428.

EU consumer law and policy

fronts. That body of criticism has grown in the last 15 years as the EC's role as an actor in the field of private law has become ever more high-profile. EC law has always affected private law. For example, it is very old news, stemming from the original Treaty of Rome which came into force in 1958, that a contract entered into in breach of Article 81(1) is automatically void. In some circumstances the rules governing free movement in the Treaty affect private law, especially those (such as the law governing free movement of persons) which the European Court has interpreted to be capable of direct application to the activities of private parties.[31] But the adoption of Directive 93/13 on unfair terms in consumer contracts was probably the moment at which most national private lawyers truly appreciated for the first time just how deeply the EC was apt to intrude into their cherished home territory in the name of legislative harmonization. In the wake of Directive 93/13 in particular the debate has intensified.

Any attempt to offer a summary of the diverse strands of the debate is vulnerable to criticism as misguidedly superficial. But, with that caveat in mind, it is submitted that understanding can be advanced by appreciating that some of the criticism is aimed at the – in short – economic justifications which have been advanced in support of the development of a common set of contract law rules for Europe, while other criticism is targeted at the more intangible notion that Europe is culturally impoverished by the suppression of local regulatory autonomy under a blanket of legal homogeneity. The two strains of criticism – the economic and the cultural – are sustained by different anxieties but they are joined by a feeling that Europe is better served by taking a more sceptical line in assessing the benefits of harmonization combined with a more positive attitude to the calculation of the benefits found in maintenance of diversity.[32]

THE ECONOMIC CASES FOR AND AGAINST HARMONIZATION

From the economic perspective, there are (at least) two strains of criticism. The first is that the programme of harmonization of contract law in the EU is based on a misconception. The relevant Directives routinely claim that diversity among national contract law regimes distorts competition in the market. A retort is that this has simply not been satisfactorily demonstrated to be true. So harmonization is not needed. The second thematic criticism is connected. It

[31] See, e.g., Case C-415/93 *URBSFA* v. *Bosman* [1995] ECR I-4921; Case C-281/98 *Roman Angonese* [2000] ECR I-4139.
[32] Cf. S. Weatherill, 'Why Object to the Harmonisation of Private Law by the EC?' (2004) 12 *European Review of Private Law* 633.

holds not merely that harmonization is unnecessary but, worse, that it is damaging because it suppresses the possibility of different solutions being selected in different jurisdictions, from which one may learn the advantages of competing approaches to fixing the rules of contract law.

Why would one suppose that diversity between contract law systems damages the process of economic integration? A standard thesis would hold that traders seeking to piece together a common commercial strategy for Europe would be confronted by the costs of having to adapt to the peculiarities of each jurisdiction. They will need to explore what is and is not allowed or required locally, and then shape their contracts accordingly – and differently. The process will demand investment of time and money. This would create 'transaction costs'. All firms are faced with such burdens, but big firms will tend to have the experience and expertise required to absorb them as painlessly as possible. By contrast small and medium-sized businesses may be especially likely to be deterred by such a pattern of legal heterogeneity, and consumers too may suffer, deterred from shopping (actively or passively) across borders because of unfamiliarity with local law.

Accordingly the argument runs that transaction costs will be reduced by eliminating legal diversity in favour of a single rule that can be relied on for the whole territory of the EU. The point relates to selling goods and services generally, where traders are forced to find out about and comply with the rules of all the states in which they plan to operate, but it is apt to operate with extra force where the transaction is itself defined by the law of the state of sale – consider, for example, a contract of insurance.

It would be enormously helpful to gather empirical evidence of the costs associated with legal diversity. This, however, is hard to acquire and regrettably it has not been the past practice of the Commission to assemble such data when advancing legislative proposals for harmonization in order to cure such perceived distortion in the market.

As already suggested above, part of the reason for the claims made for harmonization as a method to eliminate competitive distortion is found in the constitutional requirement that the EC show a valid legal base for proposed legislation. There is no competence conferred by the Treaty to harmonize laws *per se*. Article 95, the commonly chosen base, is more limited than that. In so far as it is unconvincing to claim that an absence of harmonization is commercially detrimental to the creation of an integrated market, constitutional questions are raised about available competence. But also at stake is the more general normative question of why harmonization should be pursued with such vigour. Simply to treat diversity among laws as an inevitable engine of 'distortion' in competition is inadequate. The more reticent the EC political and judicial institutions are in identifying 'distortion' requiring cure, the more space is left to state regulatory autonomy – and to diversity within the EU.

Hugh Beale has called for EC intervention to focus on 'hidden traps' – circumstances in which national law will present unforeseen obstacles to parties seeking to adopt a common commercial strategy across the territory of the EU.[33] This is a helpful contribution to the quest to pin down what 'added value' the EC can bring to contract law in Europe.[34] In this vein the Commission's documents of 2001, 2003 and 2004 are, viewed in their most positive light, attempts to elucidate how much is needed from the EC in the field of contract law in order to squeeze maximum economic benefit from the internal market project. It is to be welcomed that past assumptions that legal diversity distorts conditions of competition appear now to be set aside as intellectually and empirically inadequate foundations for EC intervention.

The objection that harmonization of contract law is not merely superfluous in the cause of economic integration but rather potentially damaging is primarily driven by proponents of 'inter-jurisdictional regulatory competition' as a model for the EU. This perspective would damn harmonization itself as anticompetitive. Why should there not be regulatory variation among Member States, with the market, populated by consumers of regulation, *inter alia* commercial firms, dictating which approach is 'best' by selecting the jurisdiction judged most hospitable, and using that as a base to supply the wider market? This, one might argue, is not state laws causing a distortion of competition – it *is* competition! The counter-argument would assert – *inter alia* – that markets for regulation are no more immune from failure than any other market. Transnational harmonization of laws may cure flaws such as the imposition of external costs that are associated with unduly decentralized models of rule-making. This is close to the rich literature surveying the economics of federalism and invites argument about whether mutual recognition of divergent standards and unlimited market access to host state markets of goods and services complying with home state requirements is a better way to proceed than the imposition of common standards of mandatory substantive regulation.[35]

This economic approach to regulatory competition has associations with the topical interest in securing greater respect in the EU for the virtues of decentralization. Although – as the history of the EC's approach to consumer contract law reveals – the EC's legislative instinct has been much more favourably inclined to harmonization initiatives than to the idea of preserving

---

[33] H. Beale, 'Finding the Remaining Traps instead of Unifying Contract Law', in Grundmann and Stuyck (eds), *An Academic Green Paper*, note 16 above.

[34] See also H. Collins, 'Transaction Costs and Subsidiarity in European Contract Law', and A. Schwartze, 'Design for an empirical data investigation into the impact of existing law harmonisation', both in Grundmann and Stuyck, *An Academic Green Paper*, note 16 above.

[35] See, much more fully, D. Esty and D. Geradin, *Regulatory Competition and Economic Integration* (Oxford: Oxford University Press, 2001).

competition among jurisdictions, this attitude may be changing as the value of diversity attains greater prominence in the debate about the shaping of the EU. Wolfgang Kerber has illuminatingly observed that 'if we want simultaneous mobility and decentralization, then we must accept interjurisdictional competition and we must think about ways to make competition processes workable'.[36] Untrammelled local regulatory autonomy is antagonistic to mobility, but central regulatory competence damages local choice and the prospects for inter-jurisdictional competition.

The literature is beginning to examine what 'distortion' can and should imply in the context of legal diversity within the EU and to explore the case for and against regulatory competition in particular sectors, not only contract law[37] and tort,[38] but also labour standards,[39] environmental policy[40] and company law.[41] Sector-specific inquiry is appropriate. Ultimately the key insight is that one may find flaws in a pattern of decentralized rule-making but this does not of itself constitute an adequate case for centralized rule-making. Centralizing power may be even more flawed. Put another way, the benefits of harmonized rules – most prominently, reduction in transaction costs – must be carefully weighed against the benefits of regulatory diversity – most prominently, the consequent scope for regulatory experimentation and unrestricted choice combined with the reduced risk that powerful interest groups may come to dominate the single centralized rule-maker. One should add too that in practice it is not readily evident that regulatory competition has much role to play in the matter of contract law, not least because of the impediments to mobility caused by *inter alia* linguistic variation and, from the perspective of the consumer in particular, the very real practical problems of obtaining effective access to justice when a transaction concluded away from home territory goes sour. That is to say, 'shopping around' for a different, more favourable regime of contract law is unlikely to be common. Even if it were, one should

---

36 In 'Interjurisdictional Competition within the European Union' (2000) 23 *Fordham International Law Journal* S217, S221, S249.

37 G. Wagner, 'The Economics of Harmonization: the Case of Contract Law' (2002) 39 *Common Market Law Review* 995; R. Van den Bergh, 'Forced Harmonisation of Contract Law in Europe: Not to be Continued' in Grundmann and Stuyck, *An Academic Green Paper*, note 16 above. For a more extended exploration, see E.-M. Kieninger, *Wettbewerb der Privatrechtsordnungen im Europäischen Binnenmarkt – Studien zur Privatrechtskoordinierung in der Europäischen Union auf den Gebieten des Gesellschafts- und Vertragsrechts* (Tübingen: J.C.B. Mohr (Paul Siebeck), 2002).

38 M. Faure, 'Toward a Harmonized Tort Law in Europe? An Economic Perspective' 8 *Maastricht Journal of European and Comparative Law* 4 (2001) 339.

39 E.g. C. Barnard, 'Social dumping and the race to the bottom: some lessons for the European Union from Delaware?' (2000) 25 *European Law Review* 57.

40 E.g. M. Faure, 'Regulating Competition vs Harmonization in EU Environmental Law' in Esty and Geradin, *Regulatory Competition and Economic Integration*, note 35 above.

41 E.g. J. Wouters, 'European Company Law: *Quo Vadis?*' (2000) 31 *Common Market Law Review* 257.

be cautious in assuming that harmonization merely on paper is adequate. A certain degree of reshaping of the judicial administration of civil matters in Europe seems an unavoidable implication of a harmonization process that delves into private law.[42]

The Commission's recent documents do not develop any explicit analysis of the prospects for regulatory competition in the field of contract law. However, there is plainly a concern to focus more closely on the economic rationales for harmonizing. For example, the 2001 Communication explicitly addresses the possibility of higher transaction costs flowing from disparate national laws.[43] This suggests a – welcome – interconnection between the constitutional dimension governing the scope of harmonization and the policy question of when harmonization is economically the way for Europe to go.

HARMONIZATION AND CULTURE

One cannot easily attack harmonization if one's alternative is disharmony. One can attack harmonization much more compellingly if one's alternative is tolerance of cultural difference.

This strand of objection to harmonization is driven by the perception that legal culture, represented in part by the shape of private law, has undergone a long-term, frequently unplanned evolution in the Member States, reflecting a range of influences. To confine such richness within the straitjacket of harmonization is to rob Europe of its past. It is to sacrifice a multi-textured private law tradition to the narrow demands of economic integration built on regulatory homogeneity. A harmonized private law will not display the susceptibility to local preference that is the preserve of a more decentralized system. More broadly still, stretching far beyond the domain of private law, this dissenting vein is nurtured by the profound belief that Europe is strengthened by its diversity.

In the private law field Pierre Legrand has acquired a reputation as the most outspoken of critics. He is closely associated with the thesis that epistemological gulfs between lawyers brought up in different systems make convergence unfeasible. Whether or not one favours the creation of a common European private law, it simply cannot be done. An obvious focus of such scepticism is the divide between common law and civil law method, but Legrand's wider contempt for harmonization has never been more vividly captured than in this onslaught:

---

[42] Wagner, 'The Economics of Harmonization', note 37 above, and see similarly W. Snijders, 'Building a European Contract Law: five fallacies and two castles in Spain', *Ius Commune Lectures of European Private Law No 9* (METRO, Maastricht, June 2003).

[43] Note 7 above, para. 31.

Nowadays, there is only one way in which one can be a 'good European' and it is to support the suppression of local particularism. Any expression of doubt in favour of cultural diversity, any critique of centralising legal integration processes is rapidly construed as inimical to the grand European project ... Another German leader opined that after Auschwitz it was no longer permissible to be 'against Europe'. [A footnote reference here adds: J. Laughland, *The Tainted Source*, London: Little, Brown, 1997, p. 9. By 'Europe' must inevitably be meant, in a significant way, the immensely profligate bureaucratic and regulationist nightmare concocted and nurtured by unelected officials sitting in Brussels (with the promise of worse to come)].[44]

Legrand is very likely correct to claim that the EC cannot bring about a convergence in the literal sense. National legal orders will not be harmonized so that they converge on the same end point.[45] Law is resistant to such unification. However, law is also not static. Legrand's work has been subjected to criticism *inter alia* for its unwillingness to take adequate account of how national laws evolve over time in the context of the EC's harmonization programme. Legal systems are dynamic creatures, so that they are capable of coming progressively and conspicuously closer, even if they may not converge in the literal sense.[46] And a visit to Scotland will reveal that Europe is any event already home to a legal system that displays internal manifestations of a perfectly workable, even inspiring, mix between the continent's two great legal traditions, the common law and the civil law.[47]

However one views the likelihood of law and legal thinking in different jurisdictions becoming similar over time, a different set of questions asks whether this is in any event generally desirable. One's assessment of the true depth of the anxieties that harmonization offends against Europe's diverse cultural heritage depends on inquiry into a number of features. The first question that must be addressed asks what really constitutes culture. On the one hand law and legal tradition are plainly capable of constituting culturally relevant phenomena. On the other there is a need for a focused articulation of why

---

[44] P. Legrand, 'On the Unbearable Localness of the Law: Academic Fallacies and Unseasonable Observations' (2002) 10 *European Review of Private Law* 61, 66.

[45] P. Legrand, 'European Legal Systems are not Converging' (1996) 45 *International and Comparative Law Quarterly* 52.

[46] See, e.g., J. Hage, 'Legal Reasoning and Legal Integration' 10 *Maastricht Journal of European and Comparative Law* (2003) 67; V. Zeno-Zencovich, 'The European Civil Code, European legal traditions and neo-positivism' (1998) 6 *European Review of Private Law* 349; L. Nottage, 'Convergence, Divergence and the Middle Way in Unifying or Harmonising Private Law', EUI Working Papers (Florence), Law 2000/1; W. Van Gerven, 'Harmonization of Private law: Do we Need it?' (2004) 41 *Common Market Law Review* 505; E. Truilhé-Marengo, 'Towards a European Law of Contracts' (2004) 10 *European Law Journal* 463; Special Issue: The Future of European Private Law (2004) 10/6 *European Law Journal*, ed. Collins.

[47] Cf. R. Zimmermann, *Roman Law, Contemporary Law, European Law: The Civilian Tradition Today* (Oxford: Oxford University Press, 2001).

EU consumer law and policy

(and which) aspects of a legal system transcend the mundane practicality of
setting disputes and making the market function efficiently and instead
become endowed with some wider value in society.[48] A second question asks
whether even if we characterize private law as cultural there is truly diversity
in Europe. Are not many – most – features held in common among systems
of private law in Europe? Watson boldly (and doubtlessly provocatively)
asserts that 'The private law of the countries of the EU is not all that different.'[49] One might recall the historical evolution of law in Europe, which has
only relatively recently become split into recognizably distinct national path-
ways, and observe that the current agenda is better labelled not
Europeanization but 're-Europeanization'.[50] One's perspective on this question is then relevant to the connected question whether the allegation that
harmonization is a technical process which tends to underestimate and therefore unjustifiably disturb the deep roots of national systems is well founded.[51]
The perception that the EC legal order is not systematic on the model of a
national legal order leads to the anxiety that it may therefore exert unpredictable and unplanned disintegrating influences on local law.[52] It is certainly
true that the harmonization programme has triggered domestic reform of
private law going beyond what is strictly required to comply with EC obligations, typically because wider reform is motivated by a concern to achieve a
degree of consistency between EC-influenced areas of law and matters that

[48] Cf. e.g., H. Collins, 'European Private Law and the Cultural Identity of States' (1995) 3
European Review of Private Law 353; S. Paasilehto, 'Legal Cultural Obstacles to the
Harmonisation of European Private Law', in V. Heiskanen and K. Kulovesi, *Function and
Future of European Law* (Law Faculty, University of Helsinki, 1999); C. Schmid,
'Legitimacy Conditions for a European Civil Code' 8 *Maastricht Journal of European and
Comparative Law* (2001) 277.

[49] A Watson, *Legal Transplants and European Private Law* (Maastricht: Ius Commune Lectures
on European Private Law 2, August 2000) pp. 12–13. See also A. Hartkamp, E. Hondius, M.
Hesselink, C. Joustra and C. du Perron (eds), *Towards a European Civil Code* (The Hague:
Kluwer, 2nd edn, 1998) and for a fact-specific investigation R. Zimmermann and S.
Whittaker, *Good Faith in European Contract Law* (Cambridge: Cambridge University Press,
2000).

[50] R. Zimmermann, 'Civil Code or Civil Law – Towards a New European Private Law' (1994)
20 *Syracuse Journal of International Law and Commerce* 217, 219. Cf. e.g., R. Van
Caenegem, *European Law in the Past and the Future: Unity and Diversity over Two
Millennia* (Cambridge: Cambridge University Press, 2002); A. Watson, *The Evolution of
Western Private Law* (Baltimore, MD: Johns Hopkins University Press, 2001).

[51] For discussion of the restructuring involved see C. Joerges, 'The Impact of European
Integration on Private Law: Reductionist Perceptions, True Conflicts and a New
Constitutionalist Perspective' (1997) 3 *European Law Journal* 378; D. Caruso, 'Private Law
and Public Stakes in European Integration: the Case of Property' (2004) 10 *European Law
Journal* 751.

[52] E.g. T. Wilhelmsson, 'Private Law in the EU: Harmonized or Fragmented Europeanisation?'
(2002) 11 *European Review of Private Law* 77; W.-H. Roth, 'Transposing Pointillist EC
Guidelines into Systematic National Codes – Problems and Consequences' (2002) 11
European Review of Private Law 761.

lie outwith the EC's formal reach.[53] And, more subtly, harmonization on paper may cause irritation in practice within national legal orders, something much less clean than the idea of harmonization involving instead the generation of unplanned ripples of reform.[54] So 'harmonisation' is by no means a clean-cut phenomenon. It is pertinent to appreciate that one's assessment of the extent to which a legal system can and should withstand impulses towards fragmentation is conditioned by one's intuition of the worth of coherence.[55] These considerations, however, represent a beginning, rather than an end, in the debate about whether such perceptions of the eccentricities of the harmonization programme one should induce a preference to curtail the growth of European contract law or instead to seek to grant it a more systematic – perhaps codified – character.

One's evaluation of the cultural impact of a Europeanization of private law is dictated in part by one's stance on what goals are properly pursued by private law, and on what propulsion would be provided a European dimension. For example the crafting of a general code is vulnerable to the criticism that it may cement in place traditional values that are hostile to sector-specific welfarist models, such as those associated with the modern development of consumer law.[56] Yet there may be circumstances in which the influence of 'Europeanization' is welcomed because of its propensity to influence the path of development of the private law generally in directions favoured by the commentator. So, for example, Wilhelmsson has mused on the possibility that – in short – welfarist reasoning may be imported into general contract law via the medium of treatment of former public utilities that have been converted into creatures governed (more vigorously) by the private law.[57]

Part of the debate concerns investigation of the values that private law

---

[53] On reforming German law in the light of, but beyond the formal scope of, Dir. 99/44 (Chapter 5), see H.-W. Micklitz, 'The New German Sales Law: Changing Patterns in the Regulation of Product Quality' (2002) 25 *Journal of Consumer Policy* 379. On reforming UK law in the light of, but beyond the formal scope of, Dir. 93/13 (Chapter 5), see H. Beale, 'Unfair terms in contracts: proposals for reform in the UK' (2004) 27 *Journal of Consumer Policy* 289.

[54] G. Teubner, 'Legal Irritants: Good Faith in British law or How Unifying Law ends up in New Divergences' (1998) 61 *Modern Law Review* 11.

[55] Cf W. Van Gerven, 'Codifying European private law? Yes, if . . .!' (2002) 27 *European Law Review* 156, 163–4; also H.-W. Micklitz, 'An Expanded and Systematised Community Consumer Law as Alternative or Complement' [2002] *European Business Law Review* 583.

[56] Wilhelmsson, note 3 above. See also his 'The Legal, the Cultural and the Political – Conclusions from Different Perspectives on Harmonisation of European Contract Law' [2002] *European Business Law Review* 541 and 'Varieties of Welfarism in European Contract Law' (2004) 10 *European Law Journal* 712. Cf. Study Group on Social Justice in European Private Law, 'Social Justice in European Contract Law: a Manifesto' (2004) 10 *European Law Journal* 653.

[57] T. Wilhelmsson, 'Services of general interest and European private law', ch. 7 in C. Rickett and T. Telfer (eds), *International Perspectives on Consumers' Access to Justice* (Cambridge: Cambridge University Press, 2003).

seeks to promote,[58] and an inspection of the influence exerted by the EC. More broadly the core of the cultural objection to harmonization holds that systematic intervention at European level would seek to impose what is rejected by the trajectory of sympathy for diversity and tolerance in Europe. The 'culture' that is treated here is not merely a culture inherent in the private law but rather a European culture of respect for difference.

Traces of appreciation of the cultural dimension of private law may be spotted in the Commission's documentation. The 2001 Communication links contract law 'to Member States' different cultural and legal traditions', while asserting that 'most Member States' legal regimes for contract law have similar concepts and rules'.[59] At a more detailed level, there is no elaborate exploration of the cultural content of contract law. It is pertinent to note that the Commission's desire to steer the debate away from pursuit of a fully fledged code could be taken as recognition of the need to allow space for diversity and choice. The adoption of comprehensive legislation at EC level – the most ambitious option advanced in 2001 and the most conducive to driving forward legal homogeneity – has been set aside (for the time being). There are evident connections with the Commission's stated broader strategy to adopt a more sensitive approach to regulation, which in turn forms part of its quest for superior models of governance in the EU.[60] On the other hand those who perceive the common frame of reference as apt to generate a set of principles that reflect the demands of economic integration more heavily than concern for social justice will be unimpressed by this appearance of 'soft' or 'responsive' governance.[61] Moreover, the evident preference for maximum rather than minimum rules reflects an intolerance of local diversity and a determined attempt to promote the harmonized level playing field. This trend is considered in its more general context in Chapters 1 and 3, but here it may be seen as potentially damaging to the expression of local preferences in contract law.

CONCLUSION

Ernst Steindorff has been as active as anyone in charting the rise of European private law.[62] He has commented that

---

58 For a vigorous assault on the notion that private law is or can be value-neutral see D. Kennedy, 'The Political Stakes in "Merely Technical" Issues of Contract Law' (2001) 10 *European Review of Private Law* 7.

59 Para. 12.

60 See in particular the Commission's White Paper on Governance, COM (2001) 428, which is cited *inter alios loci* at para. 71 of the 2003 Action Plan, note 9 above.

61 Cf. Study Group, note 18 above.

62 See E. Steindorff, *EG-Vertrag und Privatrecht* (Baden-Baden: Nomos, 1996).

civil law has to secure values which have been developed in Europe over more than two thousand years. The Court's case law dealing with the fundamental freedoms and – since *Cassis de Dijon* – hereby permitting the States to safeguard certain interests by national restrictive rules, could be interpreted as allocating to the Member States the task of protecting traditional values, even if hereby the exercise of a freedom should eventually be limited. This may apply to civil law too. . . . This could – in the future – lead to efforts to reconcile State and Community levels of private law where they conflict in specific situations. This should be guided by research as to where there are the major insufficiencies of law with respect to the internal market.'[63]

This is particularly helpful in the association it makes between the constitutional dimension of the objections to harmonization of laws and the wider economic and cultural context. Steindorff offers a normative perspective that touches all these concerns. It is evidently based on an assumption that local systems of law should be left undisturbed in the absence of a carefully articulated case for intervention from above in the name of centralization. In a similar, though less precise, vein of wariness about ill-considered pursuit of homogeneity, according to Article I-8 of the Treaty establishing a Constitution for Europe (which, as explained in Chapter 1, is not yet in force) the motto of the European Union shall be 'United in Diversity'. Quite what this means is far from clear, but the field of private law provides a potentially interesting testing ground. Harmonization has bitten deep into private law. The EU's stated concern with the virtues of diversity is challenged by the allegation that harmonization as a process of market-making is apt to threaten the values and the historical roots of the national rules governing the matter subject to the discipline of harmonization. The development of EC contract law has been pioneered by consumer contract law and accordingly the material contained in this book offers scope for reflection on how powerful such criticisms really are.

[63]   E. Steindorff, 'Annotation', (1999) 36 *Common Market Law Review* 191, 203.

8. Advertising law

ADVERTISING AND MARKET INTEGRATION

In modern marketing conditions, a successful commercial strategy involves more than offering a product or service for sale. Closely interwoven with the product or service is the advertising campaign which supports it. For new brands, in particular, it is scarcely conceivable that significant numbers of consumers will be induced to buy an unfamiliar product or service in the absence of investment in a strategy designed to draw consumers' attention to the qualities of the newcomer to the market. This is plainly of particular relevance to the process of European market integration. A traditional French product will be unlikely to make much headway into the German market, where it is unknown, unless accompanied by an advertising campaign and sustained by an effective distribution network. Advertising is a major feature of the modern market economy and it is indispensable in securing changes in existing market patterns.

Such introductory comments identify advertising as a method of consumer information and a basis for widening consumer choice. Adopting such a positive perspective, it should be encouraged – or at least not suppressed. Some of the case law discussed in Chapter 2 reflects this perception. In *GB–INNO–BM* v. *CCL*,[1] for example, a national law which prevented the provision of information to consumers by an advertiser was held incompatible with Article 28 (ex 30) as an unlawful obstacle to the free movement of goods. The impediment to an advertising technique affected the capacity of a cross-border trader to penetrate a new market, thereby prejudicing consumer choice. In fact, cases dealing with advertising restrictions have emerged as among the most difficult to resolve in the light of the Court's ruling in *Keck and Mithouard*,[2] which overturned earlier decisions and confined the scope of application of Article 28. Provided that the restriction on advertising affects all traders equally in law and in fact, the national measure appears to be immune from challenge based on Article 28. But where the measure prevents the out-of-state trader from constructing a strategy that will permit the realization of economies of scale

---

[1] Case C-362/88 [1990] ECR I-667.
[2] Cases C-267 & 268/91 [1993] ECR I-6097.

within an integrating market, it requires justification against the standards recognized by Community law. This suggests a grey area between regulated aspects of advertising that can be separated from the strategy for selling the product or service, which fall beyond the scope of Article 28, and aspects of advertising which, by contrast, are sufficiently connected with the product or service to allow a challenge to national measures that restrict their use to be founded on Article 28. This is a difficult distinction to draw in the light of the modern marketing mix between product/service and its associated identity constructed through advertising. The Court's case law was discussed in Chapter 2. Restrictions on the advertising of a product may diminish the volume of sales, and this restriction may be felt by imported goods. But Article 28 is engaged – and the regulating state called on to justify its rules – only if the provisions do not apply equally to all relevant traders operating within the national territory or do not affect all products in the same manner. This may occur if, as in *Konsumentombudsmannen* v. *Gourmet International Products*,[3] a total ban on the advertising of products (alcoholic drinks in Sweden) applies equally to all products 'on paper' but is shown to harm imports more severely than home-produced goods because the latter already benefit from the level of consumer familiarity which only an advertising campaign could generate for unfamiliar imported goods.

Advertising takes many forms and not all deserve favourable appreciation. Advertising may mislead; advertising may offend. For some, advertising distorts consumer preference. National laws restrict advertising for a variety of reasons and according to a wide range of techniques, differing state by state.[4] This has drawn the European Court into an assessment of the permissibility of types of national controls over advertising in so far as the required impediment to cross-border trade is shown. Whereas the restrictions in *GB–INNO–BM* were ruled incompatible with Article 28, those in *Oosthoek*, which prevented a strategy built around the offer of free gifts, were ruled lawful (Chapter 2). They served to protect the consumer from tactics that were liable to mislead and could accordingly be justified according to the standards of Community law despite the restrictive effect on cross-border trade.

It is a familiar theme of this book that the shape of 'consumer policy' in the integrating European market must be gleaned from an accumulation of random judicial opportunities to judge the permissibility of national measures that conflict with the impetus towards border-free trade combined with the incremental progress towards a legislative framework. This pattern endures in considering EC advertising law. Beyond the Court's role in shaping a 'negative

---

[3] Case C-405/98 [2001] ECR I-1795.
[4] I. Ramsay, *Advertising, Culture and the Law* (London: Sweet and Maxwell, 1996); J. Maxeiner and P. Schotthöfer (eds), *Advertising Law in Europe and North America* (Dordrecht: Kluwer, 1999).

law' approach to the permissibility of national advertising controls, the Community itself has begun to put in place a pattern of 'positive law', regulating advertising at Community level. The constitutional rationale for these Community measures in the field of advertising has been the pursuit of market integration. Attention has focused on the use of what were Articles 100 and 100a, and are now (after amendment) Articles 94 and 95, as a basis for harmonizing national laws which have, as a result of disparity, impeded the development of integrated marketing strategies. However, it is a familiar theme of this book that, in putting in place common Community rules as a basis for integration, such harmonization measures also serve to (re-)regulate the market according to Community standards.

So, in the early stages of the development of the Community, the legal regulation of advertising was the preserve of national authorities. Driven by the process of market integration, Community law became obliged to develop an approach to advertising law.[5] This process was discussed in relation to the Court's perception in Chapter 2 and some of the requirements of information disclosure discussed in Chapter 4 impinge on advertising strategy. But the remainder of this chapter considers more direct legislative action in the field. Piecemeal though the Community strategy for controlling advertising techniques may be, the theme, here as elsewhere in the book, is that, notwithstanding the pre-Maastricht absence of an explicit Title in the Treaty dealing with consumer protection, a type of policy in the field has been unavoidably developed.

MISLEADING ADVERTISING

National laws controlling misleading advertising vary in their precise shape, but it is a relatively uncontroversial proposition that misleading advertising should be subject to regulatory control. Misinformation of the consumer damages the effective operation of the competitive market system. This calls for intervention. This combination of circumstances led to the field of misleading advertising yielding the EC's first harmonization Directive in this area.

Directive 84/450 harmonizes national measures concerning misleading advertising.[6] It was adopted before the entry into force of the Single European Act and therefore it is based on Article 100 of the Treaty (Chapter 1). Variation between national laws in the field exerts a direct impact on the creation of a

---

[5] A. Vahrenwald, 'The Advertising Law of the EU' [1996] *European Intellectual Property Review* 279; B. Schmitz, 'Advertising and Commercial Communications – Towards a Coherent and Effective EC Policy' (1993) 16 *Journal of Consumer Policy* 387.

[6] *OJ* 1984 L250/17.

common market. The free circulation of goods and services is impeded by legislative disharmony. The familiar dual aim of EC measures affecting consumer protection is reflected in the Recitals to the Directive. It is asserted that misleading advertising may prejudice consumers. Support for the need for a regulatory response is drawn from the second 'soft law' programme for a consumer protection and information policy, agreed in 1981 (Chapter 1). It is added that legal regulation of marketing practices is not simply an exercise in protecting the consumer. The establishment of common standards in this area also serves to protect business people whose fair commercial practices might be undermined by those engaged in misleading practices, to the overall detriment of the efficient operation of the market.

Directive 84/450 was amended by Directive 97/55[7] to cover comparative advertising. As a result, the correct title of the Directive is now Directive 84/450 (as amended) concerning misleading and comparative advertising. Whereas misleading advertising is to be suppressed, comparative advertising is to be permitted, provided it meets the criteria stipulated by the Directive. Article 1 of the amended version of Directive 84/450 duly provides that

> The purpose of this Directive is to protect consumers, persons carrying on a trade or business or practising a craft or profession and the interests of the public in general against misleading advertising and the unfair consequences thereof and to lay down the conditions under which comparative advertising is permitted.

The core of the material dealing with comparative advertising is found in a self-contained Article 3a, inserted into Directive 84/450 by Directive 97/55. This is treated separately below.

The Meaning of 'Misleading'

The key definition of 'misleading' for these purposes is addressed in Articles 2(2) and 3 of the Directive. Article 2(2) identifies the deceptive nature of the advertising as the key element. It is plainly appropriate to take a broad view of the surrounding circumstances in assessing the misleading nature of advertising. This is reflected in Article 3 of the Directive: 'Account shall be taken of all its features.' A non-exhaustive list in Article 3 refers to the characteristics of goods or services, price, conditions of supply and the nature and attributes of the advertiser.

The notion of misleading is plainly dependent on all the circumstances of the case. Nevertheless, it is capable of being interpreted by the European Court in the context of an Article 234 (ex 177) preliminary reference in the light of 'Europeanized' considerations. This is well illustrated by the Court's ruling in

---

[7]   *OJ* 1997 L290/18, corrig. *OJ* 1998 L194/54.

Procureur de la République v. *X*.[8] The case reached the European Court as a
preliminary reference from a French court dealing with an allegation of
misleading advertising against a trader importing Nissan cars from Belgium
for resale in France, where they were advertised as new cars available at lower
prices than Nissan cars sold by the French exclusive distributor. The cars on
offer were registered, but for importation purposes only. They had never been
driven and were cheaper than French models because they possessed fewer
accessories. Did this tactic secure a desirable widening of consumer choice or
did it create an unacceptable risk that the consumer would be misled into
buying a model different from that which he or she expected to acquire? The
French exclusive distributor lodged a complaint before the competent French
court about the strategy. It was necessary to consider whether this amounted
to 'misleading' advertising within the meaning of the Directive, which should
therefore be suppressed at national level. The European Court considered that
'It is when a car is first driven on the public highway, and not when it is registered, that it loses its character as a new car.' This made it plain that the
imported cars should be regarded as new. The Court accepted that a national
court might properly find advertising to be misleading where it seeks to
conceal the fact that cars advertised as new were registered before importation
and where knowledge of this would have deterred purchase by a significant
number of consumers. The Court also considered that advertising cars as
cheaper could only be misleading where a significant number of consumers
were ignorant that the lower price was matched by the availability of fewer
accessories. The Court concluded its relatively full reply to the questions
referred to it by ruling that the Directive

> must be interpreted as meaning that it does not preclude vehicles from being adver-
> tised as new, less expensive and guaranteed by the manufacturer when the vehicles
> concerned are registered solely for the purpose of importation, have never been on
> the road and are sold in a member state at a price lower than that charged by deal-
> ers established in that member state because they are equipped with fewer acces-
> sories.

The essence of the ruling is that the marketing of the cars could not be
suppressed by the French authorities on the basis that it infringed the controls
which the Directive required Member States to put in place. This was not a
case of misleading advertising.

The Court is plainly unreceptive to a broad reading of what may mislead.
'Significant' levels of consumer confusion must be shown before the
Directive's control is activated. The Court's choice of this relatively high
threshold is probably motivated by concern to facilitate the commercial oppor-

---

[8]   Case C-373/90 [1992] ECR I-131.

tunities of a parallel importer in a sector which is notoriously marked by persisting fragmentation along national lines. Had the tactics employed by the dealer in Belgian cars been suppressed as misleading within the meaning of the Directive, then territorial protection within France would have been strengthened. It is plausible that the Court's interpretative approach to required levels of misapprehension among consumers took account of the ultimate consumer advantage that would flow from integration of the car market, yielding wider consumer choice. Advocate General Tesauro was explicit in his observation that suppression of the type of advertising at stake 'would be likely in practice to hit parallel importers particularly hard'. The Court too chose to confirm this perspective, referring to the privileged position in Community law of parallel importers 'because they encourage trade and help reinforce competition'. So the chance of some consumer confusion was not adequate to treat the advertising practices as 'misleading' within the meaning of the Directive. Underlying the ruling is an assumption that a sufficient majority of consumers is sufficiently well informed to exercise a choice between different types of car. Here too Mr Tesauro was explicit: 'the average consumer, who I am convinced is not wholly undiscerning, is inclined . . . to make a careful comparison of the prices on offer and to enquire of the seller, sometimes very meticulously, about the accessories with which the vehicle is equipped'. This may be taken as a further illustration of the Court's use of the informed consumer as a lever to achieve market integration, in this instance occurring against the background of a Directive rather than the primary Treaty rules examined in Chapter 2. The consumer provided with the stipulated information cannot be regarded as misled.

Here, as in other circumstances surveyed at more length in Chapter 2, the issue centres on the delicate question of when beneficially wider choice in a more competitive market shades into prejudicially intransparent market conditions in which confusion, not choice, will greet the consumer. In such cases the Court's stance is perceived to be generally favourable to the consumer interest in competitive markets achieved through a deregulatory emphasis in the interpretation of Treaty provisions and relevant secondary legislation. This may be an accurate summary of the Court's predilections, although it should be appreciated that it is for the regulating state to show a justification for rules that restrict cross-border trade. This is frequently either not forthcoming or advanced in wholly unpersuasive terms.

Minimum Harmonization

The Court's capacity to set the terms for parallel trade by restricting the possibilities for national action under the Directive is to some extent limited by Article 7 of the Directive. This contains the minimum harmonization formula.

It permits Member States to set stricter rules than those contained in the Directive should they so wish. Those stricter rules must be compatible with the Treaty. In so far as they impede the free movement of goods they must comply with Articles 28–30. So, using the example of *Procureur de la République* v. *X*, the Directive, as a minimum measure, would not prevent France adopting stricter laws controlling advertising, but it seems probable that such restrictions would be held incompatible with Article 28 EC. This was not made explicit by the Court, but it was the view expressed by the Commission in its submissions in *X*. Moreover, analogies with rulings such as *Rocher* and *Clinique*, examined in Chapter 2, in which the Court found national restrictions on advertising to be unlawful, suggest that it would be difficult for stricter rules to be justified. The minimum clause in Article 7 of Directive 84/450 was addressed directly by the Court in *Herbert Karner GmbH* v. *Troostwijk GmbH*.[9] This concerned Austrian controls over advertising. The Court found these were not excluded by the Directive, because of its minimum nature. It then tested them against the requirements of Article 28, but found that because of the absence of any special impact on imports the rules did not constitute trade barriers within the meaning of Article 28.[10] Accordingly they required no justification.[11]

It is explained in Chapter 3 that more recent judicial practice – most prominently visible in *Tobacco Advertising*[12] – has cast doubt on the validity of the model of 'minimum harmonization'. This matter has not been tested in relation to Directive 84/450.

The broad scope of the regime suppressing misleading advertising creates potential problems of overlap. It is provided in Article 7 that 'The provisions of this Directive shall apply without prejudice to Community provisions on advertising for specific products and/or services or to restrictions or prohibitions on advertising in particular media.' Accordingly Directive 84/450 does not allow for the setting aside of sector-specific rules. Article 7 of Directive 84/450 was amended by Directive 97/55 to cater for the different position applicable to comparative advertising. The Directive does not set minimum standards for comparative advertising. This is considered further below.

COMPARATIVE ADVERTISING

As mentioned above, Directive 84/450 on misleading advertising was

---

[9]   Case C-71/02 judgment of 25 March 2004.
[10] See Chapter 2 for discussion of the scope of Article 28 in the light of the ruling in Cases C-267 & 268/91 *Keck and Mithouard* [1993] ECR I-6097.
[11] Although the Court – illogically – proceeded to express the view that they were justified.
[12] Case C-376/98 [2000] ECR I-8419.

amended by Directive 97/55 to cover comparative advertising.[13] Article 3a of Directive 84/450 sets the terms on which comparative advertising is allowed, and it is considered below. But this measure was a long time coming.

The Commission's first draft proposal in this area was released in 1978 and covered misleading, unfair and comparative advertising.[14] The first two types of advertising were to be controlled, the third, comparative, was to be liberalized. However, the adopted version of Directive 84/450, discussed above, excluded provisions concerning unfair and comparative advertising, and dealt only with control of misleading advertising. This reflects the difficulties of achieving a satisfactory harmonized regime against a background of legal heterogeneity.[15] Although the notion of unfair advertising as an aspect of unfair competition between traders is relatively well understood in several continental European systems, English law recognizes no developed notion of a law against unfair competition. The matter re-emerged on the legislative agenda as late as 2003, and is considered below. Differences in legal tradition similarly explain the exclusion of comparative advertising from the agreed text of Directive 84/450. This technique has long been tightly controlled in several Member States, including Germany, as an aspect of unfair competition, whereas it is largely seen as unexceptionable in other states, including the United Kingdom where a liberal attitude is taken other than in response to trade-mark infringement.

The Commission persisted in its attempts to widen the scope of the EC's secondary legislation concerning advertising beyond the misleading brand. It is important to appreciate that legislative proposals do not exist in isolation from evolution in other areas of Community law. National restrictions on comparative advertising were not immune from decisions of the European Court on the scope of application of Article 28. This proved to be a route towards liberalization even in the absence of legislative action. In *GB–INNO–BM* v. *CCL*, discussed in Chapter 2, restrictions on comparative advertising imposed in Luxembourg were shown to be incompatible with Article 28 because of their inhibition on the free circulation of products capable of being marketed with the support of such techniques. The Commission made explicit reference to this ruling in its June 1991 proposal for a Directive concerning comparative advertising. This would have amended and extended Directive 84/450 and, in particular, was largely designed to require that comparative advertising be permitted, subject to qualifications which were principally directed to ensuring the fairness of the

---

13 Note 7 above. P. Spink and R. Petty, 'Comparative Advertising in the European Union' (1998) 47 *International and Comparative Law Quarterly* 855.
14 *OJ* 1978 C70/4, amended proposal *OJ* 1979 C194/3.
15 B. Ludwig, *Irreführende und vergleichende Werbung in der EG* (Baden-Baden: Nomos, 1995).

comparison made.[16] In view of the challenge to national laws which restricted comparative advertising which was presented by Article 28 in the wake of the ruling in *GB–INNO–BM* v. *CCL*, the need to liberalize comparative advertising by introducing positive Community law was diminished. Moreover, the vigour of the Court's intervention brought home to states determined to resist legislative reform of comparative advertising by the EC that their restrictive rules were imperilled even in the absence of the adoption of a Directive.

Nevertheless adoption of the Commission's 1991 proposal by the Council remained politically unfeasible. At this time the subsidiarity principle gained prominence in the political atmosphere surrounding existing and proposed Community legislative activity (Chapter 1). The Commission declared that it had reviewed the proposal on comparative advertising in the light of the demands of the subsidiarity principle. It published an amended proposal in 1994.[17] The thrust in favour of controlled liberalization of the practice of comparative advertising was maintained and the adjustments to the original proposal were relatively modest.

Eventually the political mood changed. Sufficient support for the adoption of a measure liberalizing comparative advertising was forthcoming. In 1997 Directive 97/55 was adopted, taking Article 100a and harmonization in pursuit of market-making as its legal base. It amends Directive 84/450.

Directive 97/55 makes the economic case in favour of comparative advertising in its Preamble. Such practices can stimulate competition between suppliers of goods and services to the consumer's advantage by permitting an objective and informed basis for selection between available products. The Preamble ties the liberalization of comparative advertising explicitly to the perceived importance of providing consumers with information, which was first recognized in the resolution on a preliminary programme for a consumer policy published as the EC's first 'soft law' incursion into the consumer field in 1975 (Chapter 1). Consumer information is an enduring theme in EC consumer law and policy. Yet information may mislead. The claim that comparative advertising will liberate objective assessments by consumers is unsettling, given that the source of the information is traders, whose job is not to act as dispassionate observers in the market. What matters is that comparative advertising be confined within appropriate boundaries. The Preamble recognizes that in order to prevent the anti-competitive and unfair use of comparative advertising 'only comparisons between competing goods and services meeting the same needs or intended for the same purpose should be permitted'.

Comparative advertising is defined broadly, to cover all its forms.[18] The detailed rules which govern the assessment of where lie the limits of permit-

[16] *OJ* 1991 C180/1.
[17] *OJ* 1994 C136/4.
[18] Case C-112/99 *Toshiba Europe* [2001] ECR I-7945.

ted comparative advertising are set out in a new provision inserted by Directive 97/55 as Article 3a into Directive 84/450.

In the first place, comparative advertising must not mislead within the meaning of Directive 84/450.

Beyond this fundamental precondition, comparative advertising is permitted provided that it compares goods or services meeting the same needs or intended for the same purpose; that it objectively compares one or more material, relevant, verifiable and representative features of those goods and services, which may include price; that it does not create confusion in the marketplace between the advertiser and a competitor or between the advertiser's trade marks, trade names, other distinguishing marks, goods or services and those of a competitor; that it does not discredit or denigrate the trade marks, trade names, other distinguishing marks, goods, services, activities, or circumstances of a competitor; that for products with designation of origin, it relates in each case to products with the same designation; that it does not take unfair advantage of the reputation of a trade mark, trade name or other distinguishing marks of a competitor or of the designation of origin of competing products; that it does not present goods or services as imitations or replicas of goods or services bearing a protected trade mark or trade name.

This is a bulky list, and embedded within it are several complex notions which can be understood only in application to particular problems that arise in practice. None the less, a central question is also a familiar one. Which perspective should one adopt in determining whether the preconditions are met or not? How much 'confusion in the market place' is required before comparative advertising is not entitled to the shelter of this permissive legal regime? The question returns once again to the image of the consumer that drives this system of rules.

In *Pippig Augenoptik* v. *Hartlauer*[19] Hartlauer had advertised its spectacles on the basis of their relatively low prices when compared with Pippig's goods. Pippig sought to suppress the comparative advertising as misleading. The Court dealt first with the pre-emptive effect of the Directive, which is considered below. It then proceeded to provide interpretative advice on the circumstances in which comparative advertising might be considered to be impermissible under the Directives. It referred to a test of whether the presumed expectations of the average consumer would be upset. In adopting this formula it made an explicit connection with the relevant case law arising under Article 28 EC, where the benchmark of the average consumer plays a central role in judging the permissibility of national trade restrictions.[20]

---

[19] Case C-44/01 [2003] ECR I-3095.
[20] Case C-220/98 Estée Lauder, mentioned in para. 55 of the judgment in Case C-44/01 and considered in Chapter 2 of this book.

Article 3a(2) adds a separate regime to cover special offers. These shall indicate

> in a clear and unequivocal way the date on which the offer ends or, where appropriate, that the special offer is subject to the availability of the goods and services, and, where the special offer has not yet begun, the date of the start of the period during which the special price or other specific conditions shall apply.

The Nature of the Harmonized Regime Governing Comparative Advertising

Article 7 of Directive 84/450 applies a rule of minimum harmonization to misleading advertising. But Article 7 of Directive 84/450, as amended by Directive 97/55, makes different provision for the phenomenon of comparative advertising. Member States may not apply stricter provisions against comparative advertising as far as the comparison is concerned. Put another way, comparative advertising that complies with the Directive may be pursued throughout the territory of the EU market and a Member State cannot insist on a local need for more rigorous rules. This maximizes the contribution of the Directive to the integration of the market.

The sole exceptions envisaged by the Directive concern the possibility that Member States may choose to ban comparative advertising regarding goods or services connected with the exercise of a commercial, industrial, craft or professional activity (Article 7(4)). Article 7(5) performs a similar function in the case of the advertising of professional services.

The exclusion of a 'minimum' approach to the regulation of comparative advertising in the EU was strongly emphasized in the Court's ruling in *Pippig Augenoptik* v. *Hartlauer*.[21] Hartlauer had advertised its spectacles on the basis that they were cheaper than Pippig's. Pippig took legal action to suppress the comparative advertising as misleading. The preliminary constitutional question for the Court was whether stricter national provisions on protection against misleading advertising could be applied to suppress comparative advertising of the type envisaged and allowed by the Directives – that is, treated as not misleading for EC purposes. The Court began its analysis by observing that the objective of Directive 84/450 as amended by Directive 97/55 is 'the establishment of conditions in which comparative advertising must be regarded as lawful in the context of the internal market'. Article 7(1) of Directive 84/450 allows Member States to apply stricter national provisions in that area, to ensure greater protection of consumers in particular, but Article 7(2) of Directive 84/450 expressly provides that Article 7(1) does not apply to comparative advertising so far as the comparison is concerned. The aim of

---

[21] Case C-44/01, note 19 above.

Directive 97/55 is 'to establish conditions under which comparative advertising is to be permitted throughout the Community'. The Court concluded that this was an instance of 'exhaustive harmonization'. The lawfulness of comparative advertising throughout the Community is to be assessed solely in the light of the criteria laid down by the Community legislature. There is no room for national provisions that are less tolerant of comparative advertising.

ENFORCEMENT OF DIRECTIVE 84/450 ON MISLEADING AND COMPARATIVE ADVERTISING

The practical impact of the Directive within national legal orders is naturally dependent on patterns of enforcement. The Directive is not content simply to leave it up to national authorities to choose how to implement the prohibition against misleading advertising. It makes specific reference to the type of institutional structures that must be established. The relevant provisions were amended by Directive 97/55 to cope with the consequences of adding the liberalization of comparative advertising to a regime previously targeted solely at suppressing misleading advertising.

Article 4(1) obliges Member States to 'ensure that adequate and effective means exist to combat misleading advertising and for the compliance with the provisions on comparative advertising in the interests of consumers as well as competitors and the general public'. Legal provisions shall enable persons or organizations regarded under national law as having a legitimate interest in prohibiting misleading advertising or regulating comparative advertising to pursue one or both of two stipulated routes: first, the taking of legal action against such advertising; second, the bringing of such advertising before an administrative authority competent either to decide on complaints or to initiate appropriate legal proceedings. Article 4(2) requires courts and administrative authorities to be empowered to take stipulated forms of action, including the making of cessation orders, in the event of offending advertising.

These arrangements were carefully crafted at the time of the negotiation of Directive 84/450. The policy which underpins this structure is directed at the perceived need to permit states the option of retaining administrative structures as adequate regulation in the area. The United Kingdom, in particular, was concerned to avoid the imposition of a judicial structure. It was also unwilling to see the exclusion of its self-regulatory structure, which the government viewed as satisfactory. Article 4(3) of the Directive requires that where the administrative option is taken the authorities shall be *inter alia* impartial (therefore, not dominated by advertisers) and that, where the powers are the exclusive preserve of the administrative authority, decisions shall be reasoned and shall be subject to judicial review in the event of impropriety or unreasonableness. Article 5 emphasizes the receptivity of the structure to extra-legal enforcement. Article 5 makes it clear that voluntary control of misleading and comparative advertising by self-regulatory bodies is not excluded, although proceedings of this nature must be additional to, not in substitution for, the court or administrative route established by Article 4.

The pattern of enforcement has been supplemented by Directive 98/27 on injunctions for the protection of consumers' interests.[22] This measure is examined at more length in Chapter 10, which provides a wider appreciation of EC law's contribution to effective enforcement of the agreed rules. Where violations of *inter alia* the advertising Directives occur and where the *collective* interests of consumers are damaged, the rules of Directive 98/27 governing actions for an injunction before national courts come into play. Where an infringement originates in a Member State, any qualified entity from *another* Member State where the interests protected by that qualified entity are affected by the infringement may bring the matter before a court or administrative authority designated pursuant to the Directive. For this purpose Member States are required to inform the Commission of the name and purpose of the qualified entities within their jurisdiction. This institutes a type of 'mutual recognition' of enforcement agencies which is motivated by the anxiety that traders may be tempted to exploit weaknesses in law enforcement in the border-free market by locating in one state and targeting unlawful practices at the consumers of another Member State.

TOBACCO ADVERTISING

In EC law, the very phrase 'Tobacco Advertising' immediately conjures up concern about the constitutional limits of the Community's competence to harmonize laws. The Court's ruling in the *Tobacco Advertising* case[23] was mentioned in Chapter 1 and examined more fully in Chapter 3 and it is of fundamental constitutional importance. But the substance of the relevant rules that have escaped annulment by the Court also merits attention. The EC has a role in setting standards that must be met by those engaged in the business of advertising tobacco products. These are of significance to both commercial operators and to consumers. Intervention in this sector is notoriously politically sensitive.[24]

Over the last three decades or so tobacco advertising has been the subject of increasingly intensive control in most Member States in response to the

[22] *OJ* 1998 L166/51.
[23] Case C-376/98 *Germany* v. *Parliament and Council* [2000] ECR I-8419.
[24] F. Duina and P. Kurzer, 'Smoke in your eyes: the struggle over tobacco control in the European Union' (2004) 11 *Journal of European Public Policy* 57.

growing awareness of the health risks for both smokers and non-smokers associated with tobacco consumption. In line with much of the legislative activity surveyed in this book, the diversity of regulatory responses among the Member States provides a ready rationale for Community legislative intervention in the field based initially on Article 100a and, since the entry into force of the Amsterdam Treaty in 1999, Article 100a's amended successor, Article 95. The Community's intervention has affected both advertising displayed on the packaging of tobacco products and more general advertising physically separate from the tobacco products themselves. The associated constitutional context is not the same in both cases. This draws attention to the fundamental constitutional principle found in Article 5(1) EC that the Community acts only within the scope of the competences conferred on it by its Treaty.

Directive 89/622 was the EC's first adventure into this field. It concerned the labelling of tobacco products and it took Article 100a as its legal base.[25] The Directive was adopted in November 1989 by qualified majority vote in Council. The United Kingdom, which had preferred to employ a voluntary approach in this sector in the past, voted in vain against the measure. It provided that products shall carry a general warning, which in English shall read 'Tobacco seriously damages health'. Furthermore, manufacturers were required to select from a list of additional warnings to be printed on packets of cigarettes. The Directive stipulated that the warnings should cover at least 4 per cent of the relevant surface area.[26] Directive 89/622 was amended by Directive 92/41, which was also based on Article 100a.[27] This provided that the additional warnings must be applied to all tobacco products, not just cigarettes. Moreover, a prohibition was imposed on certain tobacco products for oral use.

Directives 89/622 and 92/41 survived until they were repealed and replaced by Directive 2001/37, which harmonizes laws concerning the manufacture, presentation and sale of tobacco products.[28] Its legal base is Article 95.[29] It deals with rules governing warnings on packets, as well as the maximum tar yield of tobacco products,[30] and insists in its Preamble on the need for harmonization of such matters in order to advance the smooth functioning of the internal market. The protection of health is also cited as an objective with reference to the demands of Article 95(3).

---

[25]   *OJ* 1989 L359/1.

[26]   States must admit on to their market imported packets which carry a warning covering 4 per cent of surface area, but they remain free to impose stricter rules on home production; Case C-11/92 *R* v. *Secretary of State, ex parte Gallaher Ltd* [1993] ECR I-3545.

[27]   *OJ* 1992 L158.

[28]   *OJ* 2001 L194/26.

[29]   The Dir. also cites Art. 133 EC but the Court ruled this incorrect in Case C-491/01 *R* v. *Secretary of State ex parte BAT and Imperial Tobacco* [2002] ECR I-11543, considered below. Art. 95 EC constitutes the only appropriate legal base.

[30]   In respect of which it replaces Dir. 90/239, *OJ* 1990 L137/36.

In the present inquiry into EC advertising law, it is the rules stipulated by Directive 2001/37 to cover warnings and labelling, rather than those governing tar yield, that are of most direct consequence. These are found in Article 5 and are relatively detailed. Tar, nicotine and carbon monoxide yields of cigarettes shall be printed on one side of the packet in the official language or languages of the Member State where the product is marketed, so that at least 10 per cent of the corresponding surface is covered.[31]

Packets of tobacco products (excepting only tobacco for oral use and other smokeless tobacco products) must carry both a specified general warning, printed on the most visible surface of the packet, and an additional warning selected from a menu set out in Annex I to the Directive, which shall be printed on the other most visible surface of the packet.

Article 8 forbids the marketing of tobacco for oral use, though this is stated to be without prejudice to Article 151 of the Act of Accession of Austria, Finland and Sweden. Such tobacco products for oral use that escape prohibition shall nevertheless carry the warning that 'This tobacco product can damage your health and is addictive', which shall be printed on the most visible surface of the packet. The same applies to smokeless tobacco products.

Article 5(5) contains detailed rules governing the size of warnings. The general warning and the warning for smokeless and oral tobacco products shall cover not less than 30 per cent of the surface of the packet on which it is printed.[32] The additional warning required shall cover not less than 40 per cent of that surface.[33] The Directive goes so far as to specify in Article 5(6) matters associated with the typeface, background and the point size of the font.

Tobacco companies play for high stakes and they are among the most litigious of commercial operators. A challenge to the validity of Directive 2001/37 was initiated before the English courts. An Article 234 preliminary reference was made to Luxembourg asking the European Court to rule on this question of validity. In *ex parte BAT*[34] the Court concluded that the Directive was validly adopted on the basis of Article 95 EC. It insisted that measures of harmonization adopted pursuant to Article 95 must be intended to improve the conditions for the establishment and functioning of the internal market and must genuinely have that object. Moreover, Article 95 EC may be deployed to prevent the emergence of future obstacles to trade resulting from diverse development of national laws, provided that the emergence of such obstacles

[31] That percentage rises to 12 per cent for Member States with two official languages and to 15 per cent for Member States with three official languages.

[32] This rises to 32 per cent for Member States with two official languages and 35 per cent for Member States with three official languages.

[33] This rises to 45 per cent for Member States with two official languages and 50 per cent for Member States with three official languages.

[34] Case C-491/01, note 29 above.

is likely. This test was satisfied in the case. There was sufficient evidence to persuade the Court that the increasing attention devoted by public authorities in the Member States to control of tobacco products made it likely that the adoption of diverse rules would impede the functioning of the internal market. EC harmonization was therefore valid.

The Court also checked the Directive for compliance with the principle of subsidiarity, which is found in Article 5(2) EC. It concluded that the objective of the measure was to set common standards, and that the Community could better achieve this than the Member States, and that accordingly the subsidiarity threshold was crossed. As explained in Chapter 1, this appears to allow little scope in practice for effective judicial review of common rule-making against the standards set by the principle of subsidiarity.

The Court was not deterred by the obvious public health component in Directive 2001/37. It cited Articles 95(3) and 152(1) EC as authority for the proposition that 'provided that the conditions for recourse to Article 95 EC as a legal basis are fulfilled, the Community legislature cannot be prevented from relying on that legal basis on the ground that public health protection is a decisive factor in the choices to be made'. It also made light of the submission that since there was already a harmonized regime at EC level the legislature could not validly use Article 95 to make it more restrictive. The Court upheld a discretion available to the EC legislature to upgrade the standard of protection promised by common rules, not only because of prompts from progress in scientific knowledge but also on account of 'other considerations, such as the increased importance given to the social and political aspects of the anti-smoking campaign'.[35]

This combination of legislative practice and judicial approval maps out a role for the EC legislature in setting the permissible terms of advertising and labelling which is physically attached to packets of tobacco products. The Commission long maintained the view that the scope of Community action in the field should be extended. A proposal for a much more ambitious Directive was issued in 1991. This envisaged the introduction of a complete ban on advertising throughout the EU, save within tobacco retail outlets.[36] Had the Commission wished to advance this measure as a public health measure, it would have been confronted by the problem that the Treaty conferred such a competence only with effect from 1993, the entry into force of the Maastricht Treaty. More fundamentally the relevant provision, which is now Article 152, does not envisage harmonization of laws. But the 1991 proposal, like its predecessors concerned with warnings on packets, was based on Article 100a. The Commission insisted on the contribution the Directive would make to the

[35] Para. 80 of the judgment.
[36] *OJ* 1991 C167/3.

elimination of the distortive effect of different national laws in the field, and referred also to the reference to a high level of health protection found in Article 100a(3), now Article 95(3). It was also able to refer to relevant 'soft law' – the 1986 Council Resolution on an EC programme of action against cancer.[37]

The approval of the Parliament was received in February 1992, although the Parliament suggested amendments which would have rendered the controls still more rigorous. The Commission then redrafted its proposal to accommodate some of these amendments and issued a fresh proposal in April 1992.[38] But it proved impossible to secure an adequate majority in Council to ensure the adoption of the proposed wide-ranging harmonized ban on tobacco advertising. Suspicions that this measure was in truth predominantly dedicated to public health concerns and not to market-making remained no more than dark whispers, devoid of practical significance in the light of the lack of adequate political support.

This changed in 1997. The Conservative administration in the United Kingdom had been opposed to the Commission's proposal. The incoming Labour government in the United Kingdom was supportive. There was a qualified majority in Council in favour. Directive 98/43 was duly adopted on the basis of Articles 100a, 57(2) and 66 (now 95, 47(2) & 55), which are directed at integrating goods and services markets.[39] It banned the advertising of tobacco products throughout the EC, including on ashtrays, parasols used in street cafés and billboards, allowing only small exceptions, for example for advertising at the point of retail. The question of whether the EC was even competent to act to suppress advertising in this way became one of the highest practical significance. Germany, a member of the outvoted minority in Council, brought the matter before the European Court. The Court annulled the Directive. It was not validly based on Articles 100a, 57(2) and 66 (now 95, 47(2) & 55).

The constitutional salience of *Tobacco Advertising* is discussed in its broader context in Chapters 1 and 3. The Court has vigorously insisted that the Treaty does not envisage a competence to harmonize *per se*. Fixing and understanding the threshold the Court imposes before recourse to Article 95 is valid and is very important to determining the reach of the EC as a 're-regulator' of the internal market, *inter alia* in the field of consumer protection. The issue in this chapter is the specific issue of EC regulation of advertising.

The Court in *Tobacco Advertising* was unpersuaded that harmonizing rules governing the advertising of tobacco products on ashtrays, parasols and bill-

---

[37]   *OJ* 1986 C184/19.
[38]   *OJ* 1992 C129/5.
[39]   *OJ* 1998 L213/9.

boards made any demonstrable contribution to the functioning of the internal market. But it went out of its way to make plain that it was not ruling out the possibility of using Article 95 to harmonize national rules governing advertising; nor that the content of such a harmonized regime might be highly restrictive of commercial freedom. Correctly so. After all, the EC has long possessed harmonized rules requiring the suppression of misleading advertising and there is no reason in principle why it cannot act to harmonize rules suppressing the advertising of tobacco products – provided the necessary contribution to the functioning of the internal market is demonstrated. The Court offered as an example the case of periodicals, magazines and newspapers which contain advertising for tobacco products. It is likely that national rules will increasingly forbid such advertising which, in so far as legisative diversity proliferates within the EU, will lead to obstacles to the free movement of press products. A Directive prohibiting the advertising of tobacco products in periodicals, magazines and newspapers could be adopted on the basis of Article 95 EC.[40] And the Court fully acknowledged that the Treaty requires policy integration between market-making delivered *inter alia* through harmonization and matters of public health and consumer protection, enshrined in Articles 95(3), 152(1) and 153(2).

The lesson of *Tobacco Advertising* is that the EC must shape its strategy on the regulation of advertising with more careful regard for its absence of any general legislative competence. The annulment of Directive 98/43 was followed by the adoption of a much more limited measure of harmonization which revealed that the legislature has taken the Court's advice. Directive 2003/33 on the approximation of laws relating to the advertising and sponsorship of tobacco products is explicitly presented as having been prepared in the wake of the annulment of Directive 98/43.[41] It is based on Articles 47(2), 55 and 95 and its deadline for implementation by the Member States is 31 July 2005. It confines the scope of the harmonized regime to advertising of tobacco products in the press and other media. The content of that regime is robust. Advertising is prohibited. This prohibition is directed at the press and other printed publications, radio broadcasting, information society services, and tobacco-related sponsorship, including the free distribution of tobacco products. Exceptions are made only for publications intended exclusively for professionals in the tobacco trade and for publications which are printed and published in third countries, where those publications are not principally intended for the Community market. The constitutionally important connection between the Directive and the project of market integration is stated in Article 1(2). The Directive is 'intended to ensure the free movement of the

---

[40] Paras 97–8 of the judgment in Case C-376/98.
[41] *OJ* 2003 L152/16.

media concerned and of related services and to eliminate obstacles to the operation of the Internal Market'. The corollary is stated by Article 8. 'Member
States shall not prohibit or restrict the free movement of products or services
which comply with this Directive.' Such a 'market access' clause was missing
from Directive 98/43, which provided one of the Court's reasons for annulling
that measure.

The wider ambitions of Directive 98/43 have therefore been expunged from
the EC's legislative record. They went beyond the reach of the competence to
harmonize pursuant to Article 95; the public health provisions in the Treaty are
textually too weak to support such harmonization. But the Council
Recommendation on the prevention of smoking and on initiatives to improve
tobacco control[42] suggests that what may not be done by binding legal act may
none the less re-emerge in the form of 'soft law'. The Recommendation cites
Article 152(4) EC, concerning public health, and 'recommends' that Member
States do a number of things that had been required under the annulled
Tobacco Advertising Directive, including acting to prohibit the use of promo-
tional items such as ashtrays and parasols and the use of billboards for advertising.

The EC has therefore established a system of advertising regulation applicable to tobacco products which governs their labelling and packaging and also
severely confines the circumstances in which they may be advertised in press
products and other media. In line with the general theme of this book
addressed to the evolving nature of EC consumer protection, what is at stake
here is a form of public health policy emerging as an incidental effect of a
policy aimed at integrating markets in Europe. The Treaty makes plain *via*
Articles 95(3), 152(1) and 153(2) that the EC is not indifferent about the
content of the harmonized regime. However, there exists competence to
harmonize, and then to take account of the quality of the regulatory environment, only provided an adequate contribution to market-making is made. This
is the enduringly important contribution of the *Tobacco Advertising* judgment.

TELEVISION BROADCASTING

Directive 89/552 harmonizes national laws concerning the pursuit of television broadcasting activities.[43] Its legal base was Articles 57(2) and 66 EC and
its primary purpose is the removal of obstacles to free movement of television
broadcasting services within the Community. It is the so-called 'Television
without Frontiers' Directive. Laws differ between Member States and thereby

---

[42]   *OJ* 2003 L22/31.
[43]   *OJ* 1989 L298/23.

act as impediments to trade. The Directive lays down the minimum rules needed to guarantee freedom of transmission. The structure of the Directive provides that the originating state then bears responsibility for ensuring that the broadcasts are in conformity with the law and that secondary control in the receiving state shall normally not be imposed. Directive 89/552 was amended by Directive 97/36, *inter alia* in order to sharpen up some awkward definitional question about jurisdiction.[44] Directive 97/36 also acted as a response to technological advance, for example by bringing the phenomenon of 'teleshopping' within the scope of the Directive.

Chapter IV of the Directive, comprising Articles 10–21, is entitled 'Television advertising, sponsorship and teleshopping'. From the point of view of the consumer, the most significant provisions of the Directive are those directed at the control of advertisements for tobacco, medical products and alcoholic beverages.

Article 13 prohibits 'all forms of television advertising and teleshopping for cigarettes and other tobacco products'. According to Article 17(2) television programmes may not be sponsored by undertakings whose principal activity is the manufacture or sale of cigarettes and other tobacco products. Directive 2003/33, considered above, is explicitly stated to operate without prejudice to this system.

Article 14(1) prohibits 'television advertising for medicinal products and medical treatment available only on prescription in the member state within whose jurisdiction the broadcaster falls'. This is supplemented by Article 14(2), which provides that teleshopping for medicinal products which are subject to an EC marketing authorization and teleshopping for medical treatment shall be prohibited. Sponsorship of television programmes by undertakings active in the field of manufacture or sale of medicinal products and medical treatment may promote the name or the image of the undertaking but they may not promote specific medicinal products or medical treatments available only on prescription in the Member State within whose jurisdiction the broadcaster falls.

Article 15 adopts a more nuanced approach to advertisements for alcoholic beverages. There is no outright prohibition, but the Directive controls such advertising through a list of six criteria with which advertising shall comply. Article 16 is directed at the protection of minors from advertisements. Chapter V of the Directive (Article 22) deals with this matter in the context of broadcasting generally.

These provisions reveal an explicit concern on the part of the Community legislature to take account of the interests of particularly vulnerable groups of

---

[44]   *OJ* 1997 L202/60. C.A. Jones, 'Television without Frontiers' (1999–2000) 19 *Yearbook of European Law* 299.

consumers. Although it may be true as a general proposition that the EC concept of the consumer assumes and/or promotes an active, questioning, self-aware consumer, the regulatory picture is not without nuance.

The 'Television without Frontiers' Directive provides a good illustration of the re-regulatory bargain inherent in the programme of legislative harmonization. Anxieties which previously prompted a plurality of market-fragmenting national restrictions on broadcasting freedom are now addressed by common Community rules. Although the primary constitutional purpose of these restrictions on commercial freedom is the making of a transfrontier market in this sector, Article 3(2) of the Directive makes plain that these are nevertheless duties of 're-regulation' imposed on home states, in return for which host states have surrendered the competence to set stricter rules.

As in the case of tobacco advertising, here too there arise questions about constitutional limitations that apply to the capacity of the Community legislature to restrict advertising. In the judgment in *Tobacco Advertising* the Court went out of its way to confirm the validity of use of the harmonization legal base to adopt this restriction. In suggesting the scope of a Directive prohibiting the advertising of tobacco products in periodicals, magazines and newspapers adopted on the basis of Article 95 EC it drew an analogy with Article 13 of Directive 89/552's prohibition on television advertising of tobacco products as a means to promote the free broadcasting of television programmes.[45]

Directive 89/552 (as amended) establishes rules of exhaustive harmonization. Stricter rules are not permitted. In fact, this model of 'home state control' is strengthened by provisions that preclude host states acting directly even in cases of violation of the agreed rules save in exceptional circumstances. These are set out in Article 2a(2). They arise in the event of a breach of Article 22 relating to impairment of 'the physical, mental or moral development of minors' and/or Article 22a forbidding broadcasts containing 'any incitement to hatred on grounds of race, sex, religion or nationality'. But the power to suspend services is available only where the infringement is manifest, serious and grave, there must have been at least two prior infringements in the preceding 12 months and the receiving state must have engaged in consultation of a defined type with broadcaster, Commission and transmitting state.[46] The assumption is that normally the home state carries responsibility for enforcing the rules against 'its' broadcaster. This model contrasts with most other Directives considered in this book which assume that the host state may – and

---

[45] Paras 97–8 of the judgment in case C-376/98 note 40 above.
[46] The Commission's 3rd report on the application of Dir 89/552, covering mid-1997 to end-2000, reports only one instance, COM (2001) 09, p. 12; the 4th report, covering 2001 and 2002, also records only one instance, COM (2002) 778, p. 15.

often must – take action in the event of violation of the agreed standards of protection.[47] The elimination of multiple regulation in favour of home state control is central to the strategy for achieving an integrated market in a sector which is technologically well suited to transfrontier growth. Market access is to be maintained in all but extreme cases.[48]

Fixing the precise scope of the Directive remains important. The Court drew a distinction between action under the Directive against a broadcaster and (the greater scope for) action against an advertiser in *Konsumment-ombudsmannen* v. *De Agostini Forlag*.[49] It ruled that the Directive does not preclude a Member State from relying on its general legislation against misleading advertising to take steps backed by financial penalties against an advertiser, provided that those measures do not prevent the retransmission on its territory of television broadcasts (which include the advertisements) origi-nating in another Member state. This interpretation ensures that on this point a remnant of 'host state' control is preserved.

Remaining aspects of the host state's freedom to regulate were also respected in *Bacardi* v. *TF1*.[50] This concerned the *Loi Evin*, pursuant to which France required that television broadcasts in France by French broadcasters of sports events occurring in other Member States should not feature advertise-ments for alcohol. This created severe difficulties in the case of games taking place in states where shirt or poster advertising of alcoholic drinks was permit-ted. The French law restricted the free movement of services within the mean-ing of Article 49 EC. The Court was asked whether Directive 89/552 applied to the *Loi Evin*. It ruled that it did not. This was advertising by an indirect route: it did not meet the Directive's definition of 'television advertising'. The question therefore became whether the restrictions on advertising could be justified – the orthodox way of handling cases involving the EC Treaty's free movement rules (Chapter 2). The Court found the rules to be a justified contri-bution to the protection of public health.

UNFAIR COMMERCIAL PRACTICES

Advertising is an important element in successful marketing of goods and services. But there is a wider scope to the range of commercial practices that may be deployed by traders. In 2001 the Commission published a Green Paper on Consumer Protection which tracked the heap of diverse national laws that

---

47   See, e.g., the rules on product safety considered in Chapter 9.
48   E.g. Case C-14/96 Paul Denuit [1996] ECR I-4115.
49   Joined Cases C-34/95, C-35/95 & C-36/95 [1997] ECR I-3843.
50   Case C-429/02 judgment of 13 July 2004.

are relevant to the regulation of marketing practices.[51] It described the sheer number of legal obligations that arise in the Member States as 'off-putting' to 'nearly all businesses but those who can afford to establish in all Member States', and, in addition, as a brake on consumer confidence. This was plainly intended to establish EC competence to set harmonized rules in the field pursuant to Article 95, as well as to make the substantive case in favour of an EC intervention into the regulation of marketing practices. A follow-up document in 2002 reported that consultation had showed strong support for the adoption of a framework Directive in the field.[52] This was followed by a draft Directive published by the Commission in June 2003.[53] This proposed a prohibition against unfair business-to-consumer commercial practices. In accordance with the orthodox 'dual impact' of harmonization of laws (Chapter 3), the adoption of a common EU-wide regime was stated to be designed both to eliminate barriers to trade caused by diverse national approaches to the regulation of unfair practices and to achieve a high level of consumer protection. In April 2004 a supportive legislative resolution was adopted by the Parliament[54] and in May 2004 the Council reached a political agreement on the Directive[55] which was welcomed by the Commission.[56] In November 2004 the Council reached a common position on the adoption of a Directive, which was transmitted to the Parliament.[57] Adoption of a Directive on unfair commercial practices some time in 2005 seems likely.

From the perspective of both trader and advocate of consumer protection the vital question is what is envisaged by an 'unfair' commercial practice. The text sets out two general conditions to apply in determining whether a practice is unfair: first, that the practice is contrary to the requirements of professional diligence; second, that the practice materially distorts consumers' behaviour. The benchmark is the 'average consumer' to whom the practice is directed.

Two particular categories of unfairness are envisaged: misleading and aggressive practices. A commercial practice may mislead either through action or omission. No attempt is made to define a comprehensive list of information to be positively disclosed in all circumstances. The duty imposed on businesses is not to omit 'material' information which the average consumer needs

---

[51]   COM (2001) 531, 2 October 2001. See H.-W. Micklitz and J. Kessler, *Marketing Practices Regulation and Consumer Protection in the EC Member States and the US* (Baden-Baden: Nomos, 2002).

[52]   COM (2002) 289, 11 June 2002.

[53]   COM (03) 356, available via http://europa.eu.int/comm/consumers/cons_int/safe_shop fair_bus_pract/index_en.htm.

[54]   A5-0188/2004, 20 April 2004.

[55]   2003/0134 (COD), 25 May 2004.

[56]   IP/04/658, 18 May 2004.

[57]   2003/0134 (COD), 9 November 2004. The Commission issued a Communication concerning the common position the next day: COM (2004) 753, 16 November 2004.

to make an informed decision. Core items of information are listed (non-exhaustively). These include the main characteristics of the product, the price (inclusive of taxes) and, where appropriate, delivery charges and the existence of a right of withdrawal where one exists. The draft identifies three ways in which a commercial practice may be regarded as aggressive. These are harassment, coercion and undue influence.

Although the perceptions of the 'average consumer' serve as the benchmark in judging whether a practice materially distorts consumers' behaviour, practices likely to affect a particular group of vulnerable consumers shall be assessed from the perspective of an average member of that group. This could cover consumers characterized by mental or physical infirmity, age or credulity, provided the trader can reasonably be expected to foresee such impact. This recognition of the special status of vulnerable consumers is designed to shelter the measure from criticism that it adopts an unduly homogeneous view of consumers' ability to see through and discard unfair practices. There is room for scepticism about whether the measure is sufficiently nuanced to ensure that consumer protection is treated in such a careful and sensitive manner.

The style of this proposed regime might be thought troubling in those Member States unaccustomed to such generally phrased and potentially unpredictably applied clauses, though in the UK a report commissioned by the government and written by legal academics reached the conclusion that English law was unlikely to be found deficient in its readiness to address the key questions arising out of the embrace of a test of substantive unfairness.[58] The draft Directive's vulnerability to criticism for lack of precision is qualified by the inclusion of an Annex listing (non-exhaustively) specific types of banned commercial practice. In the bag of misleading practices one finds *inter alia* a false claim that a trader is a signatory to a code of conduct or a false claim that a code of conduct has an endorsement from a public body; use of the expression 'liquidation sale' or equivalent when the trader is not about to cease trading; an inaccurate statement that a product can be legally sold; paying for the publication of an advertisement without making clear the item is in fact an advertisement; and establishing, operating, or promoting a pyramid scheme. Aggressive practices include creating the impression that the consumer cannot leave the premises until the contract is signed or the payment made; making extended and/or repeated visits to the consumer's home and making persistent and unwanted solicitations by media including telephone, fax, and e-mail; targeting consumers who have recently suffered a family

---

[58] 'The Impact of Adopting a Duty to Trade Fairly', authored by R. Bradgate, R. Brownsword and C. Twigg–Flesner (July 2003), available via http://www.dti.gov.uk/ccp/topics1/pdf1/unfairreport.pdf.

bereavement or serious illness as a strategy to sell a product directly related to the ill fortune; demanding payment for products supplied by the trader but not solicited by the consumer. This proposes a non-exhaustive black list of unacceptable clauses.

The measure would incorporate the current provisions of the Misleading Advertising Directive but would, of course, go far beyond the phenomenon of advertising. It is stated in the text that the measure would not reach so far as to impinge on the field of contract law. However, the legal regulation of contracts already possesses a dimension aimed at pre-contractual conduct, most prominently concerning mandatory disclosure of information. This is close to the terrain that would be occupied by this measure, were it to be adopted. So the demarcation between contract law and the regulation of unfair commercial practices does not seem capable of being precisely drawn. And, more generally, the pattern of sector-specific regulation of marketing practices surveyed in Chapter 4 of this book would be supplemented by the broader control envisaged by this measure.

According to the proposals, it would be incumbent on Member States to secure the suppression of all practices falling within the scope of the Directive's prohibition, but it would be excluded that Member States could prevent the commission of practices judged fair under the standard of control envisaged by the Directive in so far as such action restricted cross-border trade in goods and services. The same rules are to apply in all Member States and traders are not to face diverse regulatory expectations once they step beyond the confines of their own Member State. Home state control prevails. In this sense the draft Directive on unfair commercial practices follows the model chosen for comparative advertising and, more generally, it conforms to the policy preferences lately embraced by the Commission in favour of this style of maximum harmonization (Chapter 1). In the spring of 2004 Denmark and Sweden expressed an intention to vote against the proposal in Council precisely because they opposed this approach. They took the view that the model of full harmonization would be likely to exert a negative impact on the level of consumer protection in specific areas where Member States already possess stricter rules than provided for in existing minimum measures. But the majority among the Member States seems to be strongly in favour of the maximum formula. This would exclude the possibility of Member States exercising a preference to suppress practices that are in conformity with the Directive, should it be adopted.

Notwithstanding the attempts made in the draft to put flesh on the skeletal concept of an unfair commercial practice, a major question asks whether one can realistically imagine that such a regime could be enforced in a uniform manner across the territory of the 25 Member States of the European Union. With this in mind the Commission's 2003 package also included a proposal for a Regulation on consumer protection co-operation.[59] Regulation 2006/2004 on co-operation between national authorities responsible for the enforcement of consumer protection laws was duly adopted in October 2004.[60] Its legal base is Article 95. It puts in place a system that is designed to ensure a sharing of information and a pattern of 'mutual assistance' between enforcement authorities in different Member States. This planned network is to start work in 2006. The measure is considered in Chapter 10 in the wider context of enforcing EC consumer protection laws.

ADVERTISING REGULATION AND FUNDAMENTAL RIGHTS

Any form of market regulation is in principle susceptible to challenge for interference with the rights of commercial operators. Advertising regulation provides a particularly lively battleground. The Court's ruling in *Tobacco Advertising* established that the scope of the EC's competence to harmonize laws is limited and may be challenged, but even where a competence is shown to exist, its exercise may be challenged for violation of the general principles of Community law. Most prominently a legislative ban on advertising may be attacked as an impediment to the freedom of expression. The notion of 'commercial free speech', whereby traders assert a constitutional right to challenge legislative inhibition on their freedom, remains relatively underdeveloped in Europe, although it has a longer pedigree in North America.[61]

In *ERT* v. *Dimotiki* the European Court interpreted the scope of the freedom to provide services 'in the light of the general principle of freedom of expression embodied in Article 10 of the European Convention on Human Rights'.[62] In that case state restrictions on broadcasting had to be justified with reference to the European Convention, which is not formally part of EC law, but which has been fed into the fabric of the general principles of Community law by the European Court. No adequate justification for the restrictions was forthcoming. A similar pattern may be observed in the law governing free movement of goods. In *Vereinigte Familiapress Zeitungsverlags- und vertriebs GmbH* v. *Heinrich Bauer Verlag*[63] the Court ruled that attempts to justify national

---

[59]   COM (2003) 443.
[60]   *OJ* 2004 L364/1.
[61]   W. Skouris (ed.), *Advertising and Constitutional Rights. in Europe* (Baden-Baden: Nomos, 1994); A.M. Collins, 'Commercial Speech and the Free Movement of Goods and Services at Community Law', in J. O'Reilly (ed.), *Human Rights and Constitutional Law* (Dublin: Butterworths, 1992).
[62]   Case C-260/89 [1991] ECR I-2925.
[63]   Case C-368/95 [1997] ECR I-3689.

restrictions on trade in magazines fell to be assessed in the light of their impact on the fundamental rights of freedom of expression enjoyed by publishers, although in this case it was less hostile to the rules. It left it to the referring national court to determine whether the aim of the rules, the maintenance of press diversity in Austria, was sufficient to outweigh the detrimental impact on traders.

The general principles of Community law apply both to national authorities in so far as they act within the scope of application of Community law, which was the situation in *ERT* v. *Dimotiki* and in *Familiapress*, and to Community institutions. It is accordingly appropriate to check the validity of *inter alia* legislative action by the Community which affects commercial free speech against these standards.

It is by no means suggested here that advertising restrictions which are tested against laws pertaining to freedom of expression would or should be necessarily invalidated.[64] It is properly recognized in Article 10(2) of the European Convention that public authorities are entitled to exercise some degree of control in accordance with what is 'necessary in a democratic society'.[65] In so far as rights to freedom of expression are transplanted from the Convention to EC law, they are accompanied by legal recognition that such rights are not absolute. This is evident in the Court's ruling in *Familiapress*,[66] concerning national restrictions, and awareness that restrictions on commercial freedom require justification but that justification may be forthcoming is also evident in the development of Community rules controlling advertising techniques.

The EC legislature has recognized that restrictions on freedom of expression generate a necessary concern to show justification for such regulatory intervention. Legislative activity in the field of broadcasting clearly recognizes the connection with principles inspired by the European Convention. The Preamble to Directive 89/552 on television broadcasting[67] declares that

> Whereas this right as applied to the broadcasting and distribution of television services is also a specific manifestation in Community law of a more general principle, namely the freedom of expression as enshrined in Article 10(1) of the Convention for the Protection of Human Rights and Fundamental Freedoms ratified by all member states; whereas for this reason the issuing of Directives on the broadcasting and distribution of television programmes must ensure their free movement

[64] Cf. A. Hutchinson, 'Money Talk: Against Constitutionalizing (Commercial) Speech' (1990) 17 *Canadian Business Law Journal* 2; R. Shiner, *Freedom of Commercial Expression* (Oxford: Oxford University Press, 2003).

[65] No violation of Art. 10 of the Convention was found in *Markt Intern and Beerman* v. *Germany*, ECHR Series A No. 165, judgment of 20 November 1989.

[66] Case C-368/95 note 63 above. See also Case C-71/02 *Herbert Karner GmbH* v. *Troostwijk GmbH* judgment of 25 March 2004.

[67] Note 43 above.

in the light of the said Article and subject only to the limits set by paragraph 2 of that Article and by Article 56(1) [now 46(1)] of the Treaty.

Subsequently the Maastricht Treaty, which entered into force in 1993, brought more explicit recognition of the place of fundamental rights protection into the EU Treaty. A provision that was Article F EU and is now, after amendment, Article 6 EU states that the Union is founded on a series of principles including respect for human rights and fundamental freedoms. It also stipulates that the Union 'shall respect fundamental rights, as guaranteed by the European Convention for the Protection of Human Rights and Fundamental Freedoms signed in Rome on 4 November 1950 and as they result from the constitutional traditions common to the member states, as general principles of Community law'. This is reflected in the Preamble to Directive 97/36,[68] which amended Directive 89/552, the 'Television without Frontiers' Directive:

> Whereas Article F (2) [now 6(2)] of the Treaty on European Union stipulates that the Union shall respect fundamental rights as guaranteed by the European Convention for the Protection of Human Rights and Fundamental Freedoms as general principles of Community law; whereas any measure aimed at restricting the reception and/or suspending the retransmission of television broadcasts taken under Article 2a of Directive 89/552/EEC as amended by this Directive must be compatible with such principles . . .

Directive 2003/33 on the advertising and sponsorship of tobacco products[69] filled part of the gap left by Directive 98/43, the measure annulled in *Tobacco Advertising*.[70] It too includes recognition in its Preamble of the need for a measure that takes away freedom to advertise to meet objections rooted in alleged infringement of fundamental rights. Recital 18 claims

> This Directive respects the fundamental rights and observes the principles recognised in particular by the Charter of Fundamental Rights of the European Union. In particular, this Directive seeks to ensure respect for the fundamental right of freedom of expression. . . .

Regulation of advertising in the EC is visibly developing in the shadow of two European legal orders, that of the EC and that of the European Convention,[71]

---

[68] Note 44 above.
[69] Note 41 above.
[70] Case C-376/98, note 230 above.
[71] D. Wyatt, 'Freedom of Expression in the EU Legal Order and in EU Relations with third countries', in J. Beatson and Y. Cripps (eds), *Freedom of Information: Essays in Honour of DGT Williams* (Oxford: Clarendon Press, 2000); and see C. McCrudden, 'A Common Law of Human Rights? Transnational Judicial Conversations on Constitutional Rights' (2000) 20 *Oxford Journal of Legal Studies* 499 for broader discussion of comparative dialogue in rights protection.

supplemented by the Charter of Fundamental Rights to which this Recital refers. The Charter was agreed at Nice in 2000 as a non-binding instrument but, were the Treaty establishing a Constitution for Europe to enter into force (Chapter 1), it would be converted into a binding document.

Naturally, legislative assertions of this type cannot amount to conclusive evidence that the restrictions on advertising envisaged by these Directives do not infringe rights to freedom of expression. Such matters may yet be brought before the Court. In *Tobacco Advertising* Germany submitted that the challenged harmonization Directive, which envisaged an almost total ban on advertising of tobacco products throughout the territory of the EU, violated principles of freedom of expression. The Court had no need to address the point, since the Directive was in any event found to lack a valid legal basis. In his Opinion in the case Advocate General Fennelly expressed the view that the restrictions were appropriate and proportionate and that they therefore did not amount to unlawful interference with commercial freedom of expression.[72] Article 10 of the European Convention on Human Rights (and therefore, indirectly, the EC legal order) envisages limitations on freedom of expression in accordance with what is 'necessary in a democratic society'. It is perfectly conceivable that advertising restrictions may be treated as validly imposed pursuant to this concession.

---

[72]   Paras 152–76 of his Opinion.

9. Product safety regulation

COMMUNITY PRODUCT SAFETY POLICY

The development of a harmonized Community system of product safety regulation 'on paper' is far less problematic than harmonization in other sectors. It is hardly controversial to assert that there should be a requirement throughout the Community that unsafe products should not be placed on the market. To this extent, progress towards Community norms governing the health and safety of consumers raises far fewer fundamental questions of legal culture and regulatory technique than arise in the field of legal action to protect the economic interests of consumers. However, once one moves beyond a basic agreement that the law should forbid the marketing of unsafe goods, a number of problems impede the practical development of an effective Community product safety. How can the notion of 'safety' be given a common meaning? One may readily suppose that different approaches prevail in different parts of the Community. There are also fundamental questions about the enforcement strategies that are required to secure effective application of the Community rules. Community legislation establishes ground rules of safety; producers are putting in place integrated Community-wide marketing strategies; yet the patterns for enforcing the law are typically tied to national- or even local-level enforcement. How can information about dangerous goods and enforcement practice strategy be shared across borders? It will be seen that the Commission has secured a relatively limited power to act in its own right; that the Community has tried to establish systems of information-sharing; but that also there have developed 'bottom–up' initiatives to elaborate a cross-border system. Nevertheless there remains a gulf between the rapid evolution of an integrated product market in many sectors and the painfully slow progress towards integrated enforcement strategies. This is a significant problem in relation to product safety as such, but also in connection with the more general management of the internal market post-1992.[1]

---

[1] H.-W. Micklitz (ed.), *Post Market Control of Consumer Goods* (Baden-Baden: Nomos, 1990); H.-W. Micklitz, T. Roethe and S. Weatherill (eds), *Federalism and Responsibility: a Study on Product Safety Law and Practice in the European Community* (London: Graham and Trotman, 1994); H.-W. Micklitz, *Internationales Produktsicherheitrecht* (Baden-Baden: Nomos, 1995); C. Hodges, *Regulation of Consumer Product Safety in Europe* (Oxford: Oxford University Press, forthcoming).

The first measure to be discussed is Directive 88/378 on toy safety.[2] This is a harmonization measure designed to facilitate the growth of an integrated toy market on terms requiring a basic level of safety in products marketed. The structure of the Toy Safety Directive finds a close parallel in the most ambitious measure in the field, the Directive on general product safety. The first such general measure was adopted in 1992, Directive 92/59,[3] and this was replaced with effect from January 2004 by Directive 2001/95.[4] More generally, these Directives are fine illustrations of the Community's preferred regulatory technique in this area, the so-called 'New Approach to technical harmonisation'.[5] In the field of harmonization of technical rules, the New Approach represents a shift in the legislative task from older practices that emphasized detailed rule-making in individual Directives to general policy articulation. The Community measure sets the broad target only, with reference to the 'essential safety requirements'. Elaboration is achieved through standards. Use of the New Approach accelerates the legislative procedure while loosening the grip on producers of over-rigid Community rules.

TOY SAFETY – THE STRUCTURE OF THE DIRECTIVE

The Toy Safety Directive took as its legal base Article 100a, which is now, after amendment, Article 95 (Chapter 1). It provides a clear illustration of how a measure which is constitutionally rooted in internal market policy as a means of harmonizing national laws plays an inevitable role in developing a Community regulatory policy in the field which it occupies. In the Recitals to the Directive, it is explained that laws governing toy safety which differ between the Member States cause barriers to trade. This is a rationale for the introduction of common rules. It is also explained that the content of the harmonized rule is related to the objectives of protecting consumer health and safety which were established by the Council in its resolution of June 1986, the third in the series of 'soft law' resolutions which provide a framework for shaping Community consumer policy (Chapter 1). This serves as a clear expression of the dual focus of EC legislation which harmonizes laws concerning consumer protection. Formally, such legislation is a means to the end of market integration, yet simultaneously it exerts a significant influence

[2] *OJ* 1988 L187/1.
[3] *OJ* 1992 L228/24.
[4] *OJ* 2002 L11/4.
[5] Council Resolution of 7 May 1985 on a New Approach to technical harmonization and standards, *OJ* 1985 C136/1. See G. Howells, *Consumer Product Safety* (Aldershot: Dartmouth, 1998), ch. 2; Hodges, *Regulation of Consumer Product Safety in Europe*, note 1 above.

on the development of Community consumer protection policy. Articles 95(3) and 153(2) EC confirm the association between both policy objectives.

The common rules governing the safety of toys which are introduced by the Directive are found in Article 2, which provides that 'Toys may be placed on the market only if they do not jeopardize the safety and/or health of users or third parties when they are used as intended or in a foreseeable way.' The corollary is laid down in Article 4, which stipulates that 'Member states shall not impede the placing on the market on their territory of toys which satisfy the provisions of this Directive.' This reflects the pre-emptive consequence of the introduction of a common Community harmonized rule; this is no minimum measure (Chapter 3). Once traders comply with the required safety level, they are entitled to access to the market of all the Member States. Consumers are thereby entitled to expect a wider choice of toys to become available, in accordance with the standard expectations of market integration. At the same time, the establishment and successful application of a basic safety level should serve to protect the consumer of toys from dangerous goods reaching the market.

Emphasis is typically placed on the rights of traders to gain access to markets by complying with the safety standards required by the Directive and the duty of states to accept such conforming goods on to their market. Nevertheless, it should not be neglected that the Directive also creates duties imposed on states to take action to forestall the marketing of unsafe goods. According to Article 3, 'Member states shall take all steps necessary to ensure that toys cannot be placed on the market unless they meet the essential safety requirements set out in Annex II.' So there is a duty cast by Community law on the Member States to secure safety standards. The protection of the consumer from unsafe goods is an aspect of the harmonization measure. This confirms the notion that Directives adopted under Article 95 (ex 100a) contribute to both market integration and market regulation.

The toy which complies with the essential safety requirements is entitled to free circulation. According to Article 7, a state which ascertains that toys bearing the CE marking are not in conformity with the requirements of the Directive shall take action in respect of the product. The state must then inform the Commission of what it has done and why. This transmission of information permits the Commission to initiate procedures for consultation provided for in Article 7(2). It is critically important that management of action against unsafe items is envisaged in a Community context, not simply a national one. The development of channels of communication between state and Community authorities forms an essential component in the process of creating a comprehensive regulatory strategy.

Toy Safety – the 'New Approach to Technical Harmonisation'

In line with the 'New Approach to technical harmonisation', the uniform Community rule refers to conformity with the 'essential safety requirements' and it is not the subject of exhaustive description in the Directive. Annex II to the Directive is entitled 'Essential Safety Requirements for Toys'. It provides an elaboration of what is intended by this notion. The emphasis of the Annex is on the overall objective to be achieved, not on specific methods whereby those objectives should be attained. This flexible style is aimed at providing incentives to manufacturers to pursue innovative techniques, to the ultimate benefit of the consumer. The finally adopted text of the Toy Safety Directive is in direct contrast to earlier drafts, which had followed a more detailed, technical style. Such proposals had not found favour with the Council.[6]

According to Article 5(1) of the Directive, compliance with the essential requirements is to be presumed in respect of toys bearing the EC mark. In technical terms, the mark in practice consists of the symbol 'CE' according to Article 11(2). Moreover, the 'EC mark' is now properly referred to as the 'CE marking' as result of the amendments of Directive 93/68.[7] The CE marking denotes conformity with national standards which implement at national level harmonized European standards. Compliance with these standards permits an assumption of conformity to the Toy Safety Directive's essential requirements. The Recitals explain that the Community recognizes CEN and CENELEC as the competent bodies for the adoption of harmonized standards.

The CE marking is applied by the manufacturer, who ascertains that the toy conforms to the required standards and therefore to the essential safety requirements. The manufacturer must ensure the product is suitable for the attachment of the mark and Article 8 of the Directive requires that relevant information be held. Supervision is then the responsibility of the Member States (Article 3) and Article 12 creates certain obligations in the sphere of inspection. However, it is fundamental to the pattern of regulation instituted by the Directive that the CE marking is *not* applied by the state. There is no system requiring prior approval of the toy. Doubtless such a system would be regarded as disproportionately expensive in the toy sector, in contrast to some other areas, such as medicinal products, where obligatory authorization before marketing plays a part in the system of supervision.[8]

In conformity with the New Approach's intention to lift inflexible regulatory burdens from traders, compliance with relevant standards is not mandatory from the point of view of the producer. There is another route for the

---

[6] *OJ* 1980 C228/10; *OJ* 1983 C203/1.
[7] *OJ* 1993 L220/1.
[8] See C. Hodges, 'Regulating Medicinal Products and Medical Devices', Ch. 14 in A. Grubb (ed.), *Principles of Medical Law* (Oxford: Oxford University Press, 2nd edn, 2004).

producer to demonstrate conformity with the essential requirements. The producer can innovate by using a new design. Under Article 5(2) of the Directive, states shall presume that toys satisfy the essential safety requirements where, after receipt of a type-examination certificate, their conformity with the approved model has been certified by the affixation of the CE marking. The procedures for obtaining this type-examination certificate are found in Article 10. Approved bodies must be established by the Member States for the purposes of type-examination in accordance with Article 9 and Annex III. The basic notion is that the approved body grants an EC type-examination certificate provided that the model complies with the essential safety requirements. There is accordingly made available an alternative route for producers to comply with the requirements of the Directive other than by simply adhering to existing standards.

THE HISTORY OF THE DIRECTIVE ON GENERAL PRODUCT SAFETY

The negotiation of the first EC Directive on general product safety generated a degree of political controversy. The Commission submitted a draft Directive in April 1989.[9] This was the subject of criticism on several levels and the Commission presented a further proposal in 1990.[10] It underwent several revisions before it was finally adopted by the Council in 1992 as Directive 92/59. Even this measure was the subject of a legal challenge before the European Court initiated by Germany, which objected to the scope of the powers granted to the Commission to take decisions in cases of emergency. The German challenge, considered below, was not successful, but the very fact that it was brought reveals the political anxiety about the shaping of product safety policy for the EC. The replacement of Directive 92/59 by Directive 2001/95 with effect from January 2004 was preceded in 2000 by a Commission report on the experience acquired in the application of Directive 92/59.[11] By this time the controversy had cooled. The adoption of Directive 2001/95 was politically relatively straightforward. The Directive on general product safety has evidently become an established feature of the Community's regulatory landscape.[12]

The legal basis for the measure has always been the Treaty-conferred competence to harmonize laws in furtherance of market integration, initially

---

[9] *OJ* 1989 C193/1.
[10] *OJ* 1990 C156/8.
[11] COM (2000) 140.
[12] C. Hodges, 'A New EC Directive on the Safety of Consumer Products' [2001] *European Business Law Review* 274.

pursuant to Article 100a and, in the case of Directive 2001/95, pursuant to Article 100a's amended and renumbered successor, Article 95 EC. As has already been commented in respect of the Toy Safety Directive, harmonization of safety laws integrates the market, by establishing common standards throughout the territory of the Community on which traders may rely, but it also regulates that market by adopting a Community standard of required safety. Once again, this emphasizes the 'dual focus' of harmonization activity.

Directive 2001/95, in common with its predecessor, Directive 92/59, follows the model of the Toy Safety Directive in the sense that it too is a classic New Approach Directive. It does not seek to harmonize detailed laws relating to a particular product, but instead seeks to establish horizontal rules setting Community standards across a wide range of products. Those standards are drafted in a flexible manner, designed to permit and to encourage technological innovation.

Products Covered

Article 2 of the Directive provides in paragraph (a) that for the purposes of the Directive 'product' means

> any product – including in the context of providing a service – which is intended for consumers or likely, under reasonably foreseeable conditions, to be used by consumers even if not intended for them, and is supplied or made available, whether for consideration or not, in the course of a commercial activity, and whether new, used or reconditioned.

According to paragraph (a) of Article 2 the Directive is inapplicable to second-hand products in two situations; where they are 'supplied as antiques or as products to be repaired or reconditioned prior to being used, provided that the supplier clearly informs the person to whom he supplies the product to that effect'. This limitation, which was carried over unchanged from Directive 92/59 into Directive 2001/95, reflects concern on the part of some Member States that the Directive might be drafted too broadly, and become an excessive regulatory burden. This is, in essence, a political value-judgment; these exclusions reduce the scope of the measure as a means of consumer protection.

Persons Covered

The terms 'producer' and 'distributor' are expanded in Articles 2(e) and 2(f) of Directive 2001/95 respectively. Obligations are imposed on such persons under Articles 3 and 5. The scope of these obligations has been expanded since the entry into force of Directive 2001/95.

Article 3(1) provides that 'Producers shall be obliged to place only safe products on the market.' This is amplified in Article 5(1), which refers to obligations cast on producers to inform the consumer about risks inherent in the product where appropriate; and to enable themselves to be informed as appropriate about risks and to act accordingly, which may include product withdrawal. Such a recall shall take place as a last resort, where other measures would not suffice to prevent the risks involved, in instances where the producer considers it necessary or where the producer is obliged to do so pursuant to a measure taken by the competent authority. Accordingly, the producer bears a legal responsibility even after the product has been marketed. This is a commercially highly significant aspect of the regulatory regime instituted by the Directive, for it implies the need for, *inter alia*, document retention and product tracking.[13] In 2004 a guide designed to assist businesses to plan corrective actions was published in the names of enforcement agencies, business and consumer interests, with the financial support of the Commission.[14]

By virtue of Article 5(2) distributors are drawn into this supervisory structure. The distributor is defined as 'any professional in the supply chain whose activity does not affect the safety properties of a product' (Article 2(f)). Such a person 'shall be required to act with due care to help to ensure compliance with the applicable safety requirements'. This extends beyond avoiding the supply of goods that are unsafe, and includes an obligation to 'participate in monitoring the safety of products placed on the market, especially by passing on information on product risks, keeping and providing the documentation necessary for tracing the origin of products, and co-operating in the action taken by producers and competent authorities to avoid the risks'. For distributors as well as producers, responsibility does not stop when the product has been sold.

Article 5(3) provides that where producers and distributors know or ought to know that a product that they have placed on the market poses risks to the consumer that are incompatible with the general safety requirement, they shall immediately inform the competent authorities of the Member States. Annex I to the Directive contains details and it is required, in particular, that action taken to prevent risk to the consumer be communicated by the relevant traders. Relevant guidelines governing the notification obligation envisaged by Article 5(3) have been published by the Commission.[15] Moreover, Article 5(4) envisages that producers and distributors shall co-operate with the competent authorities on action taken to avoid the risks posed by products which they

---

[13] Cf. Hodges, note 1 above.
[14] Available via http://www.unice.org/Content/Default.asp?PageID=290.
[15] http://europa.eu.int/comm/consumers/cons_safe/prod_safe/gpsd/notification_dang_en.pdf.

supply or have supplied. Smoothly functioning sharing of information and constructive co-operation between relevant public and private actors is simply indispensable to the successful management of the EC's regime governing product safety. This is considered more fully below.

Interrelation with Existing Rules

Fears of over-regulation of the market provided an impetus to make explicit provision for the relationship between the Directive and pre-existing Community rules of narrower substantive scope. Article 1(2) establishes a demarcation which precludes overlap between Directive 2001/95 and other more specific measures. Where specific Community law rules contain provisions with the same objective imposing safety requirements on the products which they govern, the basic provisions of Directives 2001/95 shall not apply to those products. However, in the absence of specific provisions governing safety in such sector-specific measures, the general Directive shall apply.

This is capable of giving rise to some awkward detailed questions of interpretation. In November 2003 the Commission issued a Guidance Document setting out its view of the relationship between the General Directive 2001/95 and sector-specific measures governing not only toys, considered above, but also equipment with voltage limits, personal protective equipment and cosmetics.[16] In principle, however, the position is clear. In fixing safety standards for products by Directive, there is to be neither overlap nor loophole.

There is also the question of the relationship between product safety regulation and liability rules for supply of defective products. Article 17 of Directive 2001/95 asserts that the Directive applies without prejudice to Directive 85/374, the Product Liability Directive (Chapter 6). However, in some respects Directive 2001/95 acts as a complement to Directive 85/374, for it too concerns legal responses to unsafe products. Whereas Directive 85/374 deals with the civil liability of the producer/supplier of an unsafe product and serves as no more than an indirect form of safety regulation by inducing the marketing of safe goods on pain of the imposition of private law liability owed to victims, Directive 2001/95 operates as a more direct form of regulation of the market. It seeks to impose a general obligation on traders to prevent unsafe goods reaching the market in the first place.

The Standard of Safety

The standard which products must attain is set in accordance with the style of

---

[16]   Available via http://europa.eu.int/comm/consumers/cons_safe/prod_safe/gpsd/index_en. htm.

the New Approach. There is no detailed set of specifications, which would stifle innovation. The objective is established by Article 1(1) of the Directive, which declares that 'The purpose of this Directive is to ensure that products placed on the market are safe.'

Chapter II of the Directive, comprising Articles 3 and 4, is entitled 'General safety requirement, conformity assessment criteria and European standards'. Article 3(1) declares simply that 'Producers shall be obliged to place only safe products on the market.' Reference back to Article 2(b) amplifies the notion of 'safe product'. A safe product 'does not present any risk or only the minimum risks compatible with the product's use, considered to be acceptable and consistent with a high level of protection for the safety and health of persons . . .'. Plainly this is a flexible notion which will depend on the particular circumstances of a case. However, a list of points to be taken into account in making this assessment is supplied in Article 2(b) of the Directive. It includes, *inter alia*, the characteristics of the product, including its composition, packaging, instructions for assembly and, where applicable, for installation and maintenance; the effect on other products, where it is reasonably foreseeable that it will be used with other products; the presentation of the product, the labelling, any warnings and instructions for its use and disposal and any other indication or information regarding the product. The assessment is stated to relate to 'normal or reasonably foreseeable conditions of use' (including duration), which indicates that products must be safe even if misused if that misuse is reasonably foreseeable.[17] So, for example, where a producer neglects to warn consumers that a product should not be used in a particular way that will cause harm, in circumstances where that misuse is foreseeable, it will be very difficult for a producer to claim successfully that the product is 'safe' by simply blaming the consumer for stepping beyond the bounds of normal usage. Moreover, it is explicitly provided that account shall be taken of the categories of consumers at risk when using the product. Product misuse by children (in particular) is notoriously common and, where reasonably foreseeable, it is therefore an element in safety assessment. The message for producers is that possible harm should be anticipated and either forestalled through a modification of product design or, at least, brought clearly and effectively to the consumer's attention through instructions and/or warnings.

The standard of safety required under the Directive is plainly not absolute. A saw is designed to cut. If it causes an injury, it is not necessarily properly treated as unsafe. Some safe products carry an inevitable risk of causing injury. Risk assessment and risk management are politically charged activities.[18] Naturally, in the case of risky products, traders are well advised to pay special

---

[17] This is readily comparable with the system of the Product Liability Directive, Chapter 6.
[18] C. Hood, H. Rothstein and R. Baldwin, *The Government of Risk: Understanding Risk Regulation Regimes* (Oxford: Oxford University Press, 2001).

attention to the availability of devices that can reduce the risk, including
appropriately bold warnings, since failure to take reasonable steps to minimize
the risk will be relevant to the assessment of overall safety. Article 2(b) of the
Directive provides that a product should present 'minimum risks compatible
with . . . [its] use'. Provided this requirement has been met (and it will depend
on the individual circumstances), the product is safe, notwithstanding that a
person may have been injured by it.

A band of permissible safety is envisaged. The fact that a product may be
less safe than another similar product does not automatically mean that the
first product is unsafe. This is emphasized in the final paragraph of Article
2(b), which declares that 'The feasibility of obtaining higher levels of safety
or the availability of other products presenting a lesser degree of risk shall not
constitute grounds for considering a product to be dangerous.' This is an
important aspect of the chosen regulatory regime. Were the required standard
of safety to be the highest attainable, then the apparent advantage to the
consumer of high safety standards would be offset by the absence of choice
and the raising of prices. Instead, the system establishes a safety requirement
below the highest attainable level, allowing a market in products offering
varying levels of protection from risk at (in a properly functioning market)
prices which vary corresponding (*inter alia*) to the level of safety offered.

Under Article 3(2), a product is deemed safe when it conforms to the
specific national law rules governing health and safety requirements of the
state in whose territory the product is in circulation. This is a statement of the
principle of mutual recognition, familiar from the European Court's *Cassis de
Dijon* jurisprudence (Chapter 2). Furthermore a product shall be presumed
safe as far as the risks and risk categories covered by relevant national standards are concerned when it conforms to voluntary national standards transposing European standards.

Outside these situations, Article 3(3) provides that assessment of the
conformity of a product with the general safety requirement involves taking
into account a range of factors. The list of relevant material covers voluntary
national standards transposing relevant European standards other than those
covered by Article 3(2); the standards drawn up in the Member State in which
the product is marketed; Commission recommendations setting guidelines on
product safety assessment; product safety codes of good practice in force in
the sector concerned; the state of the art and technology; and reasonable
consumer expectations concerning safety. A broad range of sources may
inform the inquiry into whether a product is safe, but no single indicator is
likely to prove decisive.

Article 3(4) establishes the competence which remains with the state into
which the product is imported. Even where a product conforms to either
Article 3(2) or 3(3), national authorities are able to restrict its access to the

market or to secure its withdrawal from the market 'where there is evidence that, despite such conformity, it is dangerous'. In this sense the core issue is compliance with the general safety requirement, and meeting a standard is merely an important method of demonstrating such compliance. In the case of conformity with national standards transposing European standards, a presumption in favour of the safety of the product is created (Article 3(2)). But the presumption is set aside if the product is dangerous. It is explained below that action taken in such circumstances by a national authority must be managed within a Community framework.

The important role of standards in putting flesh on the bones of the general safety requirement is evident from this description of the regime set up by the Directive. Article 4 of Directive 2001/95 sets out procedures which govern the making of European standards. The Commission has granted a mandate to the private standardization bodies based in Belgium, CEN and CENELEC.[19]

ENFORCEMENT BY MEMBER STATES

Implementation of the Directive by the Member States involves, *inter alia*, securing the enforcement of the pattern of obligations imposed on producers and distributors to market only safe products. One approach would have been simply to exclude from the Directive any reference to national methods of enforcement and to rely on the Member States to shape enforcement structures in line with national tradition. Patterns would vary. In several Member States the job would be done by regional or local actors, according to preferred decentralized structures.[20] Public authorities within the Member States would simply carry the general obligation of effective implementation, rooted in Articles 10 and 249 of the Treaty. However, the Directive is rather more ambitious. It makes limited progress towards the specification of the institutional support and enforcement techniques that are required as a matter of Community law. This issue caused much of the controversy in the several draft proposals which were rejected before the final successful adoption of the first general Directive in 1992.[21] The controversy had long since cooled and did not re-emerge in the negotiation that led to the adoption of Directive 2001/95. Rather the reverse. Directive 2001/95 gently amplifies the detailed arrangements which the

[19] Howells, *Consumer Product Safety*, ch. 2. See more generally H. Schepel, *The Constitution of Private Governance: Product Standards in the Regulation of Integrating Markets* (Oxford: Hart Publishing, 2005).
[20] Practice is summarized in the Commission's 2000 report into practice under Directive 92/59, note 11 above. See also Howells, *Consumer Product Safety*, note 5 above; F. Maniet, 'The transposition of the General Product Safety Directive 92/59/EC by the Member States of the European Union' [1999] *Consumer Law Journal* 15.
[21] Note 3 above.

Member States are expected to make in support of the achievement of the
objectives of the Directive, in particular in the matter of product recall.[22]

Chapter IV of Directive 2001/95 is entitled 'Specific obligations and
powers of the Member States'. Article 6(1) provides that 'Member States shall
ensure that producers and distributors comply with their obligations under this
Directive in such a way that products placed on the market are safe.' In itself,
this is little more than an application of the general obligation found in Articles
10 and 249 EC to the specific area covered by this Directive. Article 6(2) of
the Directive requires Member States to establish or nominate authorities
empowered to monitor the application of the law and to take the measures
required under the Directive. Article 7 requires that Member States shall lay
down the rules on penalties applicable to infringements and to take all
measures necessary to ensure that they are implemented. Penalties shall be
'effective, proportionate and dissuasive'. This too is a statement of the general
law governing effective implementation of EC Directives by Member States.

Article 8 stipulates that Member States shall have the necessary powers to
adopt appropriate measures to achieve a list of objectives, including, for example, safety checks, publication of warnings, product bans and product withdrawal. In respect of withdrawal or recall of dangerous products it is stipulated
that where necessary Member States shall intervene if the action undertaken
by the producers and distributors in fulfilment of their obligations is unsatisfactory or insufficient. It is stated that 'recall shall take place as a last resort',
but the Directive plainly envisages that Member States shall equip themselves
with appropriate powers to step in should action by producers or distributors
prove inadequate. This exceeds the directions made by Directive 92/59, the
first general Directive in this field. According to Article 8(3) of Directive
2001/95, competent national authorities shall also have the power to take 'with
due dispatch' the necessary action in the case of products posing a 'serious
risk'. Article 2(d) defines 'serious risk' to mean one requiring rapid intervention by the public authorities. Article 8(3) directs that it is for Member States
to judge when this arises. They shall assess each individual case on its merits,
and in doing so shall take account of guidelines referred to in point 8 of Annex
II to the Directive (considered more fully below).

Article 11 places action taken in the context of an integrating market.
Where states restrain the marketing of a product or require its recall, they shall
inform the Commission. The notification shall include an account of the
reasons for the action. If the state considers that the effects of the risk do not
or cannot go beyond its territory, it is still expected to notify its adopted
measures in so far as they involve information relevant to product safety likely
to be of interest to other Member States. Article 11(2) directs the Commission

---

[22] Hodges, *Regulation of Consumer Product Safety in Europe*, note 1 above.

to forward the notification to the other Member States, unless it concludes that the measure does not comply with Community law, when it should inform the notifying state. Article 11 thus envisages a system for sharing information which draws together Community and national authorities. The report into the operation of the first general Directive, Directive 92/59, which prepared the ground for the adoption of Directive 2001/95, was forced to concede that national authorities are 'uncertain' about how (what is now) the Article 11 procedure functions and that the Commission carries a heavy administrative burden which causes the procedure to operate slowly.[23] In April 2004 guidelines were adopted by the Commission to cover the handling of Article 11 notifications.[24] They set out the information that is to be transmitted by national authorities and include, in an Annex, a standard Notification Form. The guidelines also cover the emergency 'RAPEX' procedure and are considered further below. These arrangements are significant in opening a route to integrated cross-border enforcement strategies, needed in the wake of the accelerating product market integration which makes it increasingly improbable that problems of unsafe goods will have purely local impacts.

THE POWERS OF THE COMMISSION

Chapter V of the Directive covers 'Exchanges of information and rapid intervention situations'. Within Chapter V, Article 11, mentioned above, requires that Member States taking measures against products shall notify the Commission. It establishes a system for sharing information between national agencies and the Commission and, via the Commission, other national agencies elsewhere in the EU. But this is only a starting point. The Directive goes further in stipulating patterns of co-operation and in equipping the Commission itself with powers to intervene in particularly urgent cases.

Whereas Articles 6–8 of the Directive, examined above, assume action taken at national level and attempt to locate that action within a managed Community framework (especially via Article 11), Article 13 of the Directive confers powers on the Commission to act in the sphere of product safety.

This power is triggered where the Commission becomes aware of a 'serious risk' to the health and safety of consumers in various Member States. The notion of 'serious risk' is the subject of a (necessarily abstract) definition in Article 2(d) of the Directive: it refers to a risk 'including those the effects of which are not immediate, requiring rapid intervention by the public authorities'.

---

[23] COM (2000) 140, note 11 above.
[24] http://europa.eu.int/comm/consumers/cons_safe/prod_safe/gpsd/rapex_en.htm.

In such circumstances the Commission shall consult the Member States, and, if relevant questions arise, the competent EC Scientific Committee. It may then adopt a decision in accordance with the regulatory procedure foreseen by the EC's 1999 comitology decision.[25] A duly adopted Commission decision may require Member States to take measures from among those listed in Article 8 provided a trio of preconditions are cumulatively satisfied. First, the Member States must 'differ significantly on the approach adopted or to be adopted to deal with the risk'. Second, the risk must be incapable of being dealt with sufficiently promptly under other procedures laid down by any product-specific Community legislation. Third, the risk must be capable of effective elimination only by the adoption of appropriate EC-level measures which are apt to ensure a consistent and high level of protection and the proper functioning of the internal market. This third precondition is more or less a sector-specific application of the subsidiarity principle (Chapter 1). Member States are obliged to take all necessary measures to implement such decisions within less than 20 days, unless a different period is specified (Article 13(4)). The decision itself may validly last for up to one year, though it may be extended for further periods of up to one year. Decisions confined to specific, individually identified products or batches of products are valid without a time limit (Article 13(2)).

This procedure is important as a step beyond the notion that the Commission performs no more than a function of information transmission and general supervision of implementation by the Member States. Article 13 of the Directive place a power of administrative decision-making in the hands of the Commission. This allocation of power contains the seeds of a 'Europeanization' of product safety policy. However, such ambitious theoretical notions must be tempered by practical reality. Article 13 is subject to significant threshold criteria. One may even go so far as to suppose that the preconditions to Commission action will only very rarely be satisfied. Certainly, Article 13 confers a power to act which falls far short of more ambitious calls in the past for a 'Europeanized' control system. It is, for example, remote from the notion of a Community product recall procedure once suggested by the Consumers Consultative Committee.[26]

Institutional modesty is a deliberate choice. Choosing the shape of the Commission's powers was one of the most controversial aspects of the negotiation of the original Directive 92/59.[27] Earlier drafts had contained notice-

---

[25] Arts 14, 15(2) Dir. 2001/95.
[26] CCC/107/79, CCC/66/82.
[27] *OJ* 1989 C193/1. See D. Hoffmann, 'Product safety in the internal market: the proposed Community emergency procedure', in M. Fallon and F. Maniet (eds), *Product Safety and control processes in the European Community* (Brussels: Story Scientia/CDC, 1990); C. Joerges, 'Social Regulation and the Legal Structure of the EEC', in B. Stauder (ed.), *La Sécurité des produits de consommation* (Zürich: Schulthess, 1992).

ably less stringent criteria which had to be met before the Commission could act. For example, the Commission's 1989 draft did not require divergence between Member States on the adoption of measures. That would probably still have given rise to very few instances where the Commission would have been able to act, yet the Member States still preferred to insert extra preconditions before final adoption of the first general Directive in 1992. The acute political sensitivity surrounding the question of equipping the Commission with administrative powers in the field is highlighted by the fact that, on this point, the adoption of Directive 92/59 led to a legal challenge before the European Court.

THE GENERAL PRODUCT SAFETY DIRECTIVE BEFORE THE EUROPEAN COURT

Even the relatively narrow competence to act conferred on the Commission by the original Directive 92/59 provoked a challenge to the validity of the measure by Germany. *Germany* v. *Council*[28] involved an application for annulment of Article 9 of Directive 92/59. This was the predecessor to Article 13 of Directive 2001/95. It was rather more tightly drawn than Article 13, as explained below, but it served the same general function of supplementing state action against unsafe products with the possibility of Commission intervention. The German challenge was unsuccessful but the Court's ruling is important not least because it is one of the very few judgments of the Court dealing with institutional design under the programme of harmonization of laws. The Court accepted that what was then Article 100a EC, and is now, after amendment, Article 95 EC, has a valid role to play beyond simple harmonization of laws 'on paper'.

Germany did not express an objection to the harmonization of safety standards. Instead it challenged Article 9 of the Directive in so far as it empowered the Commission to adopt decisions requiring the Member States to take named measures in respect of products. Germany submitted that Article 9 lacked a legal base and that it violated the principle of proportionality. Germany claimed that all that could be drawn from Article 100a (now, after amendment, Article 95) was a power conferred on the Commission to check whether provisional national measures comply with Community law and not to adopt measures itself. This view is transparently driven by a narrow interpretation of the scope of the Treaty-conferred competence to harmonize laws as a means of building Community institutional power and a corresponding emphasis on the primary role of implementation at national level as a means of realizing

---

[28] Case C-359/92 [1994] ECR I-3681.

Community objectives expressed in Directives. Were such an approach to prevail, the potential for 'Europeanization' of enforcement structures would be severely circumscribed, at least via Article 95 (ex 100a). Germany's concern to fix the boundaries between Community and national competence was further reflected in its observation that Article 9 of Directive 92/59 conferred more power to the Commission than would be allowed the *Bund* at the expense of the *Länder* in the context of German federalism.

The Court rejected the German application, concluding that action at Community level of the type envisaged by Article 9 of Directive 92/59 was justified in order to protect the health and safety of consumers and to ensure the proper functioning of the market. The Court considered that Article 100a (now, after amendment, Article 95) empowered the Council to take measures aimed at the establishment and functioning of the internal market. In some sectors, particularly that of product safety, harmonization of laws alone may not be adequate to achieve this objective. The Court accepted that harmonization measures 'must be interpreted as encompassing the Council's power to lay down measures relating to a specific product or class of products and, if necessary, individual measures concerning those products'.[29] The Court was unsurprisingly unreceptive to the German suggestion that the relationship between the Community and Member State powers should be analysed with reference to national constitutional patterns. It simply observed that the relationship between Community and its Member States is not the same as that between *Bund* and *Länder*. The Court was also unpersuaded by the rather flimsy submission that Article 9 contravened the principle of proportionality. It stated that the powers conferred were appropriate to achieve the objectives pursued and did not go beyond what was necessary in relation to those objectives.

The issue underlying this litigation is political resistance in some quarters to the capacity of the Community to construct 'Europeanized' institutional structures in support of the process of market integration. The Court's ruling provides no general method for resolving such tensions; nor could the Court be expected to resolve such fundamental political questions about the development of (quasi-)federalism in Europe. Within the sector of product safety, at least, the Court's ruling in this case upholds the validity of the use of Article 100a EC (now, after amendment, Article 95) in order to move beyond a pattern of harmonization of laws which relies exclusively on national systems for implementation.

This litigation concerned Directive 92/59, which, as explained, was replaced by Directive 2001/95 with effect from January 2004. Under Article 9 of Directive 92/59, which survived challenge in *Germany* v. *Council*, the

---

[29] Para. 37 of the judgment.

powers granted to the Commission to act were more narrowly drawn than they are today, pursuant to Article 13 of Directive 2001/95. Under Directive 92/59 'a serious and immediate risk' was the necessary trigger. Moreover, there was a requirement of prior action taken against the product by at least one Member State. And a valid decision could endure for no more than three months. Directive 2001/95 has loosened these restraints. The risk need only be 'serious', not 'immediate'. Prior action taken by one Member State is no longer essential. And a decision may be adopted for up to one year.

It is submitted that despite its modestly enhanced scope Directive 2001/95 still comfortably falls within the scope of the competence to act pursuant to Article 95 EC in the matter of product safety which is mapped out in the Court's judgment in *Germany* v. *Council*. In any event its validity has gone unchallenged. It appears that the political attitude among (some of) the Member States towards building a degree of interventionist capacity at European level in the name of effective management of product safety policy has grown more favourable since the early friction caused by the adoption of Directive 92/59. This may be in part attributable to the realization that the Commission's powers were very rarely invoked. The power to intervene pursuant to Article 9 of Directive 92/59 was invoked just once by the Commission, when it intervened in the market to ban soft PVC toys intended to be put in the mouths of children under three years of age – teething rings and dummies suspected of containing toxic materials.[30] The imposition of the high hurdles set by Directive 92/59 was in any event difficult to reconcile with the perceived need for prompt action in emergencies, as the Commission itself pointed out in its 2000 report into the application of the Directive.[31] The Commission's report also stated that the authorities of seven Member States welcomed an enhanced role for the Commission.[32] It added that there were 'different opinions' – but chose not to cite any unfavourable ones! The hurdles which the Commission must cross before it is able to act were duly lowered and the procedure now envisaged by Article 13 of Directive 2001/95 is designed to offer greater scope to the Commission to act in cases of emergency than was permitted under Directive 92/59. However, even now the terms are such that it seems probable that intervention by the Commission will remain exceptional.

---

[30] Decision 1999/815 *OJ* 1999 L315/46. The ban can be temporary only (see now Art. 13(2) Dir. 2001/95) but it has been maintained by subsequent Commission Decisions, see, e.g., Dec. 2004/624 *OJ* 2004 L280/34.

[31] Note 11 above. See also Howells, *Consumer Product Safety*, note 5 above, pp. 148–54.

[32] The report names Belgium, Denmark, Spain, Greece, Italy, Luxembourg and the Netherlands.

INFORMATION-SHARING

Effective information-sharing about unsafe products in Europe is vital but difficult to achieve. Article 10(1) of Directive 2001/95 declares that the Commission
'shall promote and take part in the operation in a European network of the
authorities of the Member States competent for product safety, in particular in
the form of administrative co-operation'. Article 10(2) contains a 'wish list' of
matters that would usefully be facilitated, including the exchange of information
on risk assessment, dangerous products and test methods, the exchange of expertise and improved co-operation at Community level on tracing, withdrawal and
recall of dangerous products. Article 11, mentioned above, provides that where
states restrain the marketing of a product or require its recall, they shall inform
the Commission. As a general observation, it is plainly of fundamental importance that the growth of an integrated European product market is accompanied
by effective pan-European arrangements for information-sharing and co-operation in problem-solving. Such arrangements are not to be built solely on a
'top–down' European model, but rather on a co-operative infrastructure involving both the Commission and national and sub-national authorities, duly
equipped with relevant powers pursuant to Directive 2001/95. The challenge is
to promote an effective system of vertical (Commission/state) and horizontal
(state/state) co-operation. The risk is that cross-border trading opportunities will
not be matched by cross-border pursuit of unsafe products.

The specific issue of unsafe products presenting an urgent risk was one of
the first in which the aspiration to develop effective administrative co-ordination bore fruit. The Community first put in place a system for the rapid
exchange of information on dangers arising from the use of consumer products in 1984.[33] The system, commonly abbreviated from Rapid Exchange to
RAPEX, provides for the transmission of information about urgent measures
taken against goods at national level because of perceived serious and immediate risks to the health or safety of consumers. The state must inform the
Commission, which then forwards information to other Member States. Those
states then alert the Commission to any measures they have taken, which is
then communicated to the other states. Plainly the system reflects the need for
a cross-border dimension to effective enforcement policy in the sphere of
product safety, in the light of the cross-border commercial strategies undertaken by traders in an integrated market.

The system was initially set up in 1984 for a four-year trial period. In 1988
the Commission proposed that that period be extended to ten years.[34] It
prepared a report on the operation of the system which was broadly

---

[33] Council Decision 84/133 EEC, *OJ* 1984 L70/16.
[34] *OJ* 1988 C124/9.

favourable, although it admitted that use of the notification procedure had been rather erratic.[35] However, in December 1988 the Council decided that it would renew the system only until 30 June 1990.[36] The debate about RAPEX was conducted in the shadow of discussion of the proposed Directive on general product safety, which would be adopted as Directive 92/59 only in 1992, for it was envisaged that the legal provisions governing RAPEX would be brought within that Directive, once adopted, as part of the construction of a comprehensive Community system dealing with product safety. In 1990 it was therefore agreed in Council that the system would once again be renewed, on this occasion until the date for implementing the Directive on general product safety.[37] In 1992, when the Directive was finally adopted, RAPEX was accommodated within it and given a formal footing by Article 8, amplified by an Annex to the Directive. Decision 89/45 was repealed with effect from June 1994 by Article 18 of Directive 92/59.

RAPEX has always had two branches, covering food products and non-food products. The system relating to food is now governed by Regulation 178/2002.[38] Directive 2001/95 is the focus for other products.

The key role of RAPEX in product safety policy is fully recognized and underpinned by Directive 2001/95, which has taken over and adjusted the system previously contained within Directive 92/59. RAPEX is central to the aspiration to create an effective network within which information about serious risks can be effectively communicated throughout the territory of the EU – just as, in a border-free economic space, products can gain free access to the markets of all 25 Member States.

The trigger is action taken by reason of a 'serious risk' posed by a product. Article 12 of Directive 2001/95 provides that in such circumstances where a Member State acts to prevent or restrict marketing or use of a product on its territory it shall immediately notify the Commission under RAPEX. It shall also inform the Commission without delay of modification or withdrawal of any such measure or action. It is made explicit that the scope of the notification system extends beyond formal action taken by public authorities to include agreements reached voluntarily with traders. Moreover, notification shall also embrace the voluntary measures laid down in Article 5 of the Directive which are taken by producers and distributors (provided a serious risk is at stake). A notifying Member State which considers that the effects of the risk do not or cannot go beyond its territory is required to follow the procedure laid down in Article 11, mentioned above. It cannot simply automatically abstain from notifying.

[35] *OJ* 1988 C146/8.
[36] Council Decision 89/45 EEC, *OJ* 1989 L17/51.
[37] Council Decision 90/352 EEC, *OJ* 1990 L173/49.
[38] *OJ* 2002 L31/1.

Once in receipt of a notification, the Commission must check whether it complies with the requirements of RAPEX, and then it must forward the details to the other Member States. They in turn are expected to inform the Commission of any measures adopted. This system envisages the sharing of information in order to reduce the inefficiencies brought about where the same problem is tackled by different authorities in different states taking different approaches with different levels of available information. However, Article 12 establishes the Commission as the channel through which information is routed, not as a filter of that information nor even as an initiator. The assumption remains that the initial decision whether to intervene in the market rests with the Member State(s), albeit acting within a framework governed by substantive Community rules on product safety.

The detailed procedures which govern RAPEX are set out in Annex II to Directive 2001/95. Within the Annex, perhaps the most important feature is the statement in point 8 that the Commission is expected to draw up 'guidelines' which will amplify the patterns of management of RAPEX by the Commission and the Member States. In April 2004 guidelines were adopted by the Commission to cover both RAPEX and notifications pursuant to Article 11 of Directive 2001/95.[39] These provide practical insight into the way in which the system is intended to operate. Among relevant issues that are helpfully fleshed out in the 'guidelines' are included treatment of matters of apparently only local concern. The guidelines cite the openness of the European market as an inducement to caution to assuming a risk has no broader impact. The guidelines also devote attention to the notion of a 'serious risk', which is a precondition in the Directive to a notification pursuant to RAPEX. Risk assessment is presented as a process of risk estimation – an inquiry into the severity of outcome and the probability of its occurrence – and of grading the risk, which involves consideration of which type of consumer is likely to be affected (are vulnerable consumers at risk?) and how feasible it is to take precautions.

The Annex to Directive 2001/95 states that Member States notifying under Article 12 shall provide 'all available details'. This is rather obvious, but point 3 of the Annex proceeds to state that notification shall contain the information stipulated in the 'guidelines' and, in addition and as a minimum, information enabling the product to be identified; a description of the risk involved, including a summary of the results and conclusions of any tests; the nature and the duration of any action taken; and information on distribution chains, in particular on destination countries.

The Annex simply sets out the bare bones of what is expected. The Commission has prepared a standard form designed for use by notifying states

---

[39]   http://europa.eu.int/comm/consumers/cons_safe/prod_safe/gpsd/rapex_en.htm.

and another for states that wish to respond to notifications. Both are annexed to the guidelines. The guidelines explain more fully what is expected. Responding Member States shall inform the Commission whether the product has been marketed in their territory, and what measures they may adopt (including any differing assessment of risk, in particular if they do not propose follow-up action).

The guidelines set out an understandable aspiration for rapid and detailed transmission of information. But, of course, there are questions about how the system works in practice. Under RAPEX it is plain that levels of notification vary widely state by state, doubtless in part attributable to differing national interpretations of the threshold criteria. Moreover, the theory of a to-and-fro of information is not matched fully by practice. A 1993 Commission Report revealed that on average only seven out of (then) 12 Member States complied with their obligation to reply under RAPEX, with 89 days the average time for a reply.[40] The Commission has devoted energy to improving the practical operation of the system, emphasizing the need for improved awareness among the public authorities in the Member States of the importance of effective information-sharing. In 2000 a Commission survey allowed it to conclude that the Member States are 'in general satisfied' with the operation of RAPEX, although it was admitted that variation among states in readiness to notify coupled to a lack of precision in notifications made remained features of the system that could usefully be improved.[41] In January 2004, to coincide with the deadline for the implementation of Directive 2001/95, the Commission initiated an attempt to improve the transparency of the system by publishing weekly summaries of information received from the Member States pursuant to RAPEX.[42] The annual number of notifications ranged from 143 to 168 to 139 in 2001, 2002 and 2003 respectively and initially this pattern appeared to be enduring into 2004, as a typical week yielded two or three notifications. However, the figure has been increasing and the main factor appears to have been enlargement of the EU to 25 Member States in May 2004. Notifications from the states of Central and Eastern Europe are not uncommon. Toys and electrical appliances are the products that are most commonly involved.

The success of RAPEX depends heavily on the energy invested by Member States to ensure that notifications to the Commission are made in circumstances where action is taken at a relatively low – regional or local – level within the state. The Member States are expected to set up a single contact point for the purposes of co-operation with the Commission. The list of

---

[40] Commission Communication on the handling of urgent situations in the context of implementation of Community rules, COM (93)430.

[41] COM (2000) 140, note 11 above.

[42] IP/04/183, 9 February 2004. Documentation is available via http: //europa.eu.int/comm/ consumers/cons_safe/prod_safe/gpsd/rapex_en.htm.

contact points is publicly available.[43] Where necessary, the Member States are expected to organize an internal network which will ensure the effective transmission of information through the single contact point to the Commission and thereby on to other Member States. In states with decentralized systems for the management of product safety law and policy, this is particularly challenging. The relatively slow and erratic progress of a system such as RAPEX is only to be expected as the EC attempts to secure the development of transnational systems of information-sharing and co-ordination against a background dominated by long-established State practices which are unreceptive to cross-border law enforcement and administrative co-operation. This demonstrates the difficulties in achieving workable integration and a reliable bridging of the gap between the law of product safety on paper and its reality in practice.

TRANSPARENCY AND PROCEDURAL PROTECTION

A balance needs to be struck between potentially conflicting concerns in the management of product safety policy. The identification of a risk may point in favour of making consumers aware of a suspect product as quickly and effectively as possible. As explained, a key component of the EC product safety regime is effective dissemination of information. But this may be commercially catastrophic for a trader in the goods concerned. It is, of course, not the case that a trader would normally wish to suppress information about potentially unsafe products. Supplying unsafe goods is bad for business and may expose the trader to legal consequences both as a result of the rules that implement Directive 2001/95 and under the liability system for supply of defective goods established by Directive 85/374 (Chapter 6). None the less circumstances may arise where enforcement agencies, on the one hand, and producers and distributors, on the other, have different priorities. And the Commission's report into the practice developed under Directive 92/59, issued in 2000, revealed concern about the imprecision of the scope of requirements of confidentiality.[44]

Article 16 of Directive 2001/95 establishes a general principle favouring transparency. Information on risks available to the authorities of the Member States or the Commission 'shall in general be available to the public'. The public shall have access to information on product identification, the nature of the risk and the measures taken. One would instinctively expect such a wide-ranging principle to be subject to qualification and it is accordingly no surprise

---

[43] http://europa.eu.int/comm/consumers/cons_safe/prod_safe/gpsd/rapex_weekly/ contact_points.pdf.

[44] COM (2000) 140, note 11 above.

that the paragraph in Article 16 that follows this general principle begins with the word 'However . . .'. The proviso is that Member States and Commission shall take the steps necessary to ensure that their officials and agents are required not to disclose information 'covered by professional secrecy in duly justified cases, except for information relating to the safety properties of products which must be made public if circumstances so require, in order to protect the health and safety of consumers'. Article 16(2) provides that the competent authorities shall share information relevant for ensuring the effectiveness of market monitoring and surveillance activities, and that this is not precluded by concerns associated with the protection of professional secrecy. In such cases it rests with the authorities concerned to ensure the protection of professional secrecy.

This drive for transparency, underpinned by the range of powers that the Directive requires be vested in the public authorities of the Member States and which are available to the Commission, involves a potentially deep intrusion into the commercial freedom of traders. Accordingly Article 18 of the Directive insists on appropriate procedural protection. The parties concerned shall, whenever feasible, be given an opportunity to submit their views before the adoption of any measure. Any measure which involves restrictions on the placing of a product on the market or which requires its withdrawal or recall must state the reasons which explain its adoption. It shall be notified as soon as possible to the party concerned and shall indicate the remedies available under the provisions in force in the Member State in question and the time limits applying to such remedies. It is made explicit that there shall be a right of access to a court to challenge any measure imposing restrictions on a product or requiring its recall.

In principle it is perfectly feasible that a trader suffering commercial loss as a result of mishandling of the relevant procedures by public authorities in the Member States or by the Commission could bring an action to claim compensation. It is, however, in the nature of a policy designed to rid the market of unsafe products that traders will suffer commercial disadvantage. That does not generate a right to secure financial redress under EC law. An unlawful act on the part of the relevant administrative authorities must be shown to have been committed. In *Malagutti-Vezinhet SA* v. *Commission*[45] the Court was faced by an action for compensation by an exporter of apples from France. The Commission had been notified by the Icelandic authorities that the apples contained potentially harmful pesticide residues. The Commission duly issued an alert naming the exporter pursuant to Article 8 of Directive 92/59, which has now been superseded in adjusted form by Article 12 of Directive 2001/95. It was contended that the risk was insufficiently serious, but the Court

---

[45] Case T-177/02 judgment of 10 March 2004.

observed that such an inquiry was beyond the Commission's powers under the relevant procedure. It was also submitted that the Commission had insufficient evidence that the applicant was the exporter of the product in question. The Court concluded that the Commission had not circulated information that was 'not plausible'. It cited the precautionary principle in application to uncertainty about the identity of the trader: it seems that it is not required that a trader's responsibility for supplying the suspect goods be conclusively proved for the purposes of this regime. The Court explicitly referred to the commercial damage suffered by the applicant but held that 'protection of public health must take precedence over economic considerations'. Nor were the applicant's rights to a fair hearing and to confidentiality breached. The Commission was not guilty of an unlawful act. Accordingly the Court chose not to proceed to consider whether the Commission had caused loss suffered by the applicant. Were a case to arise in which the Commission was found to have acted wrongfully in its handling of the relevant procedures, liability would be incurred only if this causal link were also established.

BEYOND RAPEX: WIDER/ SOFTER PATTERNS OF CO-ORDINATION AND INFORMATION-SHARING

The significance of administrative co-ordination as a means of achieving both market integration and effective consumer protection in the Community cannot be overestimated. There are two distinct aspects to the role of administrative co-ordination. First, it acts as a complement to substantive rules and ensures that they may achieve their objective. Common Community rule-making must be accompanied by a pattern of common strategies for the application and enforcement of those rules. This is a matter which has gained an increasingly high profile since the completion of the internal market. Second, the development of administrative co-ordination is itself part of the process of developing a Community consumer law and policy, even where it occurs independently of the existence of specific Community initiatives.

This should be linked, at a much more general level, with the concern to put in place the appropriate structures for managing and stabilizing an internal market which, according to Article 14 EC, was to be completed at the end of 1992. 'Completion' is in this context a misleading notion. Market-building and market maintenance are processes rather than events. The Sutherland Report, published in October 1992,[46] placed emphasis on the insight that the operation of the internal market depends for its success on much greater co-operation

---

[46] *The Internal Market after 1992: Meeting the Challenge*, Report to the EEC Commission by the High Level Group on the Operation of Internal Market.

between national and Community institutions. It envisaged a growth of administrative partnership to enhance the practical application of the rules. This has served subsequently as a basis for Commission thinking. One may readily trace the anxiety to promote viable systems for co-ordination through a great many documents concerned to provide a shape for both internal market policy and consumer protection.

The Commission regularly and vigorously cites the need to generate confidence in the viability of the internal market and correctly identifies visibly effective law enforcement as a key component in delivering that trust. It has observed that 'Late transposition, bad transposition and weak enforcement all contribute to the public impression of a Union which is not delivering.'[47] Furthermore, in its Internal Market Strategy document, in which it set out priorities for 2003–2006, the Commission asserted that:

> Free movement of goods (and services) in the Internal Market is above all based on confidence. Confidence of businesses that they can sell their products on the basis of a clear and predictable regulatory framework. Confidence of Member States' administrations that the rules are respected in practice throughout the EU and that the competent authorities in other Member States will take appropriate action when this is not the case. And, of course, consumers' confidence in their rights and that the products they buy are safe and respect the environment.[48]

As part of the quest to achieve these objectives in the particular context of product safety, Article 10 of Directive 2001/95, mentioned above, envisages the establishment of a network of co-operation between product safety agencies in Europe. However, the task of making this real is daunting, and the enlargement of the Union into Central and Eastern Europe adds to its intimidatingly large dimensions. None the less the European market will not achieve its objectives unless it is underpinned by an effective system of co-ordination between responsible administrative authorities.

The objective of improving administrative co-operation in pursuit of more effective supervision of the integrating market cannot be achieved simply by 'top–down' Community legislative instruments. Co-operation has developed across borders spontaneously, as enforcement agencies find that they cannot properly perform their functions in an integrating market without establishing connections with counterparts in other states.[49]

For example, trading standards officers in the United Kingdom began to develop links with counterparts in other Member States in the late 1980s, as

---

[47] Commission's White Paper on Governance, July 2001, COM (01) 428, p. 25.
[48] Commission Communication of May 2003, Internal Market Strategy, Priorities 2003–2006, COM (2003) 238.
[49] S. Weatherill, 'Playing Safe: the UK's Implementation of the Toy Safety Directive', ch. 9 in T. Daintith (ed.), *Implementing EC Law in the UK* (Chichester: Wiley Chancery, 1995).

the project to complete the internal market took shape.[50] The Institute of
Trading Standards Administration, the trading standards officers' professional
body, established 'PRODLINK', a database which contains information *inter
alia* about dangerous products which are found on the market. Subscribers
include British trading standards authorities, but also agencies in Sweden,
Norway, the Netherlands and the Republic of Ireland. LACORS (the Local
Authorities' Co-ordinators of Regulatory Services) has pursued several routes
for enhancing knowledge on how to co-operate across borders.

It is however realistic to conclude that contributing towards the solution of
European trans-border consumer problems and complaints seems likely to be
a long haul. Such 'bottom–up' initiatives may be patchy in their geographical
coverage; they may by-pass the Commission and even central government
within individual Member States. Partly as a consequence of the essentially
informal nature of these linkages between administrative agencies in different
states, an exhaustive, empirically observed description of the patterns of links
which have been established cannot feasibly be supplied. Developments are
dynamic, not static. However, they represent a significant development in
practical product safety law and policy. Indeed, it should not be overlooked
that such initiatives, driven by local knowledge and an awareness of practical
problem-solving, may produce a better-informed system than can be devised
at the more abstract level of legislative planning, remote from practical
enforcement. In so far as agencies in different states are induced to co-operate
in overcoming the obstacle of administrative heterogeneity between the
Member States, the 'bottom–up' system reflects desirable features of the
notion of subsidiarity.

ACCIDENT DATA

The accumulation of statistical data about accidents is a desirable feature in
the development of any coherent consumer safety policy. Empirical evidence
about where accidents occur should be part of the decision-making process on
how to target scarce resources to rule-making and to enforcement.

In contrast to some jurisdictions around the world,[51] the EC has been relatively slow to establish mechanisms for collecting such statistical data about
accidents arising from the use of consumer goods. This must in part be
explained by the prevailing constitutional inhibitions from which it suffers in
developing an active consumer policy (Chapter 1). The Council established a

[50]   S. Weatherill, 'The Reinvigoration of Community Product Safety Policy' (1991) 14 *Journal
of Consumer Policy* 171.
[51]   See Howells, *Consumer Product Safety*, note 5 above.

pilot scheme for an accident information system in 1981,[52] but Member States were able to decide how they would participate and not all chose to become involved. A breakthrough seemed to have been made in 1986 when a European Home and Leisure Accident Surveillance System (EHLASS) was established.[53] Data were collected over a five-year period from casualty departments of selected hospitals throughout the Community. The data covered all accidents in the home, whether arising from products or behaviour. Evaluation followed as part of a process of selecting priorities for accident prevention. Member States were obliged to participate in this scheme. There was resistance among some Member States to the continuation of the EHLASS project. In 1993, the Council agreed to its continuation for one year only.[54] The Commission pushed doggedly for the maintenance of the scheme and its pressure proved successful. A continuation of the scheme was agreed by the Council and Parliament in 1994 to last until the end of 1997. This measure, Decision 3092/94,[55] provides one of the few instances of an EC legal act adopted pursuant to the consumer-specific competence introduced by the Maastricht Treaty, now found in Article 153(3)(b) EC (Chapter 1). The monitoring of injuries by means of collection of data and the exchange of information on injuries is now conducted within the framework of the Community's more general policy in the field of public health. Decision 372/99 adopted a programme on injury prevention to cover 1999 to 2003.[56] The matter was then subsumed within Decision 1786/2002 adopting a general programme of Community action in the field of public health for 2003–2008, which is committed *inter alia* to improving data collection and data analysis.[57] A pessimistic view would be that the consumer-specific dimension of the collection of data on harm to physical integrity may now be lost from view, although one must concede that the EC's contribution to the scientific assessment of risk has in any event in this field been rather sporadic hitherto. A glance at its patchwork body of legislation confirms that impression.

THE SAFETY OF SERVICES

Article 2(1) of Directive 2001/95 defines the reach of the product safety regime to include any product intended for consumer use or likely to be used

---

[52] Decision 81/623, *OJ* 1981 L229/1.
[53] Decision 86/138, *OJ* 1986 L109/23, subsequently amended, *OJ* 1990 L296/64.
[54] Decision 93/683, *OJ* 1993 L319/40.
[55] Decision 3092/94, *OJ* 1994 L331/1 amended by Decision 95/184, *OJ* 1995 L120/36. For a Commission report see COM (98) 488.
[56] *OJ* 1999 L46/1.
[57] *OJ* 2003 L271/1.

by consumers 'including in the context of providing a service'. But Directive 2001/95 has no counterpart in the field of the safety of services. There is no general or 'horizontal' EC measure. The safety of services is governed at EC level by a small number of sector-specific measures, most prominently applicable in the transport sector, but the principal source of legislation setting safety standards for services is the national level.

In 2003 the Commission published a report on the safety of services for consumers.[58] This reveals (entirely unsurprisingly) that different Member States opt for different approaches. All possess sector-specific legislation. Some supplement this approach with a general framework; some rely in part of codes of practice and voluntary standards. The Commission concedes that it is unaware of any specific barrier to intra-Community trade in services caused by different safety standards. However, the report draws attention to scarce data collection and the consequent difficulty of conducting a reliable assessment of the risks associated with the delivery of services to consumers. It advocates a Community role in monitoring and supporting national policies, in particular in the shape of a procedure for exchange of information and the collection of data and methods for their systematic assessment. Improving the 'knowledge base' (pp. 4, 21) is the first priority. The Commission accepts that it is premature to consider harmonizing laws governing the safety of services (pp. 19–20, 21, 23). Any longer-term more ambitious measures would be conditional on gathering information about the need for such steps.

A Council resolution on safety of services for consumers of 1 December 2003 insists on the need for caution and balanced appraisal.[59] It too cites the need to improve the 'knowledge base' pertaining to safety of services while also referring to the need to consider the burdens of establishing systems of data collection. The Commission is invited to proceed with its work.

---

[58] COM (2003) 313, 6 June 2003, available via http://europa.eu.int/comm/consumers/cons_safe/serv_safe/reports/index_en.htm.
[59] *OJ* 2003 C299/1.

10. Access to justice

THE CHALLENGE OF SECURING ACCESS TO JUSTICE

In any system of consumer protection problems of securing effective access to justice loom large. Consumers are understandably reluctant to convert complaint into formal proceedings, especially where their loss is relatively small. Many consumers have only a limited grasp of the intricacies of the law. Taking legal action is in any event costly, slow and a source of stress. These problems are magnified in the cross-border environment. The detail of the law is likely to be even more unfamiliar, and the inhibitions to taking legal action all the greater. Creating an integrated market lies at the heart of EU's objectives, but there is no intent to set aside the existence of different legal jurisdictions. This presents a challenge to the promotion of an effective system of access to justice for the consumer in Europe.

Legal diversity between the Member States is reduced by the pattern of harmonization which provides the subject matter for much of this book. Although Harmonization Directives ought to act as a source of common consumer protection at national level, it is necessary to assess the effectiveness of the system for securing vindication of those legal rules. There are at least two separate elements to this inquiry. The first relates to the constitutional question of the extent to which Directives can create 'rights' on which individuals may rely before national courts. In so far as the Directive depends for its force within national legal orders on transposition by each Member State, the risk arises that variation between state compliance with legal obligations will lead to variation in practice between supposedly harmonized consumer protection laws. The second element, discussed later in this chapter, relates to more practical questions of the extent to which consumer protection law, even if properly and fully transposed on paper, offers a framework for improving the consumer's lot in everyday life. In the EC context, this second, practical matter raises particular questions about the ability of a cross-border consumer to assert legal rights against a trader located in a state other than his or her own coupled to inquiry into the possibilities for effective public enforcement of laws in a cross-border context.

THE IMPLEMENTATION OF DIRECTIVES

The text of Article 249 EC appears to exclude the possibility that Directives can create rights that are enforceable directly by individuals. Article 249 stipulates that a Directive is 'binding, as to the result to be achieved, upon each Member State to which it is addressed, but shall leave to the national authorities the choice of form and methods'. Directives appear incapable of direct effect, for their impact is conditional on national implementing measures. In unimplemented guise they seem inapt for judicial enforcement.

The obligation created by EC law rests with the state, which must secure implementation of the requirements of the Directive within the national legal order in conformity with the obligation found in Article 10 EC. This requires Member States to take all measures necessary to guarantee the application of Community law. The Court has explained that this requires that effective, proportionate and dissuasive sanctions be provided for in national law in order to underpin the measures which implement the Directive.[1] The precise details of the implementation process remain to be elaborated at national level. EC Directives provide for a form of 'indirect rule'.[2] This is the strength of the Directive as a legal instrument, in that it allows norms derived from Community law to be absorbed into established national structures, yet it is simultaneously a weakness in that the Community law origins of the legal rule may be obscured, and their impact diluted, by its indirect route into the national legal order.

Where a Member State fails to comply with the obligation drawn from Articles 10 and 249 EC effectively to implement a Directive at national level, the principal remedy explicitly envisaged in the Treaty involves Commission investigation which may ultimately lead to a ruling of the European Court that the state has failed to comply with its Treaty obligations. This is the Article 226 procedure. Since the entry into force of the Maastricht Treaty in 1993 this has been supplemented by the possibility of a fine being imposed on the defaulting state pursuant to a judgment of the European Court, although this has occurred only infrequently. This procedure is contained in Article 228 EC.

It is open to anyone, including a consumer, to complain to the Commission that EC law is being flouted and to request the Commission to act against a defaulting state. However, the Commission's resources are scarce and it deploys them according to its administrative priorities. Although specific legislative provision confers protection for the complainant in the area of

---

[1] E.g. Case 68/88 *Commission* v. *Greece* [1989] ECR 2965; Case C-213/99 *de Andrade* [2000] ECR I-11083; Case C-354/99 *Commission* v. *Ireland* [2001] ECR I-7657.

[2] T. Daintith (ed.), *Implementing EC Law in the UK: Structures for Indirect Rule* (Chichester: John Wiley, 1995).

competition policy,[3] there is no general possibility for the consumer to insist that the Commission shall investigate an alleged failure to comply with Community consumer policy. The Court has made it clear that the Commission's discretion to initiate Article 226 proceedings may not be the subject of judicial review initiated by an individual.[4] It seems that a consumer representative organization would be equally powerless. This leaves only the option of pursuing the alleged infraction of Community law through proceedings initiated at national level.

But nothing in the explicit terms of the Treaty suggests that an individual derives any right directly from a Directive, nor that an individual can challenge a state's failure to implement. This leaves the consumer, like the employee and other interested beneficiaries of legal protection envisaged under a Directive, dependent on faithful implementation by the Member State. Faulty implementation of Directives is a regrettably common phenomenon. In consequence, rights that ought to be enjoyed by individuals remain contingent on the Member State being driven to comply with Treaty obligations. Accordingly consumer rights might in practice be pitched at different levels in different states according to the prevailing patterns of implementation.

THE IMPACT OF DIRECTIVES WITHIN THE NATIONAL LEGAL ORDER

The European Court has famously developed the constitutional impact of Community law within the national legal order far beyond that envisaged by the explicit terms of the Treaty.[5] In certain circumstances an unimplemented Directive may generate legal effects within the national system which benefit the individual, including the consumer. Notwithstanding the apparent blockage caused by the need for state implementation which stands between the Community legislature and the private individual in the case of a Directive, the European Court has refused to allow a state's failure to implement to subvert entirely the intended conferral of rights on an individual. In this vein, the European Court in *Ratti*[6] held that Directives are capable of invocation before

---

3   Art. 7 Reg. 1/2003. Practice is developing under Reg. 1/2003, which entered into force only in 2004. Cf., concerning the pre-existing regime, Case T-37/92 *B.E.U.C.* v. *Commission* [1994] ECR II-285.

4   Case 247/87 *Star Fruit* v. *Commission* [1989] ECR 291.

5   E.g. C. Timmermans, 'The Constitutionalization of the European Union' (2002) 21 *Yearbook of European Law* 1; B. De Witte, 'Direct effect, supremacy and the Nature of the Legal Order', in P. Craig and G. de Burca (eds), *The Evolution of EU Law* (Oxford: Oxford University Press, 1999); F. Mancini, 'The Making of a Constitution for Europe' (1989) 26 *Common Market Law Review* 595.

6   Case 148/78 [1979] ECR 1629.

national courts. An individual acting in conformity with a Directive left unimplemented after its deadline by Italy was able to rely on the Directive to defeat a prosecution under an Italian law that should already have been repealed.

However, the Court is not prepared to allow a private individual to rely on an unimplemented Directive other than in proceedings where the other party is the state. This is vertical direct effect, of which Directives are capable, but Directives are not horizontally directly effective; that is, they may not be invoked directly in relations between private parties before national courts. The Court's refusal to countenance the horizontal direct effect of Directives was established in *Marshall* v. *Southampton Area Health Authority*,[7] a case arising in the sphere of sex discrimination. The principal objection to attributing horizontal direct effect to an unimplemented Directive was the Court's perception that it is the state, not a private individual, which is at fault and that it would accordingly be improper to interpret the constitutional reach of the unimplemented Directive in such a way as to impose obligations on an 'innocent' private party. This is a significant problem for the consumer. The consumer wishing to rely on an unimplemented Directive will succeed where the supplier is the 'state', which for these purposes is broadly interpreted to include local authorities[8] and even private entities which possess 'special powers beyond those which result from the normal rules applicable in relations between individuals'.[9] However, beyond the reach of the public sector, even broadly defined, Directives are incapable of direct effect. Typically the protection envisaged by an EC Directive in the consumer field will relate to private relationships between consumer and supplier. Accordingly the consumer will remain dependent on faithful national implementation for legal protection.

The Court made a separate advance in its campaign to attribute an impact at national level to unimplemented Directives by insisting that national courts fall under an obligation drawn from Article 10 'to interpret national law . . . in every way possible . . . to achieve the results envisaged by [a Directive]'. This notion that national courts shall secure the 'indirect effect' of a Directive applies to 'national law, whether the provisions concerned pre-date or post-date the Directive'.[10] The national court must consider national law as a whole, not simply measures transposing a particular Directive. The Court has explained in *Pfeiffer* that the requirement that national law be interpreted in conformity with Community law is 'inherent in the system of the Treaty, since it permits the national court, for the matters within its jurisdiction, to ensure

---

7   Case 152/84 [1986] ECR 723.
8   Case 103/88 *Fratelli Costazo* v. *Milano* [1989] ECR 1839.
9   Case C-188/89 *Foster* v. *British Gas* [1990] ECR I-3133.
10 Case C-106/89 *Marleasing* v. *La Comercial Internacional de Alimentacion* [1990] ECR I-4135.

the full effectiveness of Community law when it determines the dispute before
it'.[11] And logically this is treated as a persisting obligation. Even in the event
of accurate implementation it is expected that national courts will draw on the
Directive where national authorities apply national measures implementing
the Directive in a manner incompatible with it.[12] Through this technique an
unimplemented or improperly implemented Directive can penetrate the
national legal order. However, the Court's use of Article 10 in this fashion has
been criticized on several counts. It has been suggested that asking national
courts to repair the deficiencies of the legislature violates the principle of sepa-
ration of powers. At a more practical level, it is unclear whether the variety of
approaches to the obligation of interpretation which will doubtless be taken by
different courts in different states serves to instil adequate reliability and
uniformity in the (indirect) application of Community law. A perhaps constitutionally more appropriate, and potentially practically more effective, route is
to focus on the liability of the Member State which has failed to implement a
Directive to compensate private individuals who have suffered loss in consequence on the default. The European Court added this means of individual
legal protection in *Francovich* v. *Italian State*,[13] a case which arose in the
sphere of a Directive concerning employment protection but which expressed
a principle of wider application. The Court declared that

> The full effectiveness of Community rules would be impaired and the protection of
> the rights which they grant would be weakened if individuals were unable to obtain
> redress when their rights are infringed by a breach of Community law for which a
> Member State can be held responsible.

This shifts the focus of the individual's claim away from the identity of the
party (private or public) against which rights under the Directive are envisaged
towards the state as the party responsible under the EC Treaty for putting
rights in place in the national legal order. In this sense a *Francovich* claim is
a more direct method of protection for the individual prejudiced by non-implementation of a Directive, although claims based on the direct and indirect
effect of Directives are also still available. In *Francovich* the Court moved a
considerable distance beyond the explicit terms of the Treaty in its quest to
secure effective protection of Community law rights at national level.

The 'Francovich principle' has been used in the context of consumer
protection. In *Erich Dillenkofer et al.* v. *Germany*[14] the Court concluded that
consumers who had suffered loss when their package holiday organizers went

11 Case C-397/01 judgment of 5 October 2004, para. 114 of the judgment.
12 Case C-62/00 *Marks and Spencer plc* v. *Commissioners of Customs and Excise* [2002] ECR
    I-6325.
13 Cases C-6, C-9/90 [1991] ECR I-5357.
14 Joined Cases C-178/94, C-179/94, C-188/94, C-189/94 & C-190/94 [1996] ECR I-4845.

insolvent were entitled to seek compensation from the German public authorities, given that the circumstances which had arisen would have been the subject of the protection envisaged by Directive 90/314 on Package Travel (Chapter 3) – had Germany not neglected to implement the Directive properly. One can accordingly depict *Francovich* as a source of consumer rights against the state.

The line of case law initiated by *Francovich* has been extended by the Court. In *Brasserie du Pêcheur SA* v. *Germany* and *R* v. *Secretary of State for Transport, ex parte Factortame Ltd and others*[15] it was established that violation of primary Treaty provisions governing free movement, not simply of the specific obligation to implement Directives, could generate a responsibility on the part of the state to compensate an individual. The Court stipulated three conditions. First, the rule of law infringed must be intended to confer rights on individuals; second, the breach must be sufficiently serious; and, third, there must be a direct causal link between the breach of the obligation resting on the state and the damage sustained by the injured parties. Whether a breach is 'sufficiently serious' – the second criterion – involves an assessment of, *inter alia*, the margin of discretion permitted under the law to the national authorities. The wider the discretion permitted to the state, the less likely that the condition will be satisfied. In the field of consumer protection, failure to implement a Directive is likely to be the most relevant state infraction, and this is a matter where discretion has no role to play. Implementation is obligatory. A *Francovich* action would in principle succeed if the state has done nothing or nothing useful, as in *Francovich* itself and in *Dillenkofer*, but where the state that has made a genuine attempt to implement a Directive but has excusably misinterpreted its intent the claim for compensation may fail at this hurdle.[16]

More recently the Court has clarified that in appropriate, though doubtless uncommon, circumstances misapplication of EC law by the national judiciary may cause the state to incur liability in this manner.[17] And it has also determined that the principle of liability is capable of application in the private sphere, where infringement of the Treaty's competition rules is at stake. In *Courage Ltd* v. *Bernard Crehan* it pointed out that the 'full effectiveness' of the provisions would be weakened were it not open to any individual to claim damages for loss caused by practices liable to restrict or distort competition.[18] In principle this could permit a consumer to seek compensation before a national court from those engaged in anti-competitive practices condemned by

---

15 Joined Cases C-46/93 & C-48/93 [1996] ECR I-1029.
16 E.g. Case C-392/93 *R* v. *H.M. Treasury, ex parte British Telecommunications* [1996] ECR I–1631.
17 Case C-224/01 *Köbler* v. *Austria* 30 September 2003.
18 Case C-453/99 [2001] ECR I-6297.

Articles 81 and 82 EC which cause loss.[19] In practice, however, it is probable that this route would be appealing only to a consumer representative organization. The individual consumer would be unlikely to have the time, energy and resources required to proceed.

DENIAL OF HORIZONTAL DIRECT EFFECT

One element still remains absent from this pattern of legal protection: the horizontal direct effect of a Directive. An unimplemented Directive is not capable of generating rights which one private individual is able to enforce against another private individual. The Court's refusal to countenance the horizontal direct effect of Directives has been subjected to criticism, *inter alia* on the basis that it undermined effective legal protection and that it led to inequality of citizens before the law, since the impact of Directives varied across the territory of the Union depending on the patterns of implementation state by state. Yet the Court, even when faced with strong assertions by Advocates-General that the horizontal direct effect of Directives should be embraced,[20] chose to reaffirm its refusal to adopt that course in *Faccini Paola Dori* v. *Recreb Srl*.[21] This ruling was delivered in the context of the non-implementation of a Directive in the consumer field. It is therefore richly illustrative of the obstacles to consumer access to justice which flow from the Court's stance.

Italy had failed to implement Directive 85/577 on doorstep selling (Chapter 4). On Milan Railway Station, Ms Dori was lured into a contract covered by the Directive by a seller of educational material. Under the Directive, she should have been entitled to claim a right to withdraw from the deal and, having 'cooled off', she decided that she wished to exercise that right. Under Italian law no such right existed. She was thus bound to the deal unless she was able to plead the Directive before the Italian courts against the supplier, a private party. In an Article 234 (ex 177) ruling, the European Court adhered to *Marshall* and held that the Directive could not be directly effective in such circumstances. Plainly Ms Dori was denied a right which she was supposed to enjoy under a Directive. A loophole in the practical vigour of EC consumer protection law is exposed.

In refusing to accept that the consumer could rely on the terms of the Directive to defend an action brought before a national court by the supplier, the Court mentioned the availability to Ms Dori of an action against the state

---

[19]   Cf. N. Reich, 'The *Courage* Doctrine: encouraging or discouraging compensation for antitrust injuries?' (2005) 42 *Common Market Law Review* 35.

[20]   AG Van Gerven in Case C-271/91 *Marshall (2)* [1993] ECR I-4367, AG Jacobs in Case C-316/93 *Vaneetveld* v. *SA Le Foyer* [1994] ECR I-763, A.G. Lenz in *Dori* itself.

[21]   Case C-91/92 [1994] ECR I-3325.

based on *Francovich*. This may be welcome in theory, but in practice it seems unrealistic. The daunting prospect of pursuing an action against the state to recover a relatively small sum would dissuade the vast majority of consumers. The Court also mentioned the obligation of the national court to interpret national law in the light of the Directive, but the fragilities of this route have already been mentioned above; it is rather uncertain, dependent on national judicial capability and willingness. A consumer in such circumstances simply wishes to exercise a right to withdraw from a contract, involving, if necessary, a suitable defence to a claim for breach of contract where he or she refuses to pay sums due. This is the effective method of protecting consumer rights and it is the effective method of securing observance of Directives evenly throughout the territory of the Community. Yet the Court in *Dori* asserted that the Community is not competent to enact by Directive obligations for individuals with immediate effects. The Court confirmed that it is unreceptive to submissions that Directives should be regarded as capable of horizontal direct effect in *El Corte Inglés SA* v. *Cristina Blázquez Rivero*,[22] where a consumer was held unable to rely on Directive 87/102 on consumer credit (Chapter 4), which had not been implemented in Spain, in proceedings brought against her by a private lender. The Court decided that the insertion of Article 129a on consumer protection into the EC Treaty at Maastricht (now found as Article 153) made no difference to its refusal to attribute horizontal direct effect to Directives.

The denial of horizontal direct effect robs the Directive of some of its vitality as a method of creating consumer rights within the national system. It is especially damaging to the typical 'small-scale' consumer claimant in litigation with a trader, whether as plaintiff or as defendant. It also wrecks the even application of consumer law state by state. A consumer who shops in a Member State other than his or her own will not be confident that Community law has set effective standards of protection. If that state has not properly implemented the Directive, the consumer will have no directly enforceable right against a private supplier. The absence of horizontal direct effect contradicts the policy found in, for example, the Recitals to the Directive on unfair terms in consumer contracts and the Directive on sales and guarantees (Chapter 5) that consumer confidence in cross-border shopping should be engendered by the creation of Community-wide minimum standards. Where the state has failed to meet its obligation to implement, the right to 'cool off', for example, will be unavailable; so too the right to evade the enforceability of unfair terms. The consumer will be left with only the costly direct action against the state envisaged by *Francovich* and the unpredictable route of seeking to persuade the national judge to interpret existing national law in the light of the Directive, as required by Article 10 EC.

---

[22]   Case C-192/94 [1996] ECR I-1281.

PRACTICAL ACCESS TO JUSTICE

Even assuming that Directives are faithfully implemented at national level, there remain fundamental questions about the extent to which the consumer is able to derive practical advantage from them. There are doubts as to whether consumers even know of the extent of their legal rights. There are doubts whether they are able to use them in practice to persuade a reluctant trader to resolve a dispute. Literally the last thing a consumer wants to do is to go to the expense and delay of pursuing formal proceedings in court. Consumers frequently simply write off disappointing purchases. These are problems in any national system where consumer law on paper means little in practice if it is unknown or unused. The problems are magnified where the consumer meets a problem in another Member State, where, for all the progress made in legal harmonization, procedures are likely to be intimidatingly unfamiliar.

The anxiety does not concern solely the limited willingness of consumers to act vigorously in order to protect their rights. Public enforcement methods may also prove deficient. All Member States have some pattern of public enforcement of consumer law, though procedures, expectations and budgets display a huge diversity across the territory of the EU. However, as with consumers, so with administrative agencies: the bulk of experience has been gathered in a national or local context. It is unrealistic to expect that public enforcement will be readily and effectively transplanted into the cross-border environment. It is highly probable that when a problem of trading malpractice with a transnational dimension confronts an enforcement agency there will be obstacles to finding out the full background. If the source of the matter is in another Member State it will not simply be that an enforcement officer will likely require a degree of linguistic skill and legal sophistication in order to gather useful information from his or her counterpart over a border – it may be awkward even to find out who holds responsibility for the matter in another jurisdiction. The problem is, in short, that the development of an integrated European market has accelerated far ahead of any notion of an integrated pattern of European law enforcement.

IMPROVING ACCESS TO JUSTICE

The quest to improve effective enforcement of consumer law through the efforts of both private consumers and public bodies has long been on the Commission's agenda. The first Council Resolution on a preliminary programme for a consumer protection and information policy, adopted in 1975 (Chapter 1), included in its list of five basic rights both the right of redress and the right to information and education. However, the development of these rights and aims through specific measures has been limited by the absence of vigorous political support and, more fundamentally, by the constitutional deficiencies in the EC's competence to address these issues. Moreover, it is pertinent to realize that one cannot feasibly legislate 'effective access to justice' into being.

In June 1987, the Council adopted a Resolution on consumer redress which referred to the problems faced by aggrieved consumers in the integrating market.[23] It was broadly favourable to the idea of further work in the field as preparation for a possible Community initiative, although the Council remained non-committal on specific action. The Commission's subsequent investigation left it acutely aware of the difficulties that a consumer faced in securing access to justice in a state other than his or her own. It believed that this disincentive to shop across borders jeopardized the process of constructing the internal market. The 1992 Sutherland Report placed similar emphasis on the active, cross-border consumer as a potential instrument for breaking down national barriers.[24]

The Commission published a Green Paper on Access to Justice in November 1993.[25] It starts from the premise that access to justice is uniquely problematic in the EC because of the different procedures which apply in the legal systems of different Member States. There is no 'European legal space'. A consumer wishing to pursue a complaint in a jurisdiction other than his or her own will be confronted by unfamiliar rules which may deter pursuit of the grievance, which in turn may deter taking advantage of the internal market in the first place. The Green Paper followed the Sutherland Report is assuming that the prevailing pattern of private international law fell far short of an adequate solution. Relevant Conventions then in force were of relatively limited scope, and, in particular, as a consequence of their focus on passive consumers who do not leave their own state, they did little for the active, cross-border consumer whom the Commission would wish to encourage.

How to address these problems? One dimension involves improving consumer awareness of legal rights. Another concerns the facilitation of pursuit of a complaint, especially where the matter possesses a transfrontier element. The EC's role is limited. Article 153(3)(b) EC envisages that the EC may act to promote consumer protection by adopting 'measures which support, supplement and monitor the policy pursued by the Member States'. Education and matters of consumer redress remain largely national matters.

However, the field is not barren. The Commission has helped to establish European Consumer Information Centres ('Euroguichets'). These were

---

23   *OJ* 1987 C176/2.
24   *The Internal Market after 1992: Meeting the Challenge*, Report to the EEC Commission by the High Level Group on the Operation of the Internal Market.
25   COM (93) 576.

initially envisaged as advice centres for consumers in transfrontier regions. Ten of these pilot projects were established by the start of 1993. Their role has been extended, as has their geographic coverage, and today they serve both to inform consumers of general matters pertaining to the internal market and to advise and assist consumers facing a particular problem or complaint. The shift in priorities has also resulted in moving most of the offices from border areas to the capital. A list is available electronically.[26] The 'Euroguichets' also co-operate with each other and with other European networks established in order to improve respect for the rules of the internal market game. The Commission also considers that the 'Euroguichets' are capable of supplying it with helpful insights into what is required to improve the practical operation of the market.

The Commission's contributions have largely been confined to 'soft law' initiatives designed to improve consumer access to justice in the cross-border context. This is where one can most readily envisage the EC adding value to the action taken in this sphere within the Member States. The 1993 Green Paper suggested the possibility of promoting codes of conduct for self-regulatory schemes dealing with transfrontier complaints. A 1996 Communication entitled 'Action plan on consumer access to justice and the settlement of consumer disputes in the internal market'[27] stated the Commission's determination to maintain support for pilot projects designed to improve access to justice and to help with information distribution. It placed special priority on assembling a guide to legal aid practice in the Member States. It also aimed to simplify access to court procedures, although it was understandably cautious about proposing harmonization as such, preferring the notion of producing a standard European form for intra-Community disputes.

Since these initial attempts to generate a debate about the value to be gained from an EC dimension to access to justice the Commission has invested resources in improving the quality of out-of-court settlement of disputes. If achieved expeditiously and fairly, this is likely to be the consumer's preferred way to resolve a matter. Formal court procedures are best avoided, if possible. The Commission has produced a 'consumer complaint form'[28] which it hopes might facilitate the informal resolution of disputes. It has also produced two relevant Recommendations. Recommendation 2001/310 on the principles for out-of-court bodies involved in the consensual resolution of consumer disputes is constitutionally interesting for it is one of the relatively few measures which explicitly mentions Article 153 in its Preamble.[29] In content it sets out impartiality, transparency, effectiveness and fairness as the four key

---

[26] http://europa.eu.int/comm/consumers/redress/compl/euroguichet/index_en.htm.
[27] COM (96) 13.
[28] http://europa.eu.int/comm/consumers/redress/compl/cons_compl/index_en.htm.
[29] *OJ* 2001 L109/56.

guiding principles for consensual dispute resolution. The 2001 Recommendation serves as a follow-up to a 1998 Recommendation which covers only resolution involving a third party responsible for proposing or imposing a solution.[30] The 2001 Recommendation concerns broader procedures whereby the parties are brought together with a view to finding their own agreed solution. A database of out-of-court bodies notified to the Commission as responsible for settlement of consumer disputes in line with these Recommendations is available electronically.[31]

In April 2002 the Commission published a Green Paper on alternative dispute resolution.[32] This was followed in 2004 by the launch of a code of conduct for mediation which sets out recommended guiding principles.[33] The Commission's intention is that in the particular matter of mediation in consumer disputes the two existing Recommendations shall remain the principal sources of good practice.

The Commission's concern to highlight the value of resolving disputes without resort to formal legal proceedings has led it to support the creation of the European Extra-Judicial Network for cross-border dispute resolution – EEJ-Net.[34] This is a network of out-of-court redress mechanisms that can be used to settle disputes between consumers and traders in any Member State. It is particularly targeted at facilitating the resolution of cross-border e-commerce disputes. A special version directed at the financial services sector has been created in tandem – FIN-NET.[35]

It has become common for exhortations to take seriously the need for effective redress through out-of-court procedures to find a place within the text of adopted measures. So, for example, Article 14 of Directive 2002/65 on distance selling of financial services (Chapter 4) provides that Member States shall promote adequate and effective out-of-court complaints and redress procedures for the settlement of consumer disputes and that they shall in particular encourage bodies responsible for out-of-court settlement to co-operate in the resolution of cross-border disputes.

The broad assumptions underpinning these initiatives are, first, that the principal location for improving consumer redress should lie outside the courts and, second, that the EC can play a helpful role in promoting information and good practice as a supplement to national initiatives. These considerations apply with particular force to cross-border disputes. It lies beyond the scope of this book to explore more fully the extent to which the EC is developing an

---

[30]   *OJ* 1988 L115/31.
[31]   http://europa.eu.int/comm/consumers/redress/out_of_court/database/index_en.htm.
[32]   COM (2002) 196.
[33]   http://europa.eu.int/comm/justice_home/ejn/adr/adr_ec_code_conduct_en.pdf.
[34]   http://www.eejnet.org.
[35]   http://finnet.jrc.it/en/.

interest in matters of civil justice, although some of the impact will be felt in the consumer sphere. The current impetus derives from the Tampere European Council, held in October 1999. The heads of state and government of the EU Member States there agreed priorities for judicial co-operation in civil and commercial matters. The existence of different systems of civil procedure among the Member States will endure but steps are to be taken to achieve a more harmonious relationship between that diversity and the quest to create an integrated area of freedom, security and justice in the EU as envisaged by Title IV of the EC Treaty, comprising Articles 61–69. The particular focus is on enabling all relevant actors to be able to exercise their rights in a Member State other than their own. Improved access to justice is naturally part of the programme. This is considered above. The agenda also includes further progress towards mutual recognition of judicial decisions. Common rules on jurisdiction and enforcement of judgments in civil and commercial matters were first put in place by what is commonly referred to as the Brussels Convention in 1968. This was a step towards the goal of ensuring that judicial decisions handed down in one Member State should be recognized and enforced in another without the hindrance of any additional intermediate step. The system has been renovated in the 'Brussels I' Regulation, Regulation 44/2001 concerning jurisdiction and the recognition and enforcement of judg-ments in civil and commercial matters[36] and in the 'Brussels II' Regulation, Regulation 1347/2000 concerning jurisdiction and the recognition and enforcement of judgments in matrimonial matters.[37] *Inter alia* the pre-existing sharp distinction between the active and the passive consumer is set aside. Both Regulations are based on Articles 61 c and 67 EC. This route to EC lawmaking is beginning to provide a source of rules relevant to the consumer (though not only the consumer) which is distinct from the mainstream of legislative activity charted in this book which is based on Article 95 EC.[38]

Decision 2001/470 established a European judicial network in civil and commercial matters designed to improve the pattern of judicial co-operation in practice.[39] There is no question of a homogeneous law of procedure for Europe. But there is a concern to minimize obstacles encountered by those operating in the transfrontier environment and this may involve a degree of alignment achieved by legislative intervention. For example Directive 2002/8 is based on Articles 61c and 67 EC.[40] It is concerned to improve access to

[36] *OJ* 2001 L12/1.
[37] *OJ* 2001 L160/19.
[38] N. Reich, *Understanding EU Law, Objectives, Principles and Methods of Community Law* (Antwerp: Intersentia, 2003), pp. 231–8.
[39] *OJ* 2001 L174/25. Its website is at http://europa.eu.int/comm/justice_home/ejn/index_en.htm.
[40] *OJ* 2003 L26/41.

justice in cross-border disputes by establishing minimum common rules relating to legal aid for such disputes. Article 1 stipulates an entitlement to receive 'appropriate legal aid in order to ensure their effective access to justice' in circumstances falling within the terms of the Directive. This shall include prelitigation advice and legal representation and assistance in court. The Directive avoids laying down precise financial thresholds. Traces of a 'European legal space' begin to emerge.

PUBLIC ENFORCEMENT

The obstacles to the enforcement of the EC's rules on consumer protection in the hands of private consumers which were considered above provide a powerful argument in favour of providing a supplement in the form of public agencies. A model which mixes private actions with public enforcement is likely to diminish the risk that rogue traders will be able to escape the consequences of violating the rules of consumer protection.

The orthodox principle that it is for national authorities to select how to implement and enforce the provisions of EC Directives (Article 249 EC) has been eroded in part in the field of consumer protection. So, for example, Directive 93/13 on unfair terms in consumer contracts and Directive 84/450 on misleading advertising both include more specific provisions that envisage enforcement by public agencies (Chapters 5, 8). The assumption underpinning these interventions is that infringements of consumer protection law are not adequately addressed by relying on private actions nor by simply leaving the matter in the hands of national authorities according to local enforcement preferences.

Of much wider importance is Directive 98/27 on injunctions for the protection of consumers' interests.[41] This was adopted on the basis of Article 100a (now, after amendment, Article 95). It harmonizes aspects of procedures for securing injunctions against practices that harm consumers.

The Commission's 1993 Green Paper[42] noted that it is common for administrative bodies and/or consumer organizations in the Member States to have standing to take legal proceedings to suppress unlawful commercial practices. Such collective action represents an important mechanism for securing law enforcement in the light of the inability of an individual consumer relying on the private law effectively to dissuade widespread malpractice. However, such collective action tends to break down where the rogue trader is based in a different Member State from affected consumers. Agencies in the state where

---

[41]   *OJ* 1998 L166/51.
[42]   Note 25 above.

loss is suffered typically lack capacity to take legal action because they are not the national bodies of the offending country; agencies in the state whence the practice originated typically lack an interest in pursuing the matter since 'their' consumers are not affected.[43] The Commission proposed a Directive to co-ordinate national provisions relating to actions for an injunction which may be brought with regard to particular unfair commercial practices and to secure a form of mutual recognition of the entities entitled to bring such actions.[44] This attracted political support and Directive 98/27 was duly adopted.[45]

Directive 98/27 covers acts which are contrary to the batch of Directives listed in the Annex, as transposed into the internal legal order of the Member States. These designated Directives are, in short, the EC's legislative *acquis* in the field of protection of the economic interests of consumers. The list covers the measures which supply the subject matter of much of this book and it has been periodically updated since the adoption of Directive 98/27 to accommodate more recent measures of EC consumer protection.[46] Where violations of the EC's pattern of consumer protection occur and where the collective interests of consumers are damaged, the rules of Directive 98/27 governing actions for an injunction before national courts come into play.

The 'Injunctions Directive' requires that Member States shall designate the courts or administrative authorities competent to rule on proceedings commenced by 'qualified entities'. This category is defined by Article 3 of the Directive. It covers any body in a Member State which has a 'legitimate interest' in ensuring that the rules falling within the scope of the Directive are complied with. This is stated to cover in particular independent public bodies specifically responsible for protecting the relevant consumer interests in Member States in which such bodies exist and/or organizations whose purpose is to protect those interests, in accordance with the criteria laid down by their national law. It is for Member States to choose between or to combine these two options in designating qualified entities.

Cross-border action is envisaged by Article 4 of the Directive. Where an

---

[43] For an insight into the problems in practice see H.-W. Micklitz, 'Cross-border consumer conflicts – a French–German experience' (1993) 16 *Journal of Consumer Policy* 411.

[44] *OJ* 1996 C107/3, *OJ* 1997 C80/10.

[45] On the background and likely impact see P. Rott, 'The Protection of Consumers' Interests after the implementation of the EC Injunctions Directive into German and English law' (2001) 24 *Journal of Consumer Policy* 401.

[46] The original list covered Directive 84/450 on misleading advertising, Directive 85/577 on doorstep selling, Directive 87/102 on consumer credit (as amended), Directive 94/47 on time-share, Directive 97/7 on distance contracts, Directive 90/314 on package travel (all covered in Chapter 4); Directive 93/13 on unfair terms (Chapter 5); Directive 89/552 on television broadcasting (as amended) (Chapter 8); and Directive 92/28 on the advertising of medicinal products for human use. Amendment has extended it to cover Directive 99/44 on sales (Chapter 5), Directive 2000/31 on e-commerce and Directive 2002/65 on distant selling of financial services (Chapter 4).

infringement originates in a Member State, any qualified entity from another Member State where the interests protected by that qualified entity are affected by the infringement may bring the matter before a court or administrative authority designated pursuant to the Directive. For this purpose Member States are required to inform the Commission of the name and purpose of the qualified entities within their jurisdiction. The Commission publishes a list in the *Official Journal*, updated every six months. This institutes a type of 'mutual recognition' of enforcement agencies.

Article 5 permits Member States to provide that the party intending to seek an injunction can do so only after trying to bring the infringement to an end in consultation with the defendant or with the defendant and a qualified entity within the state in which the injunction is sought.

Article 7 stipulates that the Directive shall not prevent Member States from granting qualified entities – or any other person – more extensive rights to bring action at national level.

The attempt visible in this Directive to promote effective cross-border enforcement is especially laudable. As the Preamble reveals, it is motivated by the anxiety that traders may be exploiting weaknesses in law enforcement in the border-free market by locating in one state and targeting unlawful practices at the consumers of another Member State. Such strategies may be particularly hard to root out, and may seriously damage confidence in the viability of the integrated market. By improving the access of 'qualified entities' in one Member State to the courts of other Member States, Directive 98/27 aims to improve the tools available for effective cross-border enforcement without disturbing the underlying existence of different detailed procedures jurisdiction by jurisdiction.

Valuable though Directive 98/27 is, it is in a sense an admission of failure. Its rules come into play only where a violation of the law has occurred and the collective interests of consumers have been threatened. The best possible model of enforcement would be one that prevented violations occurring in the first place or, if that is wildly unrealistic, one that at least ensured effective co-ordination between enforcement authorities so that malpractice can be promptly stamped out without the need for an injunction from a court. In the cross-border context this implies an urgent need for effective channels of communication between authorities located in different Member States. Part of the problem is that a trader may seek to exploit the internal using one Member State as a base from which to use unlawful (and increasingly frequently electronic) methods to target consumers in another Member State, in the hope that the cross-border dimension may shield him or her from effective supervision. But more generally in an integrated market it is entirely plausible that a problem which crops up in one part of the EU will be a problem elsewhere too, quite independently of any degree of calculation by a trader.

Existing supervisory systems within the Member States are typically shaped by long-standing assumptions of the integrity of the national market. They are ill suited to the growth of a European market. Accordingly promoting information-sharing across borders about emerging problems is a key element in structuring an effective system for applying the EC's consumer protection rules evenly and effectively across the EU's entire territory.

The specific area of product safety (Chapter 9) provides a good example of developments of this type, involving not only information-sharing foreseen by EC acts and managed by the Commission ('RAPEX') but also 'bottom–up' co-ordination as responsible bodies discover that they must take account of the cross-border dimension in order to fulfil their tasks. The concern is to take these developments on to a broader level in order to piece together a more or less coherent strategy for law enforcement built on the diversity of practice and administrative infrastructure state by state. The Commission asserted in its Report on the Consumer Action Plan in 2001 that *ad hoc* informal administrative co-operation is not apt to generate a sufficiently comprehensive pattern to meet the demands of the internal market.[47]

In July 2003 the Commission adopted a proposal for a Regulation on Consumer Protection Cooperation.[48] The aim of the proposal was to bring national enforcement authorities into a closer working relationship with a view to sharpening co-ordinated action against rogue traders in the internal market. The initiative bore fruit.

Regulation 2006/2004 on co-operation between national authorities responsible for the enforcement of consumer protection laws was adopted in October 2004.[49] Its legal base is Article 95, and accordingly it is a rare example of a harmonization measure affecting consumer law which takes the form of a Regulation rather than a Directive. Its puts in place a system that is designed to ensure a sharing of information and a pattern of 'mutual assistance' between enforcement authorities in different Member States. Article 4 provides that each Member State shall designate the competent authorities and a single liaison office responsible for the application of the Regulation. The relevant bodies are then to be connected according to a model that empowers authorities in one Member State to obtain action by their counterparts in another. This planned new EU-wide enforcement network is to start work in 2006 according to the procedures set out in the Regulation.

According to the Preamble, 'Consumer organizations play an essential role in terms of consumer information and education and in the protection of consumer interests, including in the settlement of disputes, and should be

---

[47] COM (2001) 486, p. 15.
[48] COM (2003) 443.
[49] *OJ* 2004 L364/1.

encouraged to co-operate with competent authorities to enhance the application of this Regulation.' This is not the subject of elaboration in the text of the Regulation itself. However, the consumer-friendly motivation of the measure is well captured by Article 11(1). This provides that 'Competent authorities shall fulfil their obligations under this Regulation as though acting on behalf of consumers in their own country and on their own account or at the request of another competent authority in their own country.' The ambition motivating the Regulation is to craft a system of enforcement which retains diverse institutions and procedures state by state but which reduces to a minimum the significance in practice of the fact of an unlawful practice possessing a cross-border dimension. This is plainly a worthy ambition from the perspective of consumer protection, but achieving such seamless co-operation will be hard to realize.

ACCESS TO JUSTICE AND A TRUSTWORTHY EUROPEAN UNION

The material considered in this chapter forms part of the wider picture of a European Union moving in the direction of an area of freedom, security and justice in which, as foreseen at the Tampere European Council, a higher degree of convergence between systems of civil procedure will be required. For the consumer in particular it is the practical dimension to access to justice that is of most conspicuous importance. The Commission's initiatives, largely of a 'soft law' nature, are doubtless helpful on their own terms but reflect the limited competence attributed to the EC by its Treaty in the realms of education and access to justice. The consumer interest is strengthened by the emerging pattern of cross-border public enforcement mechanisms. It would also be improved were the horizontal direct effect of Directives to be recognized by the Court, although this seems currently improbable.

Securing effective law enforcement is, as explained, particularly challenging in the consumer sphere, but it should be appreciated that the whole issue of joining up law on paper with law in practice connects with wider concerns about perceptions of the value of the integration project itself. In its White Paper on Governance, published in 2001, the Commission commented that 'Ultimately the impact of European Union rules depends on the willingness and capacity of Member State authorities to ensure that they are transposed and enforced effectively, fully and on time. Late transposition, bad transposition and weak enforcement all contribute to the public impression of a Union which is not delivering.'[50]

[50]   Commission's White Paper on Governance, COM (01) 428, p. 25.

11. Evaluating Community consumer policy

When the first edition of this book was published in 1997 it was possible to claim convincingly that a relatively small amount of scholarship existed which took seriously the quest to understand what might and should be intended by the notion of an 'EC consumer policy'. That is no longer defensible. A rich body of work has emerged in which attempts are made to provide a systematic account of the shape of EC consumer policy. This is particularly true of the material that impinges on contract law, but it spreads more widely too.

Out of an original Treaty pattern which promised little other than the indirect fruits of the process of market integration, a network of Community policies affecting the consumer has developed. The European Court has shaped a perception of the consumer in assessing the permissibility of national techniques of market regulation, including consumer protection, which impede the integrative process. The political institutions have been responsible for a 'soft law' framework for the development of consumer policy. Moreover, the programme of harmonization of laws has involved Community legislative activity in the field of consumer protection. Although harmonization is constitutionally driven by the imperatives of economic integration, it leads to a Community pattern of laws affecting the consumer interest. Since the entry into force of the Single European Act in 1987, the constitutional link between internal market policy and consumer protection (if not the detailed elaboration of the relationship) has been beyond doubt thanks to (what is now) Article 95(3). And finally, since the entry into force of the Maastricht Treaty in 1993, any possible doubt about the legitimate claim of the EC to legislate in the field of consumer protection has been dispelled through the insertion of (what is now) Article 153. This contains the 'horizontal' clause in Article 153(2) and a textually narrow competence to legislate in Article 153(3)(b), but most of all it confirms that consumer protection belongs on the 'EU map'.

Comparable comments could be directed at the evolution of other Community policies which have an ambiguous connection with the process of market integration, in part as a result of their absence from the text of the original Treaty of Rome. Environmental policy and cultural policy provide other examples of policies that have emerged from a combination of judicial decision-making in the area of 'negative law', 'soft law' and harmonization policy before finally enjoying consecration in the Treaty itself at times of amendment. Matters such as education and training and social policy were not wholly absent from the original Treaty, but the impact of Community law in such areas has far exceeded the expectations that would be engendered by a reading of the relevant, rather bare Treaty provisions, so these sectors too offer illustrations of the tendency of Community law and policy to develop by accretion over time.

This book has portrayed this pattern of growth of consumer law and policy as inevitable in the light of the impact of the process of market integration through law on a wide range of economic and social policies pursued at national level. The explicit terms of the Treaty cannot in any formal sense effectively constrain the evolution of Community law and policy because of the dynamism which is inherent in the Community's mission expressed in the EC Treaty's Preamble 'to lay the foundations of an ever closer union among the peoples of Europe'.

However, a number of undercurrents pervade this inquiry. Although there is a collection of EC legal material which affects the consumer, is it straining analytical coherence to describe this as 'consumer policy'? Is it really no more than an erratically conceived grouping of general trade practices law? If this is so, it would not defeat the perception that there is a Community notion of the consumer, but it would suggest that this notion takes different and perhaps quite irreconcilable shapes depending on the context in which it arises, because the issue of consumer policy *per se* is unconnected with mainstream Community activity. Such an inquiry might seem especially pertinent in the light of the inclusion at Maastricht of the new Title on consumer protection, which is now to be found in Article 153. True, this provision confirms that there is legitimate scope for exploring consumer policy as more than an indirect consequence of internal market policy. But the terms of Article 153 remain rather vague and they have been little used by the legislature since their entry into force on 1 November 1993 (Chapter 1). The Court was disappointingly wholly unpersuaded by the argument that the new emphasis on consumer protection revealed by (what is now) Article 153 should cause it to accept that Directives are capable of horizontal direct effect (Chapter 10). So Article 153 has simply added a new strand to the debate about what exactly consumer policy in the EC might mean. It joins the pattern of 'soft law', the rules of free movement and competition law and, most prominent of all, the package of measures of legislative harmonization. The quest is to sieve this body of law and policy so as to identify a tolerably clear and helpful set of guiding principles, while avoiding over-pressing the thematic congruence that can be imposed on material that has developed erratically over time. Therefore the absence in this book of any attempt to define 'the consumer' is entirely delib-erate. Consumer policy in the EC is a mix of legal techniques. But the same is true of consumer policy at national level.

The variety of harmonization measures discussed in this book discloses a range of techniques and assumptions. One can classify the measures accord-ing to a number of different categories. Some have an impact on public law, others on private law. The latter category is the smaller, but of late develop-ments affecting private law have accelerated. Some Directives concern the health and safety of consumers, whereas others govern their economic inter-ests. The former category was the subject of more intense activity in the early years of consumer-related EC law, but legislation affecting economic interests has subsequently become more prevalent. Some measures introduce prohibi-tions, others adopt techniques of information provision.

Such classifications, which may be traced throughout this book, are valuable yet dangerous. Their value lies in their capacity to provide a thematic framework within which to examine the pattern of the law in detail. Their danger lies in the risk that they may lead one to overstate academically attractive thematic order where there is in practice none. It is submitted that the measures which form the subject matter of most of this book do not on their own form a comprehensive package of consumer protection law. Their uneasy relationship with the disparate patterns of national consumer law combined with their overt concern to advance market integration render such coherence inconceivable. But it is also submitted that the Community has developed policies in the consumer field which are more sophisticated than mere technical harmonization of laws. Community consumer law reflects perceptions of market failure which rob the consumer of an efficiently operating economy. Intransparency in the market, for example, prompts a legislative response through mandatory information disclo-sure, which has become a *leitmotif* of legislative policy in relation to the protec-tion of economic interests. Concern for the possible exploitation of the economically weaker party is visible in some measures.

But the 'consumer' in EC law and practice does not have a homogeneous character. He or she is frequently a commercially astute 'market citizen' – but not in all circumstances. As is explored in Chapter 2, the 'consumer' in the law of free movement is a self-aware individual who is expected to exploit the advantages of choice in the integrated market and whose need for local-level regulatory protection against confusion is commonly set aside as superfluous by the Court. But there is room for justification of trade barriers that aim at protecting the consumer – more so when the perceived risk is to health and safety rather than economic interests and especially where the national rule is shown to be carefully crafted to meet a particular concern rather than a general ill-explained intervention. The alert consumer is not invariably used in the free movement case law as a lever to deregulate national markets.

It is perilous to seek to draw precise analogies between the rules of 'negative law' examined in Chapter 2 and the EC's rules set by legislative harmonization. In the former case the EC is judging the validity of national measures whereas in the latter it has chosen its own. None the less, despite this different context, similarities are apparent. In a number of the measures considered in this book the EC legislative vision of the consumer involves an individual able to take care of him- or herself in the market by digesting and acting upon information that is mandatorily supplied and, if necessary, withdrawing from a deal on reflection after 'cooling off'. Marketing practices subject to control in the manner sketched in Chapter 4 (in particular) are not banned. They are regulated. However, this is no free-for-all, nor even a well-informed free-for-all. The EC chooses also to ban some practices. Unsafe goods (Chapter 9) and misleading advertising (Chapter 8) are relatively uncontroversial examples, while unfair terms in consumer contracts and consumer sales (Chapter 5) are also subject to direct regulation of the content of the bargain, not simply the way in which it is made. Moreover, the accusation that EC consumer law is built on a homogeneous notion of the robust consumer can be countered by identification of respect in particular measures for the concerns of groups of vulnerable consumers. For example, the position of minors is explicitly recognized in the Distance Selling Directives (Chapter 4); so too, in the 'Television without Frontiers' Directive (Chapter 8), special provision is made for the impact of advertising on minors. The draft Unfair Commercial Practices Directive (Chapter 8) also attends to the special concerns of vulnerable consumers. On the other hand, the critic would be able to observe that these are exceptional provisions. Large parts of EC consumer protection law operate according to broadly phrased and generally applicable legal rules which may be viewed critically as inapt for the diversity of consumer experience and expectation across the 25 Member States of the Union – especially if the policy preference for maximum harmonization wins the day.

This struggle between minimum and maximum harmonization is of deep significance. The long-standing political assumption that the harmonization of laws concerning the protection of the economic interests of consumers shall be conducted at a minimum level is under severe pressure. The Commission has made clear that it does not consider that this model is apt to release the benefits of an integrated market, because leeway allowed to Member States to set stricter rules than the agreed harmonized norm breeds persisting fragmentation of the market. This, for the Commission, is detrimental to the interests of both traders and consumers (Chapter 1).

The policy preference in favour of maximum harmonization is driving current Commission proposals for legislative reform. The draft Consumer Credit Directive, considered in Chapter 4, has been presented for recasting according to a maximum model, in place of the established minimum formula. The draft Unfair Commercial Practices Directive is similarly driven in a maximum direction by the Commission (Chapter 8). The broader issue of European contract law has also been imbued with the perception that the advantages of EC intervention can be secured only where national competence in the relevant field is ruled out. Chapter 7 tracks the debate about a European contract law, where maximum rule-making is similarly on the Commission's agenda.

The Court too has made an admittedly ambiguous contribution to the new distaste for minimum harmonization. As explained in Chapter 3, in its ruling in *Tobacco Advertising* the Court criticized the challenged Directive 98/43 because it 'contains no provision ensuring the free movement of products which conform to its provisions, in contrast to other Directives allowing Member States to adopt stricter measures for the protection of a general interest'. One interpretation is that it is a condition of the validity of a measure of harmonization that it excludes the possibility of states making stricter demands of imports than are envisaged by the EC act itself, except where authorization pursuant to Article 95(4) *et seq.* has been secured. 'Minimum harmonization' would mean that the minimum can be surpassed in application to domestic products alone. If this is really what is intended – and Chapter 3 explores the ambiguity – then the Commission's policy preference favourable to maximum harmonization is supported by a strong constitutional justification.

It is submitted that one should never lose sight of the fact that the creation of a more efficient, competitive market for Europe should serve the consumer interest. However, the question is whether the clear benefits of economic integration are sufficient to outweigh the costs that flow from disallowing local sensitivity to particular regulatory needs. Minimum harmonization has long been attractive precisely because of the scope permitted for variation that is sensitive to local patterns of consumer protection. If the shift from minimum to maximum harmonization is carried through consistently, it will radically alter the pattern of consumer protection in the EU. It will mean that the nature of the harmonized standard is critical in meeting consumer aspirations to a market that is free and fair. There will be no scope for local upgrading of protection.

Another key trend in the current evolution of EC consumer law and policy is 'competence sensitivity'. Until recently there was a gulf between the principle of attributed competence and the practice of legislative harmonization. Articles 94 and 95, and, before the renumbering effected by the Amsterdam Treaty in 1999, their predecessors Articles 100 and 100a, were used to cure market distortion flowing from diverse national rules. But in some circumstances these measures of harmonization were more convincingly seen as the product of the politically agreed commitment to an EC consumer policy, advanced under the convenient camouflage of the harmonization programme given the absence of any consumer-specific legislative competence until 1993 and the presence since then (in what is now Article 153(3)(b)) of a tightly confined such competence. As tracked in Chapter 3, the *Tobacco Advertising* judgment sounded a warning. The Court set limits to legislative reliance on Article 95 using a vocabulary that was more elaborately crafted than before. And the Court showed its teeth. For the first time a measure of harmonization was annulled for want of competence under the Treaty.

Questions of whether measures of harmonization of an older vintage may be vulnerable to constitutional challenge should litigation occur are addressed on several occasions in this book. Is the Community competent to harmonize rules governing consumer credit (Chapter 4), doorstep selling (Chapter 4), unfair terms (Chapter 5) or sales law (Chapter 5)? The Court's *Tobacco Advertising* test insists on the market-making potential of measures adopted under Article 95 and some of these Directives lack carefully reasoned connections with that economic imperative. This by no means implies that they would fall if challenged. In particular, there may be scope for justifying the adoption of harmonized consumer law rules from the perspective of their contribution to promoting confidence in the functioning of the internal market. Ambiguities in the scope of legislative harmonization persist, as examined in Chapter 3. This debate is enduringly important. Moreover, the questions are not simply backward-looking. Chapter 7 reflects on the Commission's thinking about European contract law. Here too lurks 'competence sensitivity', although, as explained, the Commission has good reasons to avoid aggressive engagement with the constitutional dimension.

This second edition, like the first, tries to provide a systematic account of the shape of EC consumer policy which is duly respectful of the idiosyncratic way in which some of the law and practice has been shaped. If anything, the picture is even more colourful today. Over 30 years have passed since EC consumer policy was launched at the 'Paris Summit' in 1972 (Chapter 1). And EC consumer policy is set to enjoy deservedly close attention as it enters its mid-life, if not its mid-life crisis.

Index